It's The Beer Talking

Adventures In Public Houses

Ian Clayton

First published by Route in 2018
PO Box 167, Pontefract, WF8 4WW
info@route-online.com
www.route-online.com

ISBN : 978-1901927-74-0

First Edition

Ian Clayton asserts his moral
right to be identified as the author of this book

Photographs:
Porl Medlock and the Tony Lumb archive.

Cover Design:
GOLDEN
www.wearegolden.co.uk

Typeset in Bembo by Route

Printed & bound in Great Britain by T.J. International Ltd

*This book is dedicated to the memory of my grandad,
Ted Fletcher, who taught me how to sup ale.*

Contents

Foreword by Roger Protz   7

Spitting Feathers   13

Part I: Good Journeys Start With A Pint Of Bitter
Looking For The Perfect Pub   19
The Three Musketeers   31
The Wrong Side Of The Bar   43
What Are You?   51
Partnerstadt   59
What Time Of Day Is It Lad?   67
Steeped In History   73
What Shall We Do With The Drunken Sailor?   89
Those Who Believe Their Giraffe Is On Fire   99

Part II: Don't Get Too Much And Spoil Your Dinner
Afore The War   111
Soaking It Up In The Seventies   120
Home From Home   133
Top House Tales   140
The Palladium Of The Potteries   146
Enter Martin Stage Left   160
Saturday Afternoon Society   172
Time Gentlemen Please   184

Part III: I Raise A Glass To Them Still
Close Enough For Jazz   189
Some Pubs You Might Want To Make A Journey To   200

The Green Shoots Of Recovery   205

Progress vs Vandalism   209

Clubbing Together   219

Localism   234

Man In A Station   243

Peeling Back The Years   257

Foreword

Ian Clayton's superb book is a vivid reminder of how deeply embedded the pub is in working life. I come from a different part of the country, the East End of London, but Ian and I have a lot in common. While he supped in miners' clubs and pubs, my first drinking experiences were in dockers' pubs: like the miners, their industry has long been ripped apart and 'containerised' in the name of modernisation.

The pubs in the dockers' heartland of East and West Ham were so numerous that bus stops were named after them. A few years ago, when I left a match at the old West Ham United ground, the police announced that Upton Park station was closed due to congestion. I caught a bus and travelled along the Barking Road to Canning Town to pick up the Jubilee Line. It was a sad journey. It started at the Boleyn, named after the glorious multi-storeyed Victorian pile next to the football ground. It's still open but so many of the stops along the way have lost their pubs. 'Green Gate!' the conductor called out but, alas, the pub there is boarded-up and empty and it was the same story all the way to Canning Town.

As Ian shows, pubs and beers are inseparable. While Ian supped Tetley's and other legendary Yorkshire brews, I had the pick of Charrington, Manns, Taylor Walker and Truman's, with Ind Coope just over the border in Romford, Essex. I can still recall my first taste of Charrington IPA in a pub at Upton Park called, I think, the White Horse: a glorious pale beer rich in malt and hops. Bass bought and closed the brewery on Mile End Road even though it was brewing an impressive 750,000 barrels a year. Bass wanted to fill the several hundred Charrington pubs with such nonsense as Carling Black Label. Damn their eyes.

When I started work I joined another hard-drinking pub culture in Fleet Street, the heart of the old newspaper industry in central London. I drank Whitbread mild and bitter in the Old King Lud in Ludgate Circus or, if I crossed the road, Draught Bass in the Punch Tavern, where the satirical magazine was founded. The most famous pub in 'the street' was the Old Cheshire Cheese, once the haunt of Dr Johnson and Charles Dickens – though not at the same time. The Cheese sold more Marston's Pedigree than the rest of the London pubs the brewer supplied. On Saturday nights, there would be a long queue of hacks and inkies (printers) gagging for a pint of Ped. For some odd reason, Marston's sold the pub to Sam Smith and it lost its lustre.

In common with Ian, I've had the good fortune to travel widely in search of good beer. I've been taken to 'English pubs' in such unlikely places as Mexico City, Texas and Moscow and, of course, they are absurd parodies of the real thing. You can't uproot several centuries of history and plant it in a foreign land, complete with fake beams and over-cold beer. But there are great drinking places abroad: the swaying, boisterous taverns of Munich, the great good humour of Aussie pubs – especially when they've just beaten the Poms at cricket – and the pleasing welcome of American bars, unless as an Englishman you wander by mistake into an Irish bar in Boston.

My first few trips to what was then Czechoslovakia in the 1980s were memorable for the austerity of the communist regime, uniforms everywhere, dreadful food – and sublime beer at around tuppence a pint, served in cavernous, smoky taverns or small wood-panelled bars. Advertising and branding were outlawed and you had to ask carefully which beer you were supping in a particular hostelry but I was able to discover where to find such delights as Budweiser Budvar, Pilsner Urquell and Staropramen.

But you are never free from the pull of the British pub. I recall returning from the Munich Oktoberfest, where I had drunk magnificent lager and wheat beers, gagging for a pint of good old draught bitter. It's still around but its heartbeat, the British pub, is under threat as never before. When I started writing about beer in the mid-1970s, 80 per cent of beer was drunk in pubs. Now there are fewer than 50,000 pubs and less than half the beer we consume is on draught.

There are many reasons for the decline of the pub. One is that we don't make things any more. As a young reporter I had to cover a dispute at the steelworks in Redcar. I'd arranged to meet the shop stewards in a pub across the road from the works. I arrived early and at five minutes to six the landlord started to pull pints and line them up along the bar. When the whistle sounded, men streamed out of the works and into the pub where they downed pint after pint to remove the sweat and grime of eight hours hard graft.

We've lost the steelworks. And the mines. And the docks. Now we're in danger of losing the pubs as well. A convenience store near me has a special offer: six cans of Amstel for £4.50. That's a Dutch lager brewed by Heineken. If I go to a pub in the same town, St Albans in Hertfordshire, a pint is likely to set you back £4.50. If like me you're fussy about the beer you drink, you'll grin and bear it and fork out £4.50 for a pint. But if you are hard up, unemployed or can't afford to go to the pub, you may well plump for the fizzy emptiness of Amstel.

There are no easy answers. But we have to save the great old boozer from extinction. Ian's book is brimming with laughter, tall stories, great memories and endless rounds of wonderful beer. It's also a call to arms to save this unique institution. Abuse it and we'll lose it.

Roger Protz

'This beer's a bit thin.'
'Thy would be an' all if thy had come up
t'same pipe as that beer 'as.'
Frank Randle

Overleaf: In search of the perfect pint.

Spitting Feathers

'I liked the taste of beer, its live, white lather, its brass-bright depths, the sudden world through the wet-brown walls of the glass.' – Dylan Thomas

I believe it tasted nutty. My first drink of beer was either Bentley's Yorkshire Bitter, a long-gone and semi-mythical local brew, or Tetley bitter, another legendary beer brewed just up the road. They served both of these beers in the Sharlston Miners' Welfare Club. Memory plays tricks, alcohol washes away cells, and the story has been told so many times at family gatherings that I don't know whether I'm remembering the telling, the time or the tasting. It was on a Friday afternoon in 1963, I was four, I hadn't yet started school and I'd gone with my grandad to the pit to pick up his wages.

My grandad goes to the window of the wage clerk's office, or 'bob 'ole' as he calls it. A big, brown envelope is passed to him. He rips open the envelope while he is still at the window. He takes out the handwritten slip detailing stoppages and he scrutinises it to the nearest ha'penny. He then counts his money. When he is satisfied that the slip and the wages tally, he turns his back to the window and mutters something about the Coal Board being 'rob dogs' who are not to be trusted. He takes my hand and leads me out of the pit yard, across the road and into the miners' welfare club. On the way, he coughs, hacks and spits and then straightens his tie before opening the door to a smoke-filled room that smells of beer and disinfectant. Old colliers at the tables say 'Nah then Ted' and he says 'Nah then' back. Some say, 'I see tha's got thi little 'un wi' thee.' He says 'Aye' in return, but that is about the extent of the conversation. He goes to the bar and asks for a pint of bitter and a bottle of pop. We sit down at a table with a Formica top and shelves underneath. My grandad says, 'Don't drink it too fast you'll get colic.' He looks at his pint, raises it and takes a swig. 'By bloody hell, I was ready for that, I've been spitting feathers all morning.' He tells me to sit straight and stop swinging my legs and then picks up a copy of *The Sporting Life*.

Grandad takes out a little stubby pencil from the breast pocket of his jacket and licks the nib. He then starts writing on a little piece of paper, pressing so hard with his pencil that he breaks the nib. 'Bloody thing!' He takes out a penknife from his trouser pocket and shaves the sides of the pencil with it. 'What are you writing down Grandad?' I ask, between mouthfuls of pop and the bubbles I make in it by blowing down the straw. 'Never thee mind! And stop making bloody noises with that pop.' He writes some more, scratches the side of his head with the pencil and then shouts across to a bloke in the corner who looks like a ferret. This man is wearing a cloth cap with a frayed neb and braces over the top of a woollen pullover with holes in the front. My grandad then stands up and says, 'I'm going to t'back, don't talk to anybody and stop blowing down that straw into your pop.' He goes over to the ferret man and whispers something to him. The man nods his head vigorously and then holds out his hand. My grandad puts some money into it and the man moves off quickly. My grandad whispers a lot, I've seen him doing it in the barbers and to my gran. Sometimes he spells words out loud, I'm not old enough to know what these words are.

My grandad doesn't come straight back, instead he heads to the lavatory. When he's out of sight, I look at the beer. I reach over and pick the glass up with two hands and raise it to my mouth. When I see him coming back I suck on the flattened end of a cardboard straw that is floating in a bottle of cream soda and pretend to be looking round. In a bass baritone voice my grandfather announces, 'Somebody has been drinking my beer!' He looks across the room. The union man, Charlie Churm, is flittering about like a moth and the other old miners who are in there drinking, dominoing and puffing on pipes and Woodbines reach for their own glasses as though to lay claim to what is theirs and keep their heads down. 'I'd only taken the top off it,' he says, louder this time. Then he puts his glasses on and looks straight at me.

'It was thee wasn't it?'

'No, Grandad, I've been supping my pop!'

'Come off it, I know it was thee, I can tell by thi moustache.'

I go red. He takes his beer pot, wraps his hand around its circumference and squeezes two big fingers between the handle and the glass. 'Now watch and learn.' He tips the pot toward his mouth, sups so that I can see his big old Adam's apple move up and down and swallows the beer in a few gulps, to leave just white foam down the insides of the glass. He then bangs the pot down on the Formica-topped table, belches and wipes the back of his hand across his mouth. 'Aaaaahhh! Bloody lovely. Now that is how tha drinks a pint of beer.' He takes out a clean white hankie and says, 'Here, wipe thi top lip.'

Part I

Good Journeys Start
With A Pint Of Bitter

*We shared some ale and wine and agreed among
ourselves that we would ride together.*
Geoffrey Chaucer

Overleaf: The Jubilee Hotel, one of my early watering holes. I think this photo is from the 1920s. It didn't look much different when I started drinking there in the 1970s.

Looking For The Perfect Pub

We were in a pub. I'm not sure which one, but it might have been The Robin Hood in Pontefract. Tracey Tomlinson said, 'I'm really going to have to stop in after today, I've been out drinking for the last fourteen nights in a row.'

As a rejoinder I said, 'I've been out for the last fourteen years in a row.' Everybody laughed. Burt spat some beer out and said, 'I've done more than that.' Then I thought about it. We weren't that far out. I started enjoying pubs before I left school. By the time Tracey came out with that line in the late 1980s, I'd been in many varied pubs and supped ale in more styles, flavours and quality than you could skim a drip mat at. I supped cans of Worthington E whilst listening to Bob Dylan in a field in Hampshire, knocked open the saloon-style doors of a permit room in Bombay, filled my glass from a tap on a barrel in a cobwebbed cellar in Pontefract and knocked the top off a bottle of Anchor Steam while watching pelicans in San Francisco Bay.

I like beer and I like pubs, better still I like the stories that you bump into on the way back from the bar. Sometimes I think I have spent half of my waking life looking for the perfect pub. I don't know why that is, because in many ways I have already found it. The best pub is the one that you go back to. It's called your local. I'm lucky, I've had a lot of locals. Some of these haven't always been near where I live. I work on the premise that everywhere is local, because everybody comes from somewhere. One of my favourite locals is in Wuppertal, northern Germany. It's called Katzengold (Fool's Gold). I've been visiting that pub since it opened in 1984. It stands on a corner of a backstreet – perhaps the prettiest street in the city – a narrow, cobbled and tree-lined way called Luisenstrasse. Back in 1982, I met two brothers, Jurgen and Volker Bredebusch, who lived in Wuppertal, we've been the best of mates and drinking buddies since then. It was these two who first introduced me to the place. I like the Katzengold as much as any pub I have frequented; the beer is good, Jever Pils and Schumacher Alt, and for those with exotic tastes they have Berliner Weisse in the amber and green versions. The clientele is lively, a mixture of locals and visitors of all ages, but mainly young, hipster types, who like their music as much as their beer. The staff are also young, friendly and know how to serve a good beer; it was here where I learned that the perfect glass of pils should take seven minutes to pour.

It's hard to put a finger on why I like that pub so much or, more to the point, why I like any pub more than another. It might be as random as putting the tip of your finger on the first domino and pushing. Sometimes they fall down in a line and other times they make a pretty pattern. I like random patterns, side roads and diversions. I like to know that I might turn up somewhere I hadn't set out to go to. I like to drop on a pub in the backstreets that seems to have grown up out of where it stands. A pub is a pub at the end of the day, but the ones that are an integral part of their neighbourhood are the ones I like most of all. And local beers are right up my street. There seems to be something right about drinking Batemans in Skegness, Timothy Taylor's in Keighley and Adnams in Southwold.

The most interesting stories, the biggest lies and most of our half-forgotten memories live in plain sight in public houses. And the best public houses are the ones that have room for all of these things to carry on breathing. I know a man who goes round pubs in Castleford. He will tell anyone he gets talking to that he wrote 'Hey Jude'. He didn't of course, but he believes that he did. In a pub called The Baltic Fleet in Birkenhead I met a man who swore blind that the spear that pierced Jesus's side was stored in a secret compartment on a U-boat that was on display in a nearby dry dock. In Bavaria I met an elderly landlady who told me that Napoleon still owed her family for a bar bill they racked up when the French army swept through the village in the early part of the nineteenth century. She still had the bill to prove it. And in a bar in China, I saw bottles of Früh Kölsch, a beer I only associate with a small brew pub in Köln. I said to the bartender, 'That beer is a long way from home.' He didn't bat an eyelid, he just said, 'It's for the locals!' Then he pointed to a crowd of German motor engineers who missed their local beer so much they brought it with them. I liked that. It's to do with tradition of course, but more than that it's to do with a certain longing, what the Welsh call 'hiraeth', a longing for home or for the home that our mothers and fathers called home.

Volker and Jurgen once took me to visit their mother. She had connections to Ostfriesland, a low-lying marshy area of Germany above Holland that has as much in common with Norfolk as it has with Saxony. It's an isolated region which means it has hung onto its traditions, culture and language; it's also the butt of German jokes about ethnicity. On the way to their mother's house, Volker said, "What does it say at the top of an Ostfriesian ladder?' I said, 'I don't know, what does it say at the top of an Ostfriesian ladder?' In unison the brothers said 'Stop!' We were welcomed with a freshly-boiled kettle and rose-patterned best china. When most of Germany moved on to coffee, the Ostfriesians stuck to their tea and all the elaborate drinking ceremony that goes with it. First a lump of rock sugar was placed in each cup, then the tea was poured, and then cream added off the side of a teaspoon. I was about to stir my tea when I was told not to. Jurgen's mother said, 'When you drink a strong Ostfriesian tea, the cream should float like the clouds.' It was as nice a cup of tea as I have sampled. The lady told us that it was a cure for everything from stomach ache to hangovers. I like home-spun wisdom, barmy ritual, backstreets, pubs with good ale, preferably brewed locally, stories from history and friendship. My old mate Arnold Millard had an earthier take on it: 'Good ale and a warm fire to your arse!'

I started sneaking into pubs during that first hot summer in 1975. I was in the fifth form at The King's School in Pontefract swotting for O-levels. Half a dozen of us swapped stories and lies and shared cigarettes behind a sports pavilion at the bottom of the school fields. Some of the lads talked about the girls they knew who were prepared to 'go the whole way', others seemed preoccupied with Led Zeppelin's latest album *Physical Graffiti* and its die-cut window sleeve, and the older ones bragged about how many pints they had supped the previous weekend. I learned from them which pubs would turn a blind eye if you looked underage. There were one or two pubs in Pontefract that would serve you a pint of Double Diamond and tell you to sit at a table in the back out of the road. There was another in Castleford called The Engineers which had a youthful clientele and a fantastic jukebox, and one just down the hill from where I lived called the St Oswald Arms. The Ossies, as it was known, was a 1960s council estate pub. I can't recall getting served in the actual bar there, but they had a little out sales part where you could buy bottles of pale ale and cider to drink with your mates down by the fire station beck.

I don't think I could tell one pub from another at the time, it was all shadowy corners, drinking quick pints, moving on and trying not to get into bother with lads who'd look you up and down spoiling for a fight. The first time I came to realise that pubs were special places where you found friendship, fun and a sense of belonging, came in a grand old pub near Leeds bus station called The Palace. It's still there and going strong today – it's a kind of real ale destination, with far more beers chalked on a blackboard than you could try in one session. Back then it was a classic spit-and-sawdust place with Tetley mild and bitter and if you wanted lager or anything fancy it came in a bottle from a shelf behind the bar staff.

I came to that place by a circuitous route. I was an avid reader of the *Rugby Leaguer*, a weekly newspaper for fans of the northern game. I can't for the life of me recall what it was, but something got my goat and I decided to write a letter to the paper. I was surprised the following week when not only did they print my letter, I got pride of place on the page as 'Letter of the Week' and I won two tickets for the Player's No.6 Trophy final to be played at Headingley between Widnes and Hull. My grandad said he'd like to come with me and we went on the bus. We got off at the main bus station in Leeds.

'We've got plenty of time before the kick off, shall we walk up to Headingley?' I said.

'Well thy can if tha wants, but there's something better that folk can do when they have plenty of time before the kick off. Follow me.'

I followed him as he strode out with a real purpose all the way to the front door of The Palace. Before he opened the door, he turned to me and said, 'And if they ask thi owt about thi age, just tell them you're with me.' Whatever that meant.

The Palace was filled with smoke and mirrors and blokes in flat caps all talking loud. It was like walking into a living museum of mankind. We pushed through overcoats that smelled of spent matches and mothballs. The men wearing these overcoats hardly moved to let us by and barely skipped a beat in their tale as they gave us the merest of glances. My grandad elbowed himself room at the bar and seemed to attract the barmaid's attention by telepathy. The lady with a blonde beehive hairdo and wreathed in bacca smoke smiled at my grandad.

'Right lads, what can I get you?'

'Two pints of bitter, love.'

She pulled two frothing beers and stood them on a copper tray in front of us. Amongst all the noise and din in that tap room, it was as if there was a pocket of silence between me, my grandad and the pints we addressed as the cream swirled before settling on top. I lifted my glass to touch and say cheers, but my grandad already had his to his mouth. I watched him drink nearly half of his pint in one go. He put the glass down hard on the bar top, then looked at me.

'Well don't stand there like a fart in a trance! Get it down, that match kicks off at three and we'll want a few more of these afore then.'

I drank my beer and looked around me. I can't remember much about the rugby we saw that day, but I can vividly recall the inside of that pub and it was glorious. Wood, brass, glass, the rise and fall of the hubbub you only get in pubs, the shock of the bitterness of that brew, the laughter, the scrape of chairs, the flicking of ash, the clink of empties being removed from tables and the whoosh of pots being filled with more. I drank it all in with great glee.

The first pub I called my local was the Blackmoor Head in Pontefract. They used to say that at one time Pontefract had more pubs per head of population than any other town in the land. I don't think it's so now; The Woodman is a pizza place, The White Swan is a vet's surgery, The Flying Horse is a Wilko, The United Kingdom is a hairdressers, The Cartner's Arms is a clothes shop, The Old Castle became apartments and The Golden Lion is an office for a lettings agency, while The Bluebell stands like cheese at ninepence slowly wilting. When I started drinking in the middle of the 1970s there was still more than forty pubs within walking distance of each other. The Blackmoor wasn't a 'local' in the strict sense of the term. Nobody lived near it because by the 1970s not many people lived in the town centre. Folk gravitated towards it, first because it served a lovely pint of Tetley bitter, and second because it had plenty of room for storytellers, liars, dreamers and those who just wanted to remember stuff alike.

The pub had an impressive facade, a stone double-doorway and green-glazed bricks at ground-floor level with mock-Tudor woodwork on white plaster at the first floor. The layout of the pub inside hadn't altered since the 1920s. There was a taproom to the right as you went in. This always seemed to be filled with middle-aged men checking Templegate tickets and betting slips. To the left was a decent-sized lounge with an open fireplace, where market traders warmed their hands and backsides and pensioners sipped halves of mild. A lot of these pensioners had fought in the war and one or two had seen action, as they said, 'in the first lot'. They seemed to have reserved seats. They whiled away time teasing some of the young punks who had found their way there. There was a bloke called Bill who had one leg. Whenever you asked him how he was, he'd say, 'Ask me forty years ago.' Then he'd sing out his mantra, 'White collar, black tie, patent leather shoes, gliding across the floor at the Palais-de-Danse, aye, I was alright then kid.'

Round the corner of the bar there was a little snug; women who had been shopping sat in this room, along with the underage drinkers, who were tolerated as long as they sat quiet. The snug had push buttons round the wall from the days when you could summon a waiter in a white coat with a tray in his hand. Almost as an echo of this, the pub still employed pot collectors; there was one called 'Flash' Flanagan who would have your glass off you, washed, dried and sided back onto the shelf if you so much as looked round.

To the rear was a small area for playing pool. It was rare you could get a game because the table was dominated by half a dozen tough-looking coal miners from the Prince of Wales pit and they'd flatten you as soon as look at you. Right at the back was a function room where every Sunday night some lads from Barnsley ran a rock music disco. You always knew when it was time to go home on Sunday because they played Lynyrd Skynyrd's song 'Freebird'. It was a cue for young, long-haired men in denim jackets and 'I'm with this idiot' t-shirts to practise their air guitar skills and scream 'Oh! Lord I can't change' as they swayed onto the cobbles in the backyard in the night air. The Blackmoor seemed to cater for everybody in a way that pubs did then.

It was in the taproom at the Blackmoor that I first met Burt. We shared a similar humour, a love of books, music, the countryside and beer. Burt was as different again to me, he was privately educated at a boarding school in Leicestershire and went on to study bio-chemistry at Manchester University. He lodged in a backstreet boarding house in the arse end of Salford and that's where he discovered a taste for ale and one ale in particular, Boddingtons bitter. He swore by it. 'The finest fucking landmark in Strangeways is not the prison,' he'd tell you, 'it is the brewery made famous by Henry Boddington with its trademark bees.' This was in the days when Boddingtons was still a regional brewer, before it was taken over by Whitbread and turned by advertising people into 'The Cream of Manchester', before it added nitrogen to its recipe and put widgets into cans. By the 1990s, Boddingtons was just another part of the freshly-washed corporate face of Manchester alongside *Coronation Street*, Man United and Happy Mondays, a parody of itself and nothing like the beer Burt had been drinking every time he skipped a lecture at the university.

I never did get to know the ins and outs of why, but Burt didn't finish his studies at Manchester University. When he was drunk or that way out, he would hint that the beer had got the better of him and he was asked to leave. The upshot was that he upped sticks and left Manchester for London to find work on the building sites. On one site that was nearing completion he was asked by the foreman to salvage scrap. There was a long, electric cable and the gaffer asked him to chop it up into lengths. Burt asked him if it was switched off. The foreman said, 'Of course it is, I wouldn't ask you to cut up a live cable would I?' It wasn't switched off and a serious amount of electricity shot through Burt's body. He returned to Pontefract to stay with his mother while he nursed his wounds. When he got right he took himself off to Israel to pick oranges on a kibbutz. Then he came home again and that's when I met him one night in the Blackmoor Head.

I dropped ten pence into the jukebox, picked three songs and sat down at a table under the window. Burt was sat across from me reading a Picador copy of Richard Brautigan's book *The Hawkline Monster*. He looked over at me, 'Curved Air's "Back Street Love", good choice!' We got talking, he noticed me looking at his black hand, so he showed me his arm. His fingers were still scarred by the electricity and he had a dark hole near his elbow where the current had shot up his arm.

'I'm lucky. I spent twenty minutes looking for the bolt croppers to cut up that cable and I couldn't find them. In the end, I decided to use my hacksaw. It was the blade on that melting that saved me. If I'd found the fucking bolt croppers, I wouldn't be here now.'

When Burt finished his story, I told him that I had been electrocuted before I was born. My father had 'mended' a faulty Hoover and when my mother, who was eight months pregnant with me, switched it on to vacuum under his lifted feet, she got a belt off it that knocked her across the room. I then mentioned that while still a toddler, I had been run over by a GPO van after I fell in front of it from my tricycle. 'Well that's fuck all, I came off my motorbike on that bend in Wentbridge and...' then he stopped and started laughing. He stuck his hand out and said, 'Burt Stephens.' I shook his hand, 'Ian Clayton. Do you fancy another pint?' Burt muttered that old line about popes and bears shitting in woods. The beer in the Blackmoor Head was twenty-one pence then. I fetched two pints back to the table. We supped them and then Burt felt in his pocket. 'I've got enough for two more and that's it until Giro day.'

Burt and I met in the Blackmoor or The Green Dragon most nights after that, to swap tittle-tattle and books. He brought Brautigan, Kerouac and Franz Kafka. I brought Emile Zola, CLR James and J P Donleavy. After Burt read Jay McInerney's book *Bright Lights, Big City* he gave me a full appraisal of it, analysing it down to minute detail, even before *The New York Times* made it their book of the year. By Thursdays we were usually skint and making roll-ups from tab ends we had saved in our tins. I have phoned him many a time after my tea on Thursday and asked, 'How much have you got left?'

'About £1.48.'

'Well I've got something similar.'

'Enough for a little session then. Meet at The Robin Hood at eight and we'll have a short crawl up to The Dragon.'

Burt always wears his Belstaff biker's jacket. He has a 1954 Triumph Tiger that is his pride and joy. He carries in one of the side pockets a dog-eared copy of Robert Pirsig's book, *Zen and the Art of Motorcycle Maintenance*. In the other pocket is an equally soiled and tatty copy of *Jupiter's Travels* by Ted Simon. This is a book about the author's journey around the world on a Triumph Tiger. Burt tells us that one day he will make such journeys. He will. He's that sort of bloke. For now though he sups his pints in the Blackmoor Head and tells us wild tales about his time at Manchester University. One night they all went to a party in a terraced house in Salford. The lavatory was outside at the bottom of the yard. They were all pissed, but after a while somebody noticed that people were going to the lavatory and not coming back. They all went to investigate. Unbeknownst to anyone, the Water Board had been that afternoon to dig a big hole in the backs of the house. It hadn't got covered up properly. Everybody who went to the toilet had tumbled into the hole and couldn't get back out again.

Burt has long black hair and fingernails to match. He'll tell you, 'That fucking bike of mine has been pissing oil again.' Burt swears a lot about his motorbike. I once watched him trying to mend it in our backyard. He was at it all afternoon without respite. I took a mug of tea and a ham sandwich out for him. He wiped his hands on an oily rag and tutted as he surveyed various bits and pieces that were lying on an old blanket on the floor. I said, 'Are you making any headway?' He pulled his hair up into a rubber band and said, 'Nah! The fucking fucker's fucking fucked.'

Before the fucking fucker was fucking fucked, Burt used to let me ride pillion on evening trips out to country pubs. We liked a pub in a village out in the flatlands near Goole. It was one of those places where time didn't move. The landlord seemed to think that the war was still on. He asked us the first few times we went there if we were Germans. When he satisfied himself that we weren't, he decided that we were communist hippies and greeted us with the announcement, 'Hey up, they're here look, Sonny and Cher.' Even if there was nobody else in the pub. This landlord kept some hens in his backyard. Now and again they would leave their pecking and cluck inquisitively round the taproom before being shooed back out. I once saw the landlord try to kick a hen. He missed, but the hen was so startled it flew up, bounced around the tables, knocked two glasses off and left feathers flying everywhere. Burt said, 'What's that hen done to you?' The landlord said, 'It's my bloody hen and I'll do what I want with the bastard.' Burt thought for a bit and said, 'I'm not sure a hen can be a bastard.' The landlord came back to the bar and looked us both in the eye, 'Well that bastard is a bastard and the next time it comes in here the bastard is going to find itself necked, plucked and roasted at gas mark number 7 with some potatoes and Yorkshire puddings round it.'

We didn't react. The landlord seemed to take this as a sign that we probably disapproved of him eating his hen. 'What's up?' he said, 'Don't tell me that you're fucking vegetarians an' all!'

Burt took a big swig on his beer. 'If we were vegetarians we wouldn't be supping this beer would we?'

The landlord knitted his eyebrows. 'Why? Can't vegetarians sup beer now either!'

Burt said, 'Technically no. But you might say that a pescatarian can.' He then explained that the finings brewers used were called isinglass and sourced from the swim bladders of fish. 'They used beluga sturgeon at one time, but nowadays most of the isinglass comes from cod. The isinglass flocculates the yeast.'

The landlord knitted his brows some more and narrowed his eyes. He didn't know what to say next, so he said, 'Flock off! There's no fucking fish floating about in my beer and none of that isin isin foreign muck either.'

The next time we went to the pub, the landlord announced to a bloke in the corner, 'Hey up Tom! Them vegetarians are here!'

Burt eventually gave his Triumph Tiger up as a bad job. He bought himself a water-cooled Honda CX 500. 'It's a touring bike and it's going to do some touring I'll tell you,' he told us. He turned up at the Blackmoor Head one Saturday afternoon, parked on the pavement and pulled the bike on to its centre stand. He had a sleeping bag rolled up in plastic and fastened to the bike with some elasticated bungee straps. He pulled off his gauntlets and announced, 'I'm just having one pint and then I'm off to Yugoslavia.'

We had a mate called Norman Britton, I don't know if his parents saw the irony when they christened him. Norman said, 'As you do.'

Burt pulled out a road map of Europe and spread it on the table under the window. We stood two ashtrays and two empty pint pots on each corner of the map. We followed Burt's mucky fingernail as he described the route he would take through Belgium, France, Italy and down to Split on the Dalmatian coast.

'All good journeys start with a pint of Tetley bitter!' Burt announced. Norman fetched one for him, 'Here get that down, it'll do you good.' Burt took a big swig and then pulled out a book he was taking with him. It was a copy of *The Book of Laughter and Forgetting* by Milan Kundera. 'I'm going to find a tree every day, sit in its shade and read a chapter. Then I'm going to find a supermarket, buy some crusty bread, some cheese and some tomatoes and a bottle of wine and that will do for me.' And with that, Burt drained his glass, belched and said, 'Right. I'll see you all in a couple of weeks.'

When Burt got back from his trip he rode his bike straight to the car park at LINPAC Packaging to start a week on the night shift. On that first night back, one of his workmates said, 'Where's thy bin? I haven't seen thi for a bit.' Burt described his journey on the back routes across Europe. He talked about nights spent looking at stars while poking at the embers on a camp fire. He told about boozy sessions in little taverns in the middle of nowhere and how he had dipped a toe into the waters of the Adriatic Sea. His workmate thought for a bit and then said, 'Well I suppose it's all right for such as you, but there's been some smashing turns on at the Girnhill Lane Club and you've missed them all.'

The Three Musketeers

I don't know whether I'm coming or going. Some sunshine is glinting through broken roof slates above me. I'm covered with a grey piece of material that seems to be carpet underlay. I'm fully clothed and I've still got my boots on. At one side of me is my friend Burt. He is sleeping, mouth slightly open and snoring. On the other side is our friend Sean Tomlinson, he's covered in the same piece of carpet underlay. He's awake and looking up at the dust dancing in the sun's rays. 'Where are we?' I ask, Sean sits up, 'I don't think we made it back to the tent.' I sit up. Two old pitchforks lean up against a wooden wall opposite, a wound-up hosepipe hangs on a nail and further along are some hessian sacks slanted against each other. 'I think we're in a barn.'

'Full marks for deduction there Sherlock.' Burt stirs now and makes that smacking noise with his lips and tongue that only those with a mouth like the bottom of a canary's cage can make the morning after a drinking session. 'It was pissing it down when we came out of the ale house, so we came in here to shelter.' Like the sun filtering through the broken slates on this barn roof, it starts to dawn on me. I've got a head like a tin bucket, breath like a ferret's cage and I need to pee. 'Was it a good session?'

Sean says, 'It's to be hoped so, otherwise there wouldn't be much point waking up freezing cold in a barn, under a roll of carpet underlay.' Sean, Burt and I start to laugh. We startle some pigeons in the rafters. More dust falls down. We sit there letting it fall on us. Silence. Sean says, 'If you had a pub, what would you call it?'

Burt thinks for a bit and says, 'The Fox and Pervert.' We both look at him. He looks back at us without so much as a twitch on his face to say that he is about to embark on one of his wind-ups.

Sean and I say in harmony, 'Why's that then?' Burt thinks a bit more. 'I don't know, I suppose it's a good name for a pub.'

Burt says, 'Bacon, eggs, a grilled tomato and mushrooms sautéed in best butter and three rounds of toast and I think I'll have room service this morning.' We laugh some more. Outside the Derbyshire countryside is waking up. Some crows caw and sheep bleat. We stand up, dust ourselves off and prepare to start all over again.

During the week Burt and I labour on a building site that one day will be a glistening shopping centre in the middle of Leeds. We dig a lot of holes. We erect steel posts to reinforce the structure and scabble concrete to make it fit. We eat dust and muck and bacon and egg every morning, it's fried by a tough Irish woman called Josie. At lunchtime we walk across to a Victorian ale house called The Guildford and drink a couple of pints of Tetley bitter. There's an Irish labourer called 'The Delaney' who generally washes half a gallon down in half an hour before coming back and losing the same amount in sweat digging holes. Then there's a Cornish giant called Ianto. He's been known to sup six pints for his dinner and then erect scaffolding non-stop until going home time.

At the weekend we like to get out into the fresh air. We like the Lake District, the Yorkshire Dales and the Upper Tees Valley in Durham. Today we have come to The Old Dungeon Ghyll. It's a pub popular with walkers and climbers and it has an old-fashioned foot scraper by the front door. You are expected to knock most of the sludge off your feet before you come in, but it's a basic bar with a stone floor that seems to have not so much been built, but to have grown out of the landscape. We have pitched our tent on the edge of a field near a beck in the Langdale Valley. It is remote and beautiful.

'Let it settle first.'

'I'm spitting feathers.'

'I said let it settle.'

Burt has an unwritten etiquette about drinking his first beer of the day. He'll order the pints, watch the bar staff pull the beer and then stoop so that his eyes are level with the bar top. He likes to see the swirling patterns in the glass. 'Give it a good coat of looking at,' he'll tell you. This only happens in the north of course, where the sparkler is tight on the dispense and the foam that will eventually form the head moves around like cream. Burt doesn't like beer without a head and claims that all southern beer is flat. We watch our pints as they settle. Burt uses the outside of his index finger to remove the condensation from the glass.

'Good health.'

We raise our glasses and touch them together slightly. We take a good draught. Burt holds his first mouthful in his gob, letting it sit on his tongue for a few seconds. After he has swallowed, he says, 'That's as nice a pint of Old Peculier as I've ever tasted.' Then he lets out the beer drinkers sigh of satisfaction, 'Aaaahhhh!'

The Old Peculier is rich and heavy and has a sweetness that you don't get in a lot of the beers we normally drink. It's too strong for a session ale, so we only sup it on days out. The Lister Arms at Ilkley keeps a good pint of it and of course the White Bear at Masham does. It ought to do, they brew it there. We supped it at the Nostell Priory Festival while watching Jethro Tull. Theakston's, who sponsored the festival, claimed that the most Old Peculier ever sold in a day was sold there. I believe it, I've never seen as many hippies staggering about. I once made myself badly on it in The Black Horse at Grassington. I supped five or six pints of it on a night before we went pot holing at the Alum Pot and Long Churn Cave in Ribblesdale. The next day the combination of cave and hangover made me claustrophobic in a way that I had never experienced. That pothole has an overhanging rock called 'Buttertubs' which you navigate by means of a rope. Water rushes down beside you. I started shaking on that rope and couldn't move my arms and legs. I promised myself that if I could continue with my descent, I'd never drink Old Peculier again. I calmed down and found my feet. The 'never again' promise lasted for all of a fortnight. We were on a trip up to Bedale and The Black Swan called me to its bar.

Burt wipes the froth off his top lip with the greasy sleeve of his Belstaff jacket. 'I'm not having too many of these because I thought we might have a ride across to Teesdale tomorrow.'

'You're in charge. It's your motorbike, so it's up to you.'

'Aye, I am in charge of that fucking bike. I'm not like you, sat on the back without a care in the world. And by the way, stop fucking daydreaming! You weren't leaning very well on some of them bends this afternoon.'

I have been Burt's pillion passenger since I've known him. We go to the building site every morning at seven o'clock and come out to the countryside at least once a fortnight in the summer. He cajoles me constantly for not leaning properly, in the same way he admonishes me for not addressing a pint of beer properly. Once on the M62 in the rain, I saw a house brick fall off the back of a lorry carrying rubble. It bounced down the carriageway towards us. I tapped Burt on the shoulder hard. He swerved at the last minute. The brick went sailing by. We were still shaking when we pulled off The Headrow and onto the site near St John's church. Burt looked at me with eyes like chapel hat pegs and shook his head. To break the tension I said, 'It's a good job one of us is awake this morning.' Burt just growled. 'You want to learn to sit still, you nearly had us off.' He was like that. I was used to him. More than that, I trusted him. When you hold a suspension bolt and the bloke who is about to knock it in is wielding a lump hammer, you develop a trust.

We drink a second and a third. It is barely nine o'clock and the bar is starting to fill up. We drink a couple more. At ten o'clock, I say, 'Right are we calling it a day, it's a fair ride tomorrow and they have forecast rain.' Burt gives me one of his glares, 'What's up with you soft twat, are you made of sugar? It's your round, get them in you tight bastard.' So I get them in and we drink another.

The next morning we wake up shivering in our sleeping bags with tongues like sandpaper. I boil a little kettle and mash a couple of tea bags in two tin mugs. We warm up a can of baked beans over the Gaz stove and fry a couple of eggs and serve them on two enamel plates. We sit on a big stone and dip crusty bread into our breakfast. After we've eaten we roll a cigarette apiece and lay back on the banking. Burt lets out a fart and says, 'I beg your pardon, but better an empty house than a bad tenant.' We both laugh. We unfold a map and pick out a picturesque route to Teesdale. I follow Burt's finger from Windermere to Ambleside, over the Kirkstone Pass, down past Brotherswater, into Patterdale and then on to Penrith and the A66 eastwards. While I wash the dishes in the beck, Burt starts to pack up the camping equipment. By ten o'clock we are back on the road. I sit still and hold my hands behind me on the luggage rack. Burt has dried grass stuck to the back of his Belstaff. The countryside starts to flash by as he increases speed. I turn over in my mind some of the things we said in the pub last night. Before we have gone two miles I am lost in reverie.

At Appleby in Westmoreland Burt pulls the bike up in front of The Grapes. I get off followed by Burt who throws a leg over the saddle like Audie Murphy dismounting a pony. He takes off his helmet and gauntlets and puts them inside the helmet. 'I thought we might have a glass of shandy. I'm as dry as a bone.' The pub hasn't been open long this morning, but there is already a few in with pints lined up on the bar. Burt strides up with a purpose. 'Two pints of Pedigree please.' I knew that just as soon as he had said shandy outside that he was lying. We have a pint of Pedigree, it's smooth, full-bodied and has that ever so slight smell of sulphur about it. Halfway down his pint, Burt says, 'You can't beat a settler on a morning.' The gathered company nod their heads around the bar. We sup up and go back to the bike. We stand to look at the River Eden. I say, 'That's where the gypsies wash their horses when the fair comes here.' Burt spits into the river and says, 'Aye, well get your arse on my saddle. We've a tent to put up before it rains.'

Our favourite pub in Teesdale is The Strathmore Arms at a little hamlet called Holwick. The landlord lets you camp in a field at the back if you spend enough on his ale. We get there before he calls last orders in the afternoon and down a pint of Theakston's best bitter. After that we put the tent up and then go for a walk up to the High Force, it's the biggest waterfall in England, an impressive sight as it tumbles over a cliff in woodland. We sit smoking our roll-ups and watching the water, both now lost in reverie.

A spit of rain brings Burt and me round. 'We best have a steady walk back. Do you fancy fish and chips? We'll have a ride down to that little chippie in Middleton and then...'

'Then what.'

We look at one another and then in tandem and wishful thinking say 'Bring forth the ale and dancing women!'

The Theakston's bitter is on top form and, because it's a quiet night, the landlord joins us for a few. He even blows the dust off a few LPs he's got in a box and plays them on a portable record player in the corner. He's got The Carpenters' *Greatest Hits* and The Beatles' blue and red compilations. Burt asks for a request, 'Have you got anything by Spirit?' The landlord says that he has never heard of them. Burt teases him, 'You mean you haven't got *Twelve Dreams of Dr. Sardonicus*, one of the greatest psychedelic rock albums ever made?' The landlord thinks for a bit and then says, 'I've got an Eagles record.' Burt tells him that will do. We spend the next half hour or so with a peaceful easy feeling and then the landlord says. 'I'm putting the towels on in a minute lads, do you want a last one?' We have a last one and then the landlord guides us into the field, shining a torch onto our tent in the moonlight.

The rain has passed over now and the night sky is as clear as a bell. It's the sort of sky you only get when you're away from all the light pollution in town. We sit outside the tent and in between farting and belching Burt describes every constellation we can see. I start to doze off. Burt suddenly announces, 'So, what do you know about logical positivism?' Up to that point I don't think I'd ever sat in a damp field in the middle of nowhere and been asked that question. I look at him. He slurs badly, but I think I manage to make out, 'Right we'll start with Wittgenstein.' The word 'Wittgenstein' sounds fantastic coming from the beery lips of someone with a gallon of Theakston's inside. I have no idea what he is talking about. Somewhere in between 'the world being in facts and keeping your gob shut if you can't find the words to express what you want to say', Burt starts to drop off himself. I drag him into the tent.

Next morning when I get up to put the kettle on Burt is still snoring. He has his jeans, bike jacket and boots still on and he's underneath rather than in his sleeping bag.

'Come on wakey wakey! Rise and shine fucking Wittgenstein!'

Burt looks at me gone out and then leans on his elbow to drink his tea.

'Descartes!'

'What!'

'I'm pissed therefore I am.'

We laugh and burst into Monty Python's drunken philosopher song.

'Immanuel Kant was a real pissant, who was very rarely stable. Heidegger Heidegger was a boozy beggar, who could drink you under the table.'

Sean Tomlinson was on a welding course at Hull, so Burt and I went over to join him for a boozy weekend. We spent the first evening in a pub overlooking Hull's Pearson Park called The Queens and finished off in an old-fashioned working men's club called St. Vincent's just up the road. The club was full of trawlermen who sang some of the old sea songs to the cold night air. Sean said he would try to smuggle us back into his digs on the Beverley Road. When we got back, we could see through the window that his landlady was up sewing with the door to the living room open. We daren't try to sneak past. I don't know how or why, but we ended up trying to sleep in Sean's Hillman Avenger on the Westwood up near Beverley race course. This was in the middle of November on a bitter cold night. At three o'clock in the morning we all woke up shivering. Through the frost patterns on the windscreen we saw a flashlight bobbing up and down and then heard a tapping at the passenger side window, where Burt sat with his hands under his armpits. Burt wound the window down, a local bobby took off his helmet and poked his head into the car. He shook his head and said, 'Now then lads, what are you doing here?' Burt said, 'I'm fucked if I know officer. You tell me.' The copper grimaced and then seemed to see the funny side. He said, 'Well look, I can smell that you have been drinking, I don't know how you have got here, but I'll tell you this for nowt, do not move this vehicle or I'll have you straight down to the station.' With that he bid us goodnight and rode off on his bicycle. At seven in the morning with mist settling over the common, we ventured into town. The stallholders were setting up for the day on the old market place. We found a café with a jukebox and the smell of fried bacon wafting through the doors. Never had bacon, egg, sausage, tomatoes and mushrooms tasted so good nor been so welcome. After our third mug of tea, we walked round the market and then we found the library. Burt sat doing the *Times* crossword and occasionally looked over the top of his paper and tutted.

'What's up Burt? Has it beaten you?'

'Bloemfontein citrus fruit not in this condition.'

'I know that, it'll cost you the first pint.'

'Go on then.'

'Orange Free State.'

'Bastard! It is an' all.'

At half past ten Burt announced that he could hear the bolts being drawn back on the front doors of the market place public houses of Beverley. We walked across town and into Nellie's front parlour on Hengate. Nellie's had a model of a white horse prancing over the front door. Nellie had been gone for a few years by the time we got there but everybody called the pub after her, they still do, nearly fifty years since she left.

The pub is an institution in East Yorkshire. It's a gas-lit gem of old-fashionedness, with scrubbed wooden tables, a fireplace in every room and a coal scuttle beside each one. It has browned ceilings and wallpaper through centuries of smoking. Like a stopped clock, it doesn't alter. It's a cosmopolitan place too that attracts locals, students, tourists, business people and those in search of well-priced beer. Sam Smith's have owned the place for a while now, but in their wisdom have left the place unaltered.

It's like walking into a George Gissing novel, either that or Gormenghast. Nellie Collinson's mother first bought the pub from the church in the 1920s, but it was originally a coaching inn going back to the 1600s. Nellie ran the pub with her sisters all the way up to the 1970s. She and her sisters were the only women allowed in because Nellie refused to serve women with beer. She washed the glasses in an enamelled washing-up bowl at the back of the bar by candlelight. One of the locals told me that by the end of the night the water in the washing-up bowl was stronger than the beer. The same bloke told me that Nellie entertained a man friend by the name of 'Suitcase Johnny' and that he was called that on account of the fact that he was regularly thrown out onto the street, followed by his suitcase from an upstairs window.

In a room on the first floor full of ramshackle tables and mismatched chairs, a traditional jazz band played on instruments full of dints. Now, of course, Sam Smith don't allow music anymore. Sometimes though, to this day, if you cock an ear near the staircase, you would swear you could hear the ghost of Dixieland jazz, or maybe just Nellie calling time.

After Sean completed his welding course at Hull, he got a job at British Jeffrey Diamond at Wakefield. They were a company that made underground coal cutting machinery for the pits all over the world. I got made redundant from the building sites and Sean asked about a job for me where he worked. The only vacancy was for a clerk in the time office. I'd never worked in an office in my life, but I borrowed a tie for the interview, spoke politely to the gaffer and proved I could do mental arithmetic. I got the job. My work involved giving out sheets to the lads who worked on the lathes and milling machine. These sheets told them how long a particular task should take to do. It was skull-numbing, tedious work and involved working night shifts once every three weeks. The pay was reasonable. On the night shift we did crosswords and listened to cassette tapes that we had compiled for one another. We told jokes and wound each other up. Every Thursday a labourer called Muhammad took orders for curry and on Friday he brought in lovely food that his wife had prepared that day. As we tucked in we planned weekend trips to the countryside that would get us away from the noise, the muck and the grease.

Sean, Burt and I had become the three musketeers of boozing, 'One for all and all for another one.' We could navigate our way around the Yorkshire Dales, the Lake District, the Pennines and the Peak District by the pubs that we knew there. Our tents and sleeping bags hadn't got the time to be aired on a washing line before they were rolled up and packed for another trip.

Sean had a keen interest in rock climbing and introduced us to his hobby. Derbyshire was a favourite destination for climbing. We skinned our hands more than a few times trying to climb grit stone at Froggat, Stanage and The Roaches in Staffordshire. Most of the time Burt and I stuck to the less severe scrambling type of climbs. Sean was daring and jammed his fingers into the narrowest of cracks and fissures to haul himself up. It was never long though before someone would declare that they were thirsty.

There was a pub on a crossroads outside Tideswell that Burt loved. This was The Anchor. Burt loved it because they served Robinsons. Robinsons beer of Stockport was second only to Boddingtons in Burt's esteem. We liked the Royal Oak at Stoney Middleton as well. Again a favourite of Burt's because he discovered that it had once been a house of ill repute. This gave him the opportunity to proclaim his toast 'Bring forth the ale and dancing women' as soon as he'd had a few.

We found an ancient and isolated pub in a tiny village called Little Hucklow. This was The Old Bull's Head. We camped nearby one weekend. We pitched the tents and walked across to the pub. On the bar were two handpumps, one for mild and one for bitter. Burt turned to Sean and me and said, 'I can't drink here, we'll have to go somewhere else.'

We asked him what was up. 'The beer is called Winkles. I can't sup a beer called Winkles!'

'Don't be so bloody daft!'

'I refuse to drink a beer called Winkles and that's final.'

'The nearest ale house is miles away.'

'I don't give a bugger. I'm not drinking Winkles. I'll sup pop first.'

The landlord must have heard us. 'Actually Winkle is just the name of the man who brews it. The beer is properly called Saxon Cross.'

Burt looked at me and Sean and said, 'Right then, we'll have three pints of Saxon Cross if you please.'

Years later Sean Tomlinson became a brewer himself. He became one the best brewers in Britain. When he was setting up, we talked about what he ought to call the brewery. Burt said, 'Call it what you want, as long as it's not fucking Winkles.' He never let that one drop.

We never did get to the bottom of why Burt didn't think Winkles was a suitable name for a beer, though we were used to his ways and idiosyncrasies so we didn't pursue it. He once told us that after picking oranges on the kibbutz in Israel he had developed an aversion to orange juice. He only ever wore checked lumberjack shirts, because he said that other types of men's shirts were frivolous. Burt was also a radio ham, an expert on short wave radio transmissions. He listened in to Eastern Europe and could give you the latest facts and figures about tractor production in Bulgaria and about the harvest in the Danube basin. He seemed to have a thirst for knowledge about East European obscurity. The more obscure it was, the more he seemed to know about it. His specialised subject if he went on *Mastermind* – and we often said he should have done – would be King Zog of Albania. We were once drinking in the Horse and Jockey at Castleford. Burt gave a run down on the various attempts at assassination that had been made on King Zog's life. He then detailed the relationship he had with Benito Mussolini. The barman leant on a flap at the corner of the bar and reckoned to be reading his newspaper, all the while earwigging. Eventually he looked across at Burt and said, 'Do you know what time the 179 bus sets off back to Pontefract?' Burt said, 'I think they run every half an hour don't they?' The barman said, 'Good! I'm glad. Why don't you get on it and take your weirdness back with you.'

Burt's wife Diane was pretty and petite. She had found a way to put up with his eccentricity and called him Burty. I remember the first time they met. We all piled back to our flat after a chucking out time. I put a Doors album on the record player. Burt did a striptease to 'Riders on the Storm'. Diane told me many a time afterwards that she didn't know what the hell she had let herself in for.

Burt loved Jim Morrison. Jefferson Airplane, The Grateful Dead and The Incredible String Band. When he'd had enough beer he also unleashed a hidden passion for disco music. He liked Shakatak, Shalamar, Odyssey, Kool and The Gang and particularly Errol Brown and his band Hot Chocolate. I teased him about this one night in The Queen's Head at Troutbeck, a pub we liked up in the Lake District. He didn't bite. He just said, 'The trouble with you is you lack taste.' When I challenged him on this he gave me a lecture on what constitutes taste. He slurred, 'You suffer from common realism, you only see what's there. You need to start hallucinating more like I do. For instance, you know fuck all about Schrödinger's cat and you come telling me off about Kool and The Gang. If I want to sing "Get Down on It" for fuck's sake I'll sing it and as for you, you don't even know how to tackle a good curry.' Before he drifted off into incoherence, he said, 'It's the same with women. You wouldn't know a beautiful woman if she gave you a smacker on the lips.'

I said, 'Go on then, who is your ideal woman?' I expected a film star like Ingrid Bergman or maybe the singer Grace Slick.

He paused just for a moment and then said, 'Silke Gladisch!'

'Silke Gladisch?'

'Yep! Silke Gladisch.'

Within seconds he was snoring.

Next morning I tried to tease him again. 'So what's this with you and Silke Gladisch? You never told me that you had a fancy for East German sprinters.'

He didn't flinch. He looked at me straight in the eye and said, 'Like I have said many times before to you. There is little point in trying to explain it. If you have to ask what jazz is, you will never know. Taste cannot be taught.'

The Wrong Side Of The Bar

I met my soulmate Heather in the days of the Blackmoor Head and we started going out regularly together after a boozy trip out to The Kinsley Hotel. I was showing off as we waited for the bus back to Pontefract. I climbed onto the bus shelter roof like it was a gymnastics bar and did a tipsy dance routine, 'Look at me I am Ludmilla Tourischeva.' Somebody shouted, 'Get down before you fall down.' I fell down. Heather picked me up. I fell for her then and I still fall for her now. We have spent many happy hours travelling a journey together and stopping off at pubs along the way.

Heather and I spent our first summer together working in a hotel in Devon. On our days off we walked along the coastline to find pubs tucked away in coves. We loved one at Morthoe called The Chichester and another at Georgham called The Rock. Our favourite was one called The Grampus at a tiny village called Lee Bay. It looked like somewhere that you would find a smuggler with a hook for a hand. We learned to enjoy beers that were strange to us, like Usher's, Devenish and Badger. Heather still swears by the Badger beers and brings bottles of their Golden Glory from the supermarket every time she does the shopping. She says it tastes like peaches.

For a short time I worked as a barman at The Woolacombe Bay Hotel. It was the wrong side of the bar for me. I thought that every time someone bought you a drink that you had to sup it there and then. By last orders I was tumbling about all over the shop. I didn't last long and ended up being a wine waiter. I was twenty years old when I started and what I knew about wine could have been written on the back of a second class stamp. I'm not sure, but I don't think I'd even had a glass of wine before I went there.

The Woolacombe Bay Hotel was an Edwardian pile of a building, built to cater for early car owners who motored to the seaside in their Bentleys between the wars. By the 1970s it was part of a local empire of hotels run by a family whose daughter was a champion tennis player. It had retained a kind of refined dignity and still attracted the kind of people who wouldn't be seen dead on a package holiday to Benidorm. These were mostly middle-class retired couples, but the occasional wide boy up from London with their 'secretary' came as well. I clocked them straightaway because they would always order the dearest champagne from the list when they were within earshot in the restaurant, but then plonk for cheaper fizz when they asked me to deliver bottles to their rooms late at night. I saw some right old shenanigans when the wide boys were pissed.

I met some lovely people as well and particularly an elderly couple from Oxfordshire called Whitney-Mayo. They had been tea planters in India in the days of the Raj and carried themselves with a dignity that I had only ever seen in old black and white English films. Mr Witney-Mayo was a tall, silver-haired man who spoke with an accent straight out of *Brief Encounter*. He didn't say 'that' he said 'thet'. He was nearly ninety but he walked with a straight back and barely leaned on a silver-capped walking cane. He dressed for breakfast and smelled of expensive cologne. Many years later I was in Köln and called into the 4711 shop near the cathedral. I sprayed a sample of 4711 onto my wrist. When I smelled it, I was taken right back to the breakfast table in the bay window at that North Devon hotel. Mr Witney-Mayo would lift the chair back for his wife to sit down and I'd get a whiff of his cologne. Mrs Witney-Mayo was tiny and hopped about like a robin in a winter garden. She, like her husband, was extremely intelligent and talked about their times in the Indian hill towns near Darjeeling. She had been born when Queen Victoria was still on the throne, so some of her language was a bit dated. I once brought her some tea on a tray and she reminisced about a chai wallah she had once been fond of. Another time she drifted off in the garden and recalled her favourite ayah, 'A sweet and plump gel who giggled all the time.'

They ate bacon, kidneys and grilled halves of tomato for their breakfast each morning. On the Saturday before they left for home, they asked if I might bring them each a dish of kedgeree. The chef was a dour Glaswegian called Bill. I asked him if he might prepare the kedgeree for the old couple as a treat. I must have caught him at the wrong time. Bill wiped the sweat off his forehead with the back of his hand. 'Fuck off! What do you think it is, the Savoy? Now get these fucking grapefruits out to the tables and don't bother me with that shite again.' I told Mr Witney-Mayo that the chef sourced his breakfast menu locally and that it might be difficult to prepare a kedgeree without notice. He tapped the back of my hand and said, 'Never mind dear boy, we'll take the local kippers this morning and do remember to bring the Dundee marmalade.'

For lunch I took bowls of mulligatawny soup and a selection of sandwiches to the side of the outdoor pool for them. Mrs Witney-Mayo liked a gin and tonic mid-afternoon and her husband could down three or four halves of real ale in a thick glass with a handle on it. He told me that in the past they had always managed a three-course luncheon, but they found it lay a bit heavy these days. At dinner they could manage four or five courses every evening with a couple of bottles of wine. Mr Witney-Mayo pressed a ten pence piece into my palm every time I uncorked a bottle at the table for them. He liked the Rothschild Mouton Cadet and the Côte de Nuits-Villages wines. He knew that I hadn't a clue about the wines I was serving, but made no fuss. Some of the cockney wide boys would have me running back and forward to the dispense. At times they would decide they didn't like a wine by the look of its label. Other times they would smell at the cork and decide against it or taste a small amount with a wrinkling of their nose and say it wasn't right. Mr Witney-Mayo washed his dinner down with glee. He would belch and beg his wife's pardon. She would giggle like a little lass. Then they would leave the table clinging to one another and ask me to bring them a glass of Auchentoshan to the lounge. Mr Witney-Mayo said that Auchentoshan was the finest of all lowland malts.

I sat with Mr Witney-Mayo on the terrace one day and asked him if he might school me in wine. He said, 'But you are a boy from the north country, the beers are so good there, why do you want to drink wine?' He then tapped me on the shoulder and said, 'There is nothing that I can teach you that you cannot find out for yourself by sampling. There are very good Burgundy's and likewise very good Bordeaux wines, try them. Steer clear of the white ones and if anyone offers you rosé, decline.' Before he went home he left me a couple of bottles of Mouton Cadet. At three o'clock one morning we bribed a Welsh night porter to let us go down to the pool. Heather and I and two waitresses, one from New Zealand and one from Worcester, shared the wine with the night porter, raised a glass to the Witney-Mayos and then went skinny dipping.

For years after, I only ever accepted wine from Burgundy or Bordeaux. At parties I turned my nose up at anything else. At the time the Portuguese wine Mateus Rosé, the one in the little fat bottle that people made into table lamps, was popular. Every time I was offered it I turned it down. Likewise I ridiculed Blue Nun. I don't think to this day I've ever tasted Blue Nun. My mates called me a wine snob. I liked being a wine snob, even though I still had no idea what I was talking about.

Heather and I took ourselves off to India after that first summer in Devon. We saw a very different India to the one the Witney-Mayo's knew. We spent our time in cheap hotels in the old bazaars sharing stories with dreamers from all over Europe. We befriended a scholarly Indian man who said his name was Clive. Clive wore jam-jar bottom glasses on the end of his nose and squinted by candlelight at a little writing bureau. He had inky fingers and seemed to have pen pals all over the world. He lived his life in a small room lined with books. It was Clive who introduced us to the poetry of Rabindranath Tagore. We still treasure a copy of

Gitanjali that he gave to us. He somehow imported good cheese from Switzerland and whisky from Scotland. Clive wasn't so good on his legs, so sent us out to collect his orders from the bookshops near the Paharganj and the old railway station. If we brought back good writing paper and envelopes for him he shared his cheese and whisky with us.

There were no pubs until we got to Bombay, as it was then. One evening Heather spotted a place called Slip Disc near the Gateway of India. It was a rough old dive that purported to be a 'discothèque', in reality it was a place to sup beer and whisky away from the prying eyes of those that didn't approve. They sold a beer called Mohan Meakin Golden Eagle, a beer said to be brewed from the sparkling pure waters of the Himalayan mountains. The barman told us that a few years before, Jimmy Page and Robert Plant had done an impromptu gig in the Slip Disc and they had drunk Mohan Meakin beer. Heather said, 'If it's good enough for Led Zeppelin, it'll do for us.' The Slip Disc became our most exotic local.

We went back to work in Devon for a second summer. In the winter we took ourselves off to the Isle of Skye. At the time I claimed the isolation would help me to write a book based on my Indian journal. The reality was different. There was a pub just three hundred yards from our front door with the Gaelic name Eilean Iarmain. The taproom was frequented by some loveable rogues. Amongst them was Archie, the local coal man; they called him 'Dhub Dhub' or double-black. Then there was Lynne, an early new-age traveller who had found her way up there from Blackpool. She dressed like a medieval minstrel and played a flute while standing on one leg. Old Eddie, a ditch digger, washed his face every morning in a stream that ran past his front door. They were all great drinkers. We became great drinkers alongside them. I didn't get much writing done. We stayed up on Skye for three months in the winter of 1981. I loved it there. Heather wasn't sure. She said it was too quiet and though we enjoyed the friends we made there, she missed the mates we already had. We decided to come home.

Coming home wasn't as easy as it sounded. Heather was originally from Pontefract. She left when she was sixteen and for five years had spent more time in London and Devon than she had there. I was from Featherstone, but since I'd left my grandparents house, I'd moved from one set of lodgings to another. For a while I shared a house with a bloke called 'Trapper'. He was a roadie for rock bands. Trapper was good mates with the band called Sutherland Brothers & Quiver; they had a hit with a song called 'Arms of Mary'. We used to sing 'The light shines down the alley' every time we saw him coming. One night when he came back off a tour with Pink Floyd he left his luggage in the passage at a pub called The Ship Inn at Castleford. He hadn't had a pint of Tetley's for two years and wanted to see if it tasted as good as he remembered. He had just the one and when he came back to collect his cases he found they had been nicked, leaving him with only the clothes he stood up in. He was granted a council house on a tough estate. He didn't have a stick of furniture and next to no money so was looking for a lodger. I met him one night on the way home from a Wishbone Ash concert in Leeds. We split the rent, bought two second-hand mattresses and slept in sleeping bags. Trapper borrowed clothes from me until he got turned round a bit and we cooked our dinners on an ancient hob that I think he got from a scrapyard. Trapper and I used to drink at The Horse and Jockey and come home to listen to Joni Mitchell and Al Stewart records on a little portable record player that I'd had since I was twelve. After that I lived for a bit with a grand old lass who took in lodgers on a council estate on the edge of Pontefract. Phyllis drank her tea from a china cup and saucer and reminisced about the days when she danced with young farmers up in the Yorkshire Dales. I was living in her back bedroom when I met Heather.

Heather and I found a flat on Station Lane in Featherstone. It sat above a derelict shop. The building was in the middle of a terraced row of shops that had been built in Victorian times. Some of the shop fronts were still solid red brick from Ackton Hall pit brick yard, others had been clad with cement rendering to give a false stone effect. They stuck out like sore thumbs. The landlord was a local businessman who sold motorbikes and fishing tackle. He once boasted to me that he was a member of the local chamber of trade. He said that one day I ought to aspire to it. I said to him, 'You know that sign on Wakefield Road that tells you that you are entering Featherstone, can your eyes see much beyond that?' He tutted and walked off with his rent money. Next door was an old-fashioned butcher's shop run by John and Jim. They were grand blokes who had been apprentices together and wore identical blue and white striped smocks. Next door on the other side was Miss Rogers' pet shop. The pet shop had shut down but she still lived upstairs. Poor Miss Rogers, she had to put up with us having late-night parties and blasting out music. One night I heard a tapping on the wall. Next morning I apologised beneath the washing lines in the backyard. I said, 'I heard you knocking and I did turn it down.' She smiled and said, 'You young people and your rock'n'roll. I was actually trying to knock a few nails into an old eiderdown to soften the noise.' She was a beautiful soul was that old lady. Next door to Miss Rogers was Mrs Asquith. She was a widow who lived in a room at the back of her former husband's butcher's shop. Ralph Asquith had been a famous butcher and a winger for Featherstone Rovers. The hooks still hung in the window, but this was another shop that was closed down. Further up the row was Evan's fruit, vegetable and game shop. They hung rabbits, hares and pheasants outside on an iron rack.

Evan's was one of the last of the traditional shops. At one time you needn't go out of Station Lane for anything, you could buy everything from a suit, to a dustbin lid to a quarter of yeast. In the early eighties, Ackton Hall Colliery, our local pit, was still open, but the town was struggling and a lot of Station Lane was in decline. Family-run businesses that everybody knew were falling like dominoes. A lot of the shops were being converted into flats and bedsits. Then came the coal miners' strike and you could sense that before long the tumbleweed would be blowing up the road.

Just up from our flat in Station Lane was a pub called The Railway. This was an old pub built for navvies back in the 1840s.

They sold John Smith's, never a favourite beer of ours, but it was on handpump and they kept their lines clean, which meant it was suppable. The landlady was an angel of a woman called Irene Ferris. She cooked gorgeous homemade food and always had a lovely smile for everybody. The Railway became our local.

One midweek night, Featherstone Rovers were playing Warrington. The pub used to be heaving before Rovers home games because Post Office Road stadium was just a cock stride away. Warrington were always a big team and as a consequence were well followed. The Railway on this night was packed. I sat at the corner of the bar and watched Irene rushed off her feet. A bloke came in, we could tell from his accent that he was a Warrington lad. He asked for a pint and if there was anything to eat. Irene pulled him a pint and said, 'I'm sorry love, there's no food, can't you see how busy we are?' The lad asked for a packet of peanuts. Ten minutes later Irene came to him with a plateful of sandwiches. 'Here you are cock, get them across your chest. I remembered there was a bit of roast beef left from lunchtime. By the look of your hands and clothes you've come here straight from work, so I didn't want you supping on an empty stomach nor doing without on a cold night.' The man looked at his mucky hands, wiped them on his overalls and thanked Irene. It was a simple act of kindness. Irene was like that, she looked after her customers wherever they came from. The following season when Warrington played at Featherstone and he came back to the pub and brought Irene some flowers.

What Are You?

Every pub in Featherstone has a connection to rugby, at one time nearly all of them had their own team. At The Junction they had a team with a picturesque moniker, Purston White Horse, named, so local legend goes, after a brand of whisky. And just across from there was The Travellers Rest. A lot of the young players in the town cut their teeth at The Travellers Rest. For many years this place was run by a legendary former player and masseur called Tommy Smales. One night he organised for a famous old referee to come and tell some stories. The place was packed. Billy Thompson, the ref in question, was well loved and had officiated at cup finals and at international matches. Billy was well into his retirement by this time but maintained a keen interest in the game. He was known to rugby lovers all over the world, but there was no love lost between him and the Australians who were nearly always world champions. That night in The Travellers he told the story of how he got a phone call from the Aussie Rugby League to ask him if he would like to referee the State of Origin match between Queensland and New South Wales, a fixture well known for its brutality. Billy said he'd like that and they flew him out to Australia especially for the occasion. The players started as they meant to go along and were knocking seven bells out of each other from Billy's whistle. In the box the commentators were having a field day, 'Ooohh! this is outright war, if the referee doesn't intervene soon there's a danger of serious injury.' Billy didn't intervene at all, just let them get on with it; stiff arm tackles, biting, gouging, the lot. At half-time nearly every player was walking wounded and in the second half it got worse. At the end of the match the TV people rushed to interview Billy as he came off the field. 'Mr Thompson, that was an absolute bloodbath, can we ask you, at what point in the proceedings did you decide not to send anybody off?' Billy, undeterred, just chuckled and said, 'Last April when they phoned me!'

Perhaps the most notorious amateur rugby league pub team to come out of my home town was one called The Jubilee. The pub was a huge red-brick fortress of a building that the local good beer guide had once described as 'Colditz Castle'. The Jubilee had been built in 1897 at the time of Queen Victoria's diamond jubilee. It was a proper rough house frequented by the coal miners who mostly lived in houses nearby known as Lister Square, named for the local coal-owning toff Samuel Cunliffe-Lister, Lord Masham. The local swimming baths was in the middle of the square and to go there meant running a gauntlet. The sons of the miners who lived next to the baths would give you a good hiding and steal your trunks and towel if it looked like you didn't belong. It was the same when you graduated from the swimming baths to the pub. The first time I went in there on my own, a lad I recognised from the swimming days came up to me and said, 'What are you?' I smiled and timidly said, 'I'm not sure what you mean.'

'I said, what are you?'

'I don't know.'

'Are you a mod or a rocker?'

This was a decade after the mods had fought with the rockers on Brighton front. They were slow to catch up in The Jubilee.

'I don't think I'm either really.'

'Well you better not be one of them fucking punk rockers.'

'Why?'

'Why! Because we don't fucking like punk rockers in here.'

I sat down with my pint next to the jukebox in the corner. The lad who wanted to know what I was came over and dropped a coin in and picked 'Yes Sir, I Can Boogie' by the Spanish duo Baccara. He told me that I should pick the next song. I looked up and down the tracks. The song '2 4 6 8 Motorway' was in the charts at the time. I thought to myself, 'If it's in the charts it should be a safe enough choice.' When it came on, the lad said, 'That's not a punker is it?' I told him it wasn't.

'Well, that's alreight then.'

Never had the phrase 'Well that's alreight then' sounded so threatening and sinister.

I became a regular in The Jubilee. I liked that it was an old-fashioned boozer. It had a huge wooden bar complete with creaky handpumps serving Bass beer. There were old Victorian mirrors at the back of the bar and ancient shelves and drawers. I always got talking in there with the older end. They were great storytellers, very funny and generous. I rarely came home without fresh duck eggs, gladioli or bundles of firewood tied up with twisted steel wire. My love of old-fashioned pubs started in the front bar at that big old public house.

The Jubilee had a very good amateur rugby team, one that was feared throughout the north. They were so good that they could field a first team on Saturdays in the first division of the regional league and a second team on Sundays who played in the top division of the district league. I'd been a nippy scrum half when I played rugby union at grammar school. After school I had a trial with the colts at Featherstone Rovers, but they already had at least half a dozen scrum halves who were much better then me. After I'd been in The Jubilee a few times, I thought I would have a go at trying to play there. The Jube had a shabby brick-built changing room in the backyard of the pub next to a pigeon racing club. I turned up one Tuesday night with an Adidas bag over my shoulder and a pair of borrowed boots. At the time, The Jubilee were coached by a big man called 'Tiddler' Simpson and Vince Farrar. Vince was a living legend of rugby in Featherstone. He was not long since retired from the professional game after a career in which he had won every honour. He had scored a try in the final at Wembley, represented his country and even played in Australia. The Aussies were in awe of this tough, hard-working prop forward who was as hard as nails.

I walk into the dressing room. Twenty-odd pairs of eyes belonging to big blokes in various stages of undress look at me.

Nobody says anything. I feel as though I ought to go out and come back in again. Eventually Vince Farrar says, 'Who are you when you're at home?'

When I find my voice, I say, 'I'm Ian Clayton and I wondered if I might train with you.'

Vince weighs me up, like Albert Pierrepoint, 'Oh! Tha wondered if tha might train with us did tha? Well get stripped then. This is Kisser, this is Stinker, he's Gargoyle, him over there is Chopper and this lunatic here is Tich.' Then he gets fed up and says, 'And thy will meet the rest of 'em on the field.' Kisser, Stinker, Gargoyle, Chopper and Tich give me the slightest of nods. Then Len Sheldon, who seems to be a bit of a spokesman says, 'What shall we call thee?' Before I can answer he says, 'Tha's got long hair and a beard, thy's like Robinson Crusoe.' The name sticks from that moment. To this day, nearly forty years on, whenever I bump into the lads who played rugby for that team, they call me Robinson Crusoe. Funnier still they call Heather 'Mrs Robinson' and whistle the Simon and Garfunkel song to her.

That first training session was a shock to my system. I paired up with a bull of a man called Karl Machen who was like an engine. He could knock out any number of squat thrusts, burpees, press-ups and sit-ups without having to pause for breath. I was as stiff as a board after half an hour and when it came to the game of touch and pass I could barely move. I loosened up enough to throw a dummy that fooled one of the older forwards and I nipped through the gap to score a try. Ten minutes later I tried the same trick. The old forward didn't move and hit me full on. Every bone in my body rattled and all the air went out of me. I fell onto my arse struggling to breathe. The old forward strode up and looked down at me, 'Now look here old cock, thy made a fool of me once, but don't think I'm simple enough to fall for it twice. And think yourself lucky, because if ever thy tries it with me again, I'll break your fucking jaw!' I'm fairly sure that I didn't try it again anywhere near him.

The Jubilee trained on a field below the Ackton Hall Colliery muck stacks. The pit's three winding head gears towered above like two prop forwards and a hooker. The older end still called the pit 'Mashams' after Lord Masham, who bought it in 1890 and developed it into one of the most profitable pits in the land. Lord Masham built a bridge over the railway line so that he could tip all of the slag onto fields to the south of his colliery. These fields were where the first generation of colliers in our town had played their sport; cricket, hare coursing, walking and running races and, of course, rugby. Before it was The Jubilee, the pub was The New Inn and was the headquarters of the first Featherstone rugby team. Before they were Featherstone Rovers, they were Featherstone Trinity and so fierce was their reputation that only the strongest of clubs dare venture to our town to play them on their rough field at the back of the pub. There was a five-year period between the late 1880s and early 1890s when the Featherstone rugby players didn't lose a single home match. These men – the Johnsons, Debneys, Barracloughs and Andersons – were the great-grandfathers of the lads I played alongside at The Jubilee. They had come to our home town, then a rural village, to dig coal like Wild West prospectors. All of their saloons, The Jubilee, The Railway, The Junction and The Top House, were built in the last decade of the nineteenth century. Most of them walked here from Warwickshire, Worcestershire and Staffordshire. They were Black Country boys with big muscles and thirsts to match.

George Johnson played for Featherstone Rovers in the 1930s and for many years he kept The Junction pub. He told me that his Uncle Reuben was the first landlord at The Jubilee. He said that The Jubilee held the record for selling more ale in a week than any other pub. They went through 32 hogsheads of Tadcaster Tower ales and 400 dozen bottles of Bass and Guinness every week. I reckoned it up on the back of a beer mat and worked out that thirty-two hogsheads is 13,824 pints of beer. If the bottles are pints, you can add another 4,800.

The dressing rooms at the back of The Jubilee were not for the faint-hearted. They smelled strong of sweat and wintergreen. You got your arse lashed with a damp towel when you were least ready for it. If by chance you took up too much room on the benches or, woe betide, hung your coat on someone else's peg, you would be told to 'Fuck off'. 'Fuck off' in there meant 'Fuck off' as well. During the miners' strike, there was a prop forward who played occasionally for the second team who became a scab by going back to work to break the strike. The lads guessed what he had done because he didn't show up to training after that. Apart from me and one or two more, all the Jubilee players were coal miners. There was a young policeman who played in the backs. One training night, the policeman put his bag down and started to get stripped. He got one or two looks from some of the lads who had been out picketing. One of these lads in particular could be nasty, both with his mouth and his boot, and was never backward at coming forward when he was that way out. On the field you would want him on your side if anything kicked off, but in the dressing room he could create a menacing atmosphere even amongst his own players.

Vince Farrar was a great coach, not just in the sporting sense but also as a manager of men, he had to be. In that dressing room during the miners' strike there was a tension. It was a room full of eyes and looks and awkward body language, nervous smiles with very few backs turned. There was great team spirit, a hard-edged camaraderie around little celebrations for victories on the field and also on the picket lines, but there could also be a silence there that said everything it had to say. Nothing phased Vince and he expected everybody to be as hard as he was. I once turned up before a game to let Vince know that I might not be able to play. I had been in a fight outside a pub in Wakefield the night before and had to go to Pinderfields Hospital for four stitches put into a gash across my eyebrow. Vince addressed me in front of the lads. 'Why what's up with thee?' I pointed to the stitched-up cut. Vince said, 'Well it's only four stitches by the look of it, rub a bit of Vaseline on.' Everybody laughed. On the night the young bobby was being picked on in the dressing room, Vince just said, 'Right, let's have you all on that field, we're playing fucking rugby tonight, not keeping the pit open. And when you come back, knock the muck off your boots before you come in. It's like a fucking pig hole in here.' Nobody laughed.

One rainy Sunday morning I travelled on the team bus as part of The Jubilee's second team squad to play Flanshaw away. Flanshaw were a lowly pub team from an estate at Wakefield and we were expected to win easily. At half-time we were losing. We sat in the dressing room sucking on quartered oranges. Vince was incandescent. 'You want some bloody raw meat down you. I've never seen such a performance… weak as watter you are… weak as bloody watter!' He then went round the whole team one by one, pointing a finger in their faces and telling them how badly they were playing. 'You!' he said, 'are like a fucking lass.' Then he moved to the next in line, 'And you! I don't know why you bothered to get out of bed this morning, because you're still asleep.' Then the next one, 'I don't know why you got on to that bus, you're bloody useless.' Eventually, he got round to me. 'And you! You're worse than fucking useless.' I said, 'But Vince, I'm a substitute and I haven't even got on the field yet.' He didn't bat an eyelid. 'And I'll tell you why.' Then he couldn't think why, but without further pause for thought he said, 'Because you've got bow legs and your fucking beard's too long!'

There was another team of coal miners at a village called Upton. They played their home games on a field that was in the flattened-out bottom of an old quarry. One Sunday morning game with them was abandoned after just twenty minutes when the referee ran off the field saying, 'I've had enough, you're like fucking animals.' He had already sent five players off by then, including our player who had been intimidating the bobby. He had kicked the Upton scrum half straight in the face as he tried to retrieve a ball from the base of the scrum. The trouble carried on in the dressing room. The ref picked his clothes up in a bundle and ran to his car to drive home in his ref's kit. Both teams carried on knocking seven bells out of each other until they had had enough. Then somebody shouted that the pub was open.

At times, the bar in The Jubilee itself had that same intimidating atmosphere. The bar was run by tough landlords. When they said 'cut it out' the lads generally cut it out and if they didn't they found the bar was policed by even tougher locals. On the rare occasions when visitors came they were looked at with something between a glare and an accusation, as though being asked by body language alone, 'What the hell do you think you are doing here?' If you got past this initiation, you were welcomed warmly. After knocking out press-ups and squat thrusts and avoiding giants who threatened to break my jaw on the training field, I liked to call in to The Jubilee for a beer or two. 'Chopper' and some of the others could do a gallon of Bass before their fish and chips. Some traditions were slow to fade.

The miners' strike was a depressing time for our town, but one of the unexpected outcomes from that bitter struggle was that the players became fitter than they had ever been and The Jubilee amateur rugby league team stunned the sporting world by winning the national cup in front of a packed house at Headingley. In between turns at picketing at Orgreave and flying visits to Nottinghamshire, they trained three hours every day. Vince had them running up and down the slag heaps that were a backdrop to their ground and, because nobody had any money for ale, they were in the shape of their lives. There wasn't a bobby in the land that could have caught a Jubilee coal miner in a foot race that year. Still, it was a remarkable achievement for a pub team to be crowned the best in the land.

Partnerstadt

Roy Herrington, an old schoolmate of mine, was playing a Sunday night gig in The Packhorse, a Tetley bitter pub popular with students in the university district of Leeds. Roy was a musical genius; by his early twenties he had committed to memory almost every lick that Buddy Guy had played, he could make the guitar cry like BB King and wail like Elmore James. He knew the more obscure pieces by JB Lenoir and every note on Robert Nighthawk's *Live on Maxwell Street* album. In the audience this particular night is Jorge Petersmann, who is on some sort of exchange visit at the university. Jorge is an electric fiddle player and asks Roy if he might jam on a couple of numbers in the second set. Roy is happy to trade licks with an electric fiddle player and they get on well. Over a pint of Tetley's after the gig, Jorge says to Roy, 'Would you be interested to come to Germany? I can set up some gigs and the money will be good.' Roy told Jorge that he was playing for beer money in England and he'd be more than happy to give it a go. So, just as The Beatles and others we don't now remember did twenty years before, Roy packed his guitars and set off for Germany. He went down a storm and made loads of friends on that short first tour. As you do, if you're from the part of Yorkshire where we are from, he responded to each new friend he made by saying, 'If ever you're in England come and visit, the front door is always open.' What he didn't expect though was that nine Germans in two cars and a Volkswagen bus would turn up on his front doorstep one spring morning with a view to stopping for a fortnight over the Easter holiday. I don't know what these German friends expected to find, they might have thought Roy was a rock star who lived in a mansion. The reality was that Roy lived in the back bedroom of a terraced house in Halton Street which he shared with his brother, sister, mam and dad. His neighbours worked at the local pit and his dad drank his nightly pint at The Rat Trap working men's club.

One day Roy called to see us in our Station Lane flat. I could see he had something on his mind. I said, 'Come on spit it out, what's up?' He stammered and said, 'If some German friends of mine needed a place to get their heads down for a few nights could you put them up?' We'd not long moved into that flat and we didn't have much furniture. I said, 'Well, there's an empty back bedroom with a bare bulb in it. If they can manage in there and they've got their own sleeping bags, I'm sure we can cope. When are they coming?' Roy smiled. 'They're sat in their car in Station Lane now.' I went down to meet them. Jurgen got out of the car and said hello. He sniffed the air, I wondered what he was doing. He said, 'I think I will like it here, it smells like my childhood.' At the time, the local pit was still open and everybody burned coal. Later, Jurgen noticed the pheasants and rabbits hanging outside Evan's shop and saw blood dripping from them onto the street. He said to Heather, 'Please don't be offended, but I think this town is primitive.'

Jurgen, his then wife Barbara and her mate Ute stayed with us. Barbara and Ute were school teachers. Jurgen had almost completed a university course after going back as a mature student. Up to then he'd been a taxi driver amongst other jobs. They slept in sleeping bags on roll-up mats in our spare bedroom. I took them to the local pubs, to watch Featherstone Rovers play rugby and up to the Yorkshire Dales for the scenery. When we ate at home we had fish and chips out of paper. I told them it was traditional to eat with fingers when you had fish and chips. I didn't tell them that Heather and I didn't have enough knives, forks and plates to go round. They must have guessed though, because the next time they visited they brought as a gift some crockery, cutlery and an old enamelled stew pan, which we still have at the bottom of a cupboard.

That's how a friendship between some young people in

Featherstone, a pit village in West Yorkshire, and some young people from Wuppertal, a cultured city in North Rhine Westphalia, began and endured for going on forty years now. We called it an unofficial partnerstadt arrangement between two unlikely places. Jurgen has been to stay with us in Featherstone at least twenty times since then, his brother Volker thirty times or more. It won't be far off that number that I have been to Wuppertal.

I first travelled out to Wuppertal in September 1982 when Roy was on his second short tour of northern Germany with his blues band Stormy Monday. On a night off we met up with Jurgen and found ourselves in The Optimum, a noisy bar in Elberfeld, the trendy northern part of the city. As we came into the bar, Jurgen said, 'This is my brother, Volker.' I'd noticed him before I was introduced. He was sat at the bar behind a large glass of beer, blond hair nearly down to his shoulder and bearded. He was dressed different to everybody else in that bar. He had a pair of bib and brace overalls on, clogs and a blue workers' jacket, the sort that council workers used to wear over here back in the day. We shook hands.

'My brother told me many things about you, I'm happy to meet you.'

'Will you have a beer with me?' I offered

'I like the weizen beer here, this is hefeweizenbier.'

'Right, we'll have some hefeweizenbier then.'

Volker laughed at my pronunciation. Almost the first thing he asked me when we got talking was, 'You live near Leeds, no?' I nodded. 'Do you know where I might get a copy of John Martyn's album *Live at Leeds*. I collect all of his records and that is the most difficult one to find.' I told him that I had two albums of John Martyn myself, *One World* and *Solid Air*. Volker said, 'But they are perfect works of art, beautiful music.' The German blues outfit Black Cat Bone were playing and towards the end of the night, Volker felt in the side pocket of his workers' jacket and pulled out a selection of blues harps. He got up on stage and jammed.

Jurgen and Volker never needed much of an excuse to visit us in Featherstone. Jurgen came for his second visit when his beloved Borrusia Dortmund had a European cup match with Glasgow Rangers one Wednesday night. He bought tickets for himself, a couple of mates and me. This meant I was in the German pen at Ibrox Park, an experience in itself. We set off early for Glasgow and went the scenic route. We stopped for our first pint in The Junction at Otley and then had a couple more in The Falcon up in the Yorkshire Dales. We drove back after the match and got back in the early hours. Jurgen set off at daybreak for the ferry to get back home. He had by then left university and was about to start his new job on the Friday morning. He had obtained work at CD Walzholz, a specialised steel company. He was to be a steel trader in the southern European countries. On his first day, a workmate said to him, 'Did you see the game on Wednesday?' Jurgen smiled and said, 'Yes I was on the terraces at Glasgow.' He became a hero at his workplace within an hour of starting his job.

Wuppertal has become almost as familiar as the back of my hand. Depending on who you talk to, Wuppertal is the city of the Schweberbahn, the world's first monorail public transport system. To others it is the home of Pina Bausch's world famous contemporary dance theatre, yet others will tell you that the vanguard of the European free-jazz movement, Peter Brotzmann and Peter Kowald live there, as does the troubadour Martin Herberg. Those with knowledge of political history will mention that Friedrich Engels lived in one of those houses with lovely slate-covered walls and Brunswick-green painted window frames that are common there. Wuppertal is a great patchwork quilt of a place, albeit a long thin one, snaking through the Wupper valley, pressed in by steep hillsides. I love this city and the surrounding countryside. In Jurgen and Volker, I had good guides to show me round. Wuppertal is also home to my local pub abroad, The Katzengold. It means 'golden cat' but it also means 'fool's gold'; I think the rock in the cellars under the pub have deposits of iron pyrite. It opened its doors for the first time in the year I first visited Wuppertal. I love that bar. I've had breakfast in there, lunch and supper.

Volker spent his early life near the mediaeval walled town of Hattingen and after leaving home as a teenager, lived communally with an assortment of hippies, activists and street theatre performers. At home he worked at music promotion, but also as a joiner. He met his wife Michaela and they moved to Wuppertal to live together in the late 1970s. Michaela was beautiful, but suffered from a cruel illness, a form of arthritis that got worse day on day. Over the thirty years I knew her, I never heard her complain, apart from if we walked too fast. She loved collecting ornaments and Mickey Mouse memorabilia; the charity shops of England were like a magnet for her. While Volker fingered his way through cardboard boxes full of dusty LP records, Michaela would be picking up figurines of ladies in country gardens and little motor cars with Mickey and Minnie driving them. Her favourite English counties were Oxfordshire and Sussex.

Our friendship was forged around a love of travel, good beer, a shared political background, looking for the other, and sport. Volker was also a fan of Borussia Dortmund and we saw a good few matches at the old Westfalenstadion. Dortmund is a working-class team supported by coal miners and brewery workers and it seemed that everybody who went to their matches called for a beer beforehand in a pub called Der Trommler (The Drummer). The pub served strong Dortmunder Export beer and was famous for its pre-match snack. This was a crusty open sandwich with a dollop of raw minced beef, raw egg and raw onion on it. Jurgen told me that it was called 'tartare' and that I should try one to soak up the beer. I ordered one and it was brought to me by a burly woman who carried six plates of it in one hand and four glasses of beer in the other. I looked at her. She said, 'Nehmen!' I took one of the plates. I looked at the raw meat and then at the woman. She said, 'Essen!' I ate. It was different to the hot beef sandwich I liked in The Railway Hotel before a Featherstone Rovers game, but it did soak up the beer.

When Volker was in Featherstone, he always wanted to go to see Featherstone Rovers play and we'd turn up on the terraces half drunk after a session in The Railway Hotel and The Top

House. Then there was the music. Volker loved the English music of the late sixties and early seventies, particularly the folk-rock stuff from the extended Fairport Convention family, Pentangle and The Incredible String Band. He adored the Island record label, especially John Martyn and Nick Drake releases, and anything that had Danny Thompson playing bass on it. His knowledge of the blues went right back to the wellspring; he had somehow deciphered the lyrics of Blind Lemon Jefferson and Bessie Smith and his knowledge of old jazz stuff was second to none. I remember once on a day out to Beverley in East Yorkshire, he found in a charity shop a whole box full of Jelly Roll Morton and Fletcher Henderson LPs and he bought the lot. He also liked contemporary left-field weirdness and was a fan of the American avant-garde composer Annette Peacock. At the drop of a hat one evening he drove us from Featherstone down to Ronnie Scott's club in London to see her perform.

Volker loved adventures that involved beer, searching for history and music. A typical adventure was when we found ourselves in Budapest after Jurgen had promised to smuggle an electric piano into Hungary for an old university mate who was a pastor at the United Reformed Church. We got into a confrontation with some East German lads who had travelled there in an old Trabant car. I can't recall how the argument started, I think the East German lads had suggested that we were decadent Westerners. Jurgen took one by the scruff of the neck and said, 'You are too stupid to realise it, but we are on your side. Still, if you want to fight, we'll give you one, much better to have a drink.' We had a drink and we drank them under the table.

I once told Volker that I was a bit shy to take him to meet my grandparents. He wanted to know why, because he was very fond of the stories I'd shared with him about them. I told him that my grandparents were still a bit wary of Germans because of the war, which was still very powerful in their minds. My grandad had fought in the desert with Montgomery and my gran had lost two brothers in the second war and all of her uncles in the first. I broached the subject with them when Volker and Michaela were staying with us on a summer visit. My grandad said, 'Germans eh! How old are they?' I said that they were about my age. My grandad said, 'Well bring the buggers down to see us. It wasn't them that were trying to bloody shoot me at El Alamein was it.' My grandparents got on with Volker and Michaela like a house on fire. My grandad liked to tease Volker when he found out that he had swam butterfly for the German national team. Grandad had been a boxer and rugby league player. He admired Volker's physique but said, 'It's a bit of a soft sport though is swimming.' My gran said Michaela was beautiful. She said to me one day in the kitchen when they weren't listening, 'She's got some lovely eyes. I can read eyes like them and they're very truthful eyes they are.'

My gran and grandad lived opposite The Jubilee in their retirement flat, a pub which both Jurgen and Volker were fascinated and terrified by in equal measure. Whenever I took the brothers for a visit in those times, my grandad would tell me to take them across for a pint on the way home. I didn't take them until one day when my grandad mentioned it for about the fourth time, Jurgen said, 'Yes I would like to see inside that pub.' My grandad coughed and laughed.

'Are you sure?'

'I have seen all the other pubs in your town. I would like to see this one.'

We went across and got a pint of Bass. We stood at the bar talking. 'Ziggy' Saunders came across. Ziggy has one ear. He had the other bitten off in a fight. To be precise, Ziggy has one ear and a lobe. He has a stud in his lobe. He said to me, 'Who's thi mate, Crusoe?' I said, 'This is Jurgen.' Ziggy couldn't pronounce it. He just said, 'Oh-aye and where are you from then?'

Jurgen said, 'I am from Wuppertal.'

Ziggy was even more confused now. 'And where's that near?'

'Wuppertal is in Germany.'

'Germany eh!' Ziggy turned to his mates who were playing the one-armed bandit near the door. 'Hey up lads, we've got a German in.'

I put myself between Jurgen and Ziggy. 'Jurgen's a good friend of mine. His grandad worked at the pit in Dortmund.'

Ziggy looked at me and then across to Jurgen. He thought for a second or two. He then stuck his hand out. Jurgen went to shake it, but as he did, Ziggy pulled his hand back, put his thumb to his nose and waggled his fingers. Then he laughed. Jurgen laughed. Then Ziggy said, 'I think I'll call you George. Welcome to The Jubilee, George.'

Jurgen said, 'May I buy you a beer, Ziggy?'

Ziggy said, 'No thanks George, I've got one ear.' He pointed at the stud in his lobe. Jurgen looked flummoxed. Then the penny dropped. Amidst more raucous laughter, Jurgen said, 'I see this is an English joke, yes?'

Later that evening a fight broke out between the women's darts team and their visiting opponents. The women's darts team didn't like getting beat at home and on the last leg, there was a danger that they might lose their record. One of the Jubilee women supporters knocked the arm of one of the visitors as she was poised to throw. Within seconds both teams and their followers were going at it hammer and tongs. An older woman in the corner who had come in with a shopping bag, started to throw the contents. Jurgen ended up with three broken eggs down his shirt front and a rasher of bacon stuck to his neck. The visiting darts team ran off and were pursued halfway to the bus stop.

On the way back to our house, Jurgen said to me, 'This is a very interesting pub. It reminds me of some of the ones near to the Reeperbahn in Hamburg.' He went on to say that he had felt nervous of some of the men in there, but then realised that the women were just as tough.

I'd been in some of those Reeperbahn pubs with Jurgen and our mate Peter Kaufmann who drove taxis there. There was one called Der Goldener Handschuh (The Golden Boxing Glove), it closed for half an hour a day just so they could swill the floor with hot water and disinfectant onto the pavement outside.

What Time Of Day Is It Lad?

Heather likes to tell the story of how one Saturday afternoon I went out to the market to buy a cauliflower for the Sunday dinner. The story ends on the punch line, 'And that's the last I saw of him for two days and I've no idea what happened to the cauliflower.' It's an entertaining story of pubs and drinking, but it's not true. All right, it's partly true. Go on then, mostly true.

I did go out to buy a cauliflower and I bought a grand big one. On the way back home I dropped on a couple of mates who were going over to Holmfirth for a few pints in The Nook. 'We'll not be long, we're just having the odd one or two.' Now, anybody who knows anything about pubs and boozing will also know that the biggest lie told in ale houses starts with those four little words, 'We'll not be long.' The Timothy Taylor's beer at The Nook was on form. Many years after this I saw Madonna on the Michael Parkinson show and I heard her say that her favourite English beer was Timothy Taylor's. I found myself wondering if she'd ever supped it in The Nook. We lost track of time that Saturday afternoon. Somebody said, 'We'll just have one more and then we'd best make a move.' Anybody who knows anything at all about boozing and pubs will know that the second best lie ever told starts with the five little words, 'We'll just have one more.' In Shakespeare's *Henry IV Part 1*, there's a classic pub scene set in The Boar's Head at Eastcheap. Falstaff asks the young Prince, 'Now, Hal, what time of day is it lad?' He gets his answer:

> What a devil hast thou to do with the time of day?
> Unless hours were cups of sack and minutes capons
> And clocks the tongues of bawds
> And dials the signs of leaping houses

And the blessed sun itself a fair hot wench
in flame-coloured taffeta.

We stayed in The Nook until chucking out time. I can't remember what time I turned the key in my house door. I woke up the next morning on the sofa cuddling up to a cauliflower in a torn carrier bag. Heather makes a joke out of it now, but she wasn't best pleased at the time. She's had a lot of fun and laughter regaling folk in pubs with that tale. That Sunday morning she gave me a severe telling off, told me that I stunk and that I ought to take a long look at myself in the mirror. And that's when the third biggest lie about pubs and boozing rears its head. You look in the mirror and tell yourself, 'Never no more.' I said it that morning and by lunchtime I was ready for a 'settler'. Just the one, yeah!

I have spent a lot of my social life in a quest to find a perfect pint. The pint that tastes lovely and chimes with the atmosphere of the pub surroundings. The pint that comes at exactly the right time, one that quenches a thirst, or that comes in a glass that you clink with good friends around a table. Sometimes I think I have found what I'm looking for, but every time I think I have found the perfect pint, something else happens and off I go again.

The sports writer Willis Hall once wrote that the greatest reward lying in wait for northerners comes after your team has won the Rugby League Challenge Cup. In 1983, my team Featherstone Rovers played Hull in the cup final at Wembley. Hull were then the team of all talents, every player an international, a number of them the cream of what New Zealand had to offer. They were such hot favourites that the bookies stopped taking bets on them. Somehow, Featherstone's team of coal miners, most of whom worked at the same pit, prevailed and they won. The article I read by Willis Hall said, 'As soon as the final whistle blows and your team has won, you will head back to the centre of London and find a mythical pub that serves Tetley bitter with a proper creamy crown on it.' I rubbed my hands at the thought of it and fantasised that because this was such a special win, this pub would have prices that didn't force you to say 'How much!?'. I never did find that pub. I'd like to find it, so the quest goes on.

I've come to realise that after many years of trying, what I'm really looking for is a place where I can be myself. A place were I can find friendship and camaraderie. Of course, beer greases the tongue and helps you to speak, but the atmosphere of the pub and the people you find there is what helps the beer taste good. I've come round to thinking that there probably won't be a perfect pint, an ultimate pub or even a greatest pub moment to point to. What there will be, and perhaps have been, is a series of moments when everything comes together like a spell. I've had a lot of them in my time.

Ron Crabtree was a complete one-off, a living legend of a landlord, a brewer of fine ale, a grumpy old bugger and one of the nicest men I ever met in a pub. Ron pioneered the microbrewery revolution when he set up the West Riding Brewery in 1980. By the middle of the 1980s he had his own pub, the Sair Inn at Linthwaite. The pub sat at the top of a steep hill called Hoyle Ing and was a solid, stone-built gem of a northern English ale house that looked like it had grown out of the landscape. It had a sign above the door of a pig sitting on a wall, after a local adage that said the locals put a pig on the wall to watch the band go by. Ron brewed beer in a lean-to at the back of the pub and had a contraption in there for recycling water. During the drought he filled his bath to the top without fear.

Ron was interested in local history, so the names of his beers reflected that. One was called 'Old Eli' after a former landlord, it was also the name of his dog. He did a skull-crunching beer of ridiculous gravity called 'Enoch's Hammer' after a tool wielded by the local Luddites when they were breaking weaving machinery. There was another called 'Leadboiler' and even a stout which he cheekily named 'English Guineas'. The pub was stone-flagged, had open fires in every room and animals were not just tolerated but encouraged. On a table at the side of the bar Ron had fashioned some cardboard boxes into a Georgian-style row of terraced houses. He called this his cattery. He had a fair few cats. The front of the bar was decorated with a vine of dried hops and there was all sorts of ephemera nailed to the walls in random fashion.

I don't know how I first heard about Ron's place. Perhaps somebody said to me, 'There's a pub near Huddersfield that you would love.' One Saturday, when Heather was away on a course and for want of nothing better to do, I bought myself a Day Rover travelcard and took the train to Huddersfield and a bus out to Linthwaite.

Ron had not long been open when I walked through the front door, he was still washing glasses from the night before.

'Yes, young man.'

I looked at a row of handpumps. At least eight of them.

'I don't know what to choose.'

'Well, I'll tell you what, you take your time making your mind up. I'm here all day, so when you're ready, give me a shout, I'm off to feed my cats.'

I liked Ron from the start. I watched him pour milk for his cats. He came back. 'Right then, have you decided?'

I hadn't.

'If I might make a suggestion. Why don't you start with the bitter and work your way down the line?' He winked and twitched his moustache.

'I'll give it a go.'

Ron pulled a pint for me and let it settle on the bar top. He tossed me a coin and said, 'Go and put something on the jukebox.'

I did as I was bid. The jukebox was as eccentric as the pub; Howling Wolf, Bob Marley, The Seekers, Aretha Franklin, Free, The Rolling Stones and Leon Rosselson's 'The Man Who Waters The Workers' Beer'. I'd never seen that on a jukebox before. It was like looking at the history of popular music. I put on 'Respect' and 'Something In The Air' by Thunderclap Newman.

When I came back to the bar, Ron had pulled himself one as well. He touched my glass, 'A good landlord always samples his ale,' he said and twitched his moustache again. We sipped our beer and Ron's cats lapped their milk. By the time Thunderclap Newman came to their third verse Ron was singing, 'Hand out the arms and ammo, we're going to blast our way through here.'

I sat at that bar all afternoon. I made conversation with Ron and a series of locals as they came and went. At three o'clock Ron said he was going to shut the pub for a bit while he had a snooze, something to eat and get washed and changed. I'd got over halfway down the line of beers.

'You'll have to finish off another day.'

'I might come back tonight. Is there anywhere I can go for something to eat?' Ron pointed me to a pub down in the valley that did dinners all day. At the Rose and Crown I tucked into roast lamb, new potatoes and mint sauce. After that I really ought to have made my way home. I didn't. I went for a walk and then fell asleep on some grass near a huge old mill called The Titanic. I woke up as the sun was going down and then made my way back up the hill to the Sair.

Ron said, 'I forecast that you would come back, now, which pump were you up to and don't dawdle because I want to fill a bucket of coal.'

I carried on down the line until I got to the big daddy of Ron's beers, Enoch's Hammer. It was delicious. I must have slurred my way through more conversations with whoever came in. I can't remember much of the context, but I seem to recall some of Ron's mates egging Ron on to tell the tale of how he was nearly prosecuted for flaunting the hosepipe ban by a fastidious council inspector. Ron showed the man with the clipboard his Heath Robinson contraption of pipes, valves and stopcocks that enabled him to recycle his water and sent him away with his tail between his legs.

The locals drifted off one by one, until it was just Ron and me left chewing the fat.

He said, 'It's not very often I see someone go down the line and enjoy their beer as much as you have.' I confessed that I wasn't in the habit of doing that sort of thing. There had been just once before. Heather and I were on a day trip to Plymouth on a day off when we worked at Woolacombe. We ended up in a pub called The Swan at Devonport. They had a similar number of handpumps with a huge variety of beers. I don't know what set

71

us off, but we both ended up sampling the lot. What possessed us to visit a museum after that is anybody's guess, but we did and we fell asleep in an inglenook fireplace. A museum worker woke us up just before they closed and we sprinted back across town to catch our excursion coach.

'What time does the last bus go?'

Ron twitched his tache, 'It's gone.'

That old maxim of time flying by when you are having fun was never truer than on that Saturday night.

'What am I going to do?'

Ron said, 'I've got that in hand lad. I've got a tent, you can put it up round the back.'

He dragged a foisty smelling, mucky orange canvas wrapped in frayed rope into the parlour. It looked like something Baden Powell might have camped in. Between us we pulled it into a little bit of garden out the back.

It was freezing out. I spent nearly half an hour trying to work out how to put that tent up and gave it up as a bad job when it dawned on me that I hadn't been given enough poles. I fashioned a kind of sleeping bag out of it and crawled in. I don't know if I slept much, but as soon as the sun came up I crawled back out, folded up the canvas and left a note saying 'Struck out early'. I then walked the four miles into Huddersfield and sipped a cup of tea to the sound of church bells while I waited for the first train.

I visited Ron Crabtree's pub many times after that. I took a lot of my friends there. Ron always greeted me warmly and announced my arrival like a herald at a regal function. 'Here he is, the happy camper!' I always joked about his tent without poles and he liked to remind me that it was the first time his tent had seen action since the Bickershaw festival.

Ron fell down and broke his hip. He brought his bed down into the domino room as he couldn't get upstairs. He died not long before his eightieth birthday. If ever they gave out medals for services to pubs and brewing, Ron Crabtree would have one as big as a dustbin lid.

Steeped In History

Volker is over for a visit. We're having some dinner. I've made a vegetable and cheese bake with fresh stuff from the allotment. Volker likes his homemade food, or handmade food as he calls it. The regional news programme *Calendar* is on the telly in the background. An item about two horses comes on. One of the horses is a huge dappled grey Shire called Extra Stout; he belongs to Sam Smith's brewery. The other is a minute Shetland pony that is being looked after by an animal sanctuary. The news reporter signs off his item with the line, 'So, there you have it, Britain's biggest and smallest horses and they're both from Yorkshire.' Volker laughs his head off. He is always tickled by Yorkshire braggadocio. He says that Yorkshire is the Bavaria of Britain.

A conversation about 'Extra Stout' the Shire horse leads us on to talk about Sam Smith's brewery and this develops into an idea for an afternoon out the following day in Tadcaster. We call for a pint in The Greyhound at Saxton and then go on to The Angel and White Horse in Tadcaster. At the bar we overhear an old man say that two of his mates haven't turned up for the brewery trip. He wonders if their might be a chance of reselling the tickets. We offer to buy them. Volker is in his eyeholes. Sam's is his favourite beer and the thought of a trip around the brewery is music to his ears. Especially when I tell him that the ticket price includes complementary beer at the end of the tour.

The bloke leading the tour is knowledgeable and boring. He wants, as my old Aunt Alice used to say, 'To tell the far end of the fart and which way the stink went.' He is particularly proud of the Yorkshire slate squares. 'Samuel Smith's is Yorkshire's oldest brewery and this system of brewing has been used here for well over two hundred years. In all that time the water for the brewing has been drawn from our own well many yards below our town.'

One or two people are stifling yawns and Volker whispers to me, 'I wonder what time the bar opens.'

'What you are looking at, at this moment in time, is the yeasty head that forms over the fermenting wort, which lies in a chamber below.'

And on and on it went. The old bloke who we got the tickets off was wisecracking behind us all the way round. 'I wonder if he's got another record to put on?' Then, just as we thought it might never end, the tour guide says, 'And now it's time to sample some of our produce, complementary of course,' and he pushes open a door to a comfortable lounge. The old bloke rubs his hands, 'Oh! How lovely, I thought you might never ask.'

The beer is like velvet. The old bloke fetches his pint over to where we are sitting. 'Do you know boys, it goes down like a silk stocking on a freshly shaved leg.' We sup up in no time and wonder if we might be allowed a second. Volker says to the tour guide, 'This beer is very fresh and delicious. May we pay for another?' The tour guide isn't sure what to say, but we see he wants to stick to the rule book in his mind. 'Well, we generally allow our guests half an hour to enjoy their beer. That's usually enough time for people to drink a pint, but I suppose if you would like another, it should be alright, though we don't have facilities for paying in here.'

Volker's eyes become twice as big as his belly at that precise moment. He goes over to the bar and fetches three more pints back. One for me, one for him and one for the old wisecracker. He winks at me. 'I believe we have approximately twenty-four minutes, how many do you think we can drink?'

Without more ado, the old lad drinks his second pint straight off, belches and says, 'By! It didn't even touch the sides! I'm up for it lads if you are.'

I don't know how many more we manage before we are politely told that the complementary bar is now closed. We come downstairs and into The Angel and White Horse by the back door. The old lad is still on our tail. He nudges Volker in the ribs and says, 'You're not rushing off lads are you? It'd be a shame not to have one for the road, I'm in the chair.' So we finish off with another in the bar. I mention to Volker that when the Australian cricket team flew to England for the Ashes series, they say the Tasmanian wicket keeper David Boon supped fifty cans before the plane touched down in London. The old lad dives straight in and says, 'Aye well, he'll have been on Foster's lager, it's like piss. He wouldn't be able to do it with Samuel Smith's Old Brewery Bitter. I bet I've spilt more ale down my waistcoat than them Aussie cricketers have supped.'

Volker reminisces now about a time when he had seen the Belgian anarchist folk singer Ferre Grignard in concert in Antwerp. 'He drank a bottle of Duvel for every song he sang and ended up with "What Shall We Do With The Drunken Sailor".'

Our pal finishes his pint. 'Right then lads, I'll bid you goodnight. I like to be up early me.'

We shake his hand. Volker says, 'Are you retired?' The old lad says that he has been retired for a long time. 'I'm nearly eighty kid, but I like to be up on a morning. I'm out walking before seven, then I have a good breakfast and I'm generally knocking on the back door at The Howden Arms by eleven. I had a session in there this afternoon with my mates, I think that's why they haven't shown up tonight. Young 'un's these days, they can't take their ale.'

Volker smiles. 'Where did you work?'

The old lad smiles. 'I'm from Tadcaster son. I worked where everybody else works in this town.' Then he put his cap on and tottered off.

Volker looks at me. 'Do you think he might have worked in the brewery?'

Volker has a real sense of history and tradition and a respect for older people that knows no bounds. I once did a brief job up in Buckie in the far north of Scotland and Volker decided he would accompany me and drove us there in his beloved Dodge van. We met an elderly school teacher with a beautiful Doric Scots accent and Volker became smitten by her. One day she invited us for a lunch of homemade Cullen Skink, a traditional smoked fish soup, and served it with three different types of oat biscuit. Volker lapped it up and wanted to know the entire history of the different oat biscuits. When the lady explained what she knew in her lovely voice, Volker asked her to go through it again just so he could listen to her. He loved language and the little nuances of it. But to hear language in the place where it came from was to him sublime. He especially liked to find the link between old Anglo-Saxon words and their modern English equivalent. One day at my gran's house, he heard her say to me, 'Sam that bit of cotton off the rug for me Ian.' Volker studied for a moment and then said, 'This verb sam, does it mean to gather?' I said that it probably did but had never given it much thought. Volker was as pleased as Punch. 'It comes from our word "sammeln" and it means the same thing.' Then he turned to my gran and said, 'You speak old German Mrs Fletcher.' My gran said, 'Bloody hell old lad.'

Volker decides that he wants to find a village in Poland where his ancestors came from. The village is barely on the map in a region the Germans call Schlesien. Volker has never been there before but believes it to be a kind of well spring. He is like an eel trying to navigate streams and becks to get back to the Sargasso Sea. We turn up in this village as dusk falls in a big, black Mercedes that crunches the gravel road under its thick tyres. We pull up outside of a low, breeze-block building. This building houses a convenience store that sells everything from washing powder to garlic, and it has a cobbler and a bar. We all troop inside. There's me, Jurgen, Volker and Marius, a Polish gastarbeiter who works alongside Volker and has become a good friend. In the bar are five blokes, two of them look like farm labourers, one is a painter and decorator and the other two look like they are retired. They have grey moustaches and are leaning on sticks. A young blonde woman greets us and tells us to sit at a table. She clears some glasses from it and gives it a wipe with a mucky dishcloth. We sit down and nod across to the blokes at the other side of the room, they nod back. The young woman brings a bottle of vodka and four small glasses. We haven't asked for it, but assume that's what happens here. She twists the top off the bottle and then throws the cap into a tin litter bin at the side of the bar. I laugh and say, 'It doesn't look like the cork goes back in the bottle in here.' Marius pours a little bit of the vodka onto the side of his hand between his thumb and forefinger and smells it. He then pours some into all four glasses and says, 'Na zdrowie.' We all chorus his toast. We down it in one. It is like fire. Marius says, 'It is a good one,' and pours us all another. He tells us that in some places you must be careful because the vodka is sometimes cut with industrial spirit, but he can always smell it when it touches his skin.

An old-fashioned bell tinkles over the door. Two old blokes with scythes over their shoulders walk in. They lean their scythes up against the wall and sit down next to the old lads leaning on sticks. It feels like we are in a Jacques Tati film. A transistor radio on a shelf behind the bar plays the Charles Trenet song 'Boum'. Above the radio is a calendar with a picture of a naked model with a snake draped round her neck. The dates on the calendar that have passed have been marked with a black cross, as though someone is counting down to something. Next to the calendar is a photo of the football team Górnik Zabrze. The players have moustaches and sideburns and the substitutes are dressed in old-fashioned tracksuits, the sort with a white stripe down the arm and baggy bottoms. The only other ornament to take the eye is a Chinese paper lantern. I can't put my finger on why, but I feel very comfortable in this place. It's just a spartan room full of blokes drinking and telling the tale. Most of them are dressed like my uncles in work clothes, it might be that that makes me feel at home. The young barmaid comes over again. This time she brings a chipped carving plate filled with crusty bread, cheese, pickled gherkins and salami. We haven't asked for that either, but we tuck in.

The locals cast the occasional glances towards us, talk about us in low voices and let out the odd laugh. I say to Marius, 'I don't want to go against local etiquette, but do you think we might order a beer to wash this lovely food down.' Marius talks to the young woman. She brings a tray full of beer.

One of the old blokes leaning on his stick can bear the suspense no longer. He wants to know what this group of strangers are doing in his local. Marius tells him that Volker's great-grandmother walked from this village back in the 1910s to find work in Germany. The old man's eyes light up and he asks Marius a few questions. Marius translates the conversation from Polish into German for Volker and Jurgen, then Volker puts it into English for me. Volker pulls out a photograph of his great-gran and shows it to the blokes around the table. The girl comes from behind the bar to look. She rests her hands on the shoulders of one of the scythe carriers to lean in and see. Five gnarled index fingers with blackened nails point at the image and the little house and orchard that is in the background. One of the men says that we should talk to the oldest lady in the village. He is sure that because she is nearly one hundred years old she will know something about the photograph. The old lady lives on her own in a cottage on the edge of the village that backs onto the woods. We decide to pay her a visit, but before we go we have another.

Jurgen pulls out his wallet. He tells the barmaid he would like to pay for the vodka, the beer, the food and another round for everybody in the bar. The barmaid puts her finger to her lips and shushes Jurgen. She then tells him through Marius that he can pay for the vodka and beer, but that the food is complementary. She also tells him that he shouldn't buy any drinks for the locals because they would then feel obliged to buy one back and they didn't have any money. Jurgen gives that wink and a nod of the head that cuts across all language barriers and means 'Don't worry, I get your drift'. He pays for our drinks and puts a bit on top. He whispers that she should put another bottle on the locals' table when we have gone. She winks back. We drink our drink alongside the locals. It's a complicated conversation in three languages, with me being the last to know what they are talking about. One of the old lads points at me with his stick and says something with a smile on his face. Through Marius and Volker they tell me that the old lad wants to know if I like Poland. For want of something better to say, I mention that I was a big fan of the 3,000-metre steeplechaser Bronislaw Malinowski. I pronounce the name wrong, the old man laughs and corrects me. We shake hands. Then we all shake hands with each other and go off to find the oldest lady in the village.

The oldest lady in the village lived in a Hansel and Gretel cottage. When she opened the front door we could see dried herbs hanging from her low-ceiling beams. She recognised Volker's great-grandmother and said that they had been friends when they were young, in the years before the First World War. We took another photograph with her in it, then left her with her memories. The Mercedes crunched the gravel outside of her house as we set a course for Zabrze.

Zabrze is a coal mining town. It's where Marius is from originally. We parked up outside a tenement block where his auntie lived. The auntie kept pigeons in a loft in the backyard. She also had half a dozen hens scratching in a pen. As we came round the corner she was collecting eggs from a nesting box and putting them into a small wicker basket. She put her eggs down to embrace Marius and then said hello to us. She saw that I was looking at the eggs in the basket. She took one out, took hold of my wrist and placed the egg into the palm of my hand. It was still warm. She then took out another egg, tapped it on a fence post and swallowed the raw contents whole. She indicated for me to do the same. I joked that I'd seen my grandad do that when he wanted to put a lining on his stomach before a drinking session. She waited for me to follow her example. I said I'd save my egg for my breakfast.

Marius's auntie had a table in the middle of the kitchen with a vinyl tablecloth on it and some candles. She lit the candles and then brought out plates full of pickled gherkins and salami. She reached inside the sideboard and brought out a bottle of vodka with a slight greenish tinge to it. Marius told us that this was Zubrowka, Bison vodka, and that it got its colour from a blade of grass from the wild European bison fields. He said that his auntie always kept a special bottle for when guests came. The working-class manners of where I am from demand that whenever I am offered special treatment or gifts I must at first decline. 'Oooh! No I couldn't! Oooh! Please no. No, you're spoiling me.' The working-class manners of coal-town Poland mean that you don't take no for an answer. Marius's auntie listened to my protestations and tutted. She opened the bottle. She breathed on a glass with an audible sigh and wiped it by lifting her pinny. I put my hand over the glass and measured an amount by turning my thumb and forefinger into a small bird's beak. The auntie knocked my hand away with a firm swipe and poured a glass full to the brim. Then she stood with her bottle poised and waited for me to take a drink. I took the daintiest of sips and told Volker to tell Marius to tell his auntie that it was lovely. The auntie laughed and made an action to suggest that I should drink it straight off. She said something to Marius. He said, 'My auntie asks me if you are a girl and wonders if you would like apple juice in it?' I drank the Zubrowka straight down. The auntie slapped me on the back and poured me another. She then put some salami onto a piece of bread and fed it into my mouth with her fingers, like I was a baby bird in a nest.

Not long after that trip Jurgen and Volker paid us a visit at home. We went to Bradford for a curry at The Kashmir. After the curry somebody took us for a drink in the Polish Ex-Servicemen's Club. On a wall there was a photograph of Górnik Zabrze Football Club. That team must have had a very successful year sometime in the early 1970s. Volker said, 'I think we have seen that picture somewhere before.' We sipped vodka and looked around the room at a lot of stocky old blokes in flat caps and overcoats.

At some time in the middle of the 1980s, Volker and Jurgen took me to a bar in the Bergisches Land called Restauration. The pub had been in the same family for over a century by then. In 1905, Wilhelmine Kupper, a daughter of a local brewing family, married Fritz Römer Senior. They ran the Restauration until old Fritz died in 1931. His son Fritz took over then and didn't alter a thing. The pub I walked into with Volker was exactly the same as the one Fritz became landlord of all that time before. He even used the same hand-painted beer glasses. Volker told me that they were an old German measure from the days before the metric system. I found out later that Germany had adopted a metric system in the 1870s so those glasses must have been very old. The beer was Wickuler Pils and came out of a porcelain font dispenser that was the centrepiece of a free-standing mahogany bar from the art nouveau times.

Fritz was an early pioneer of motorbike racing. He rode a Norton and regularly visited the Isle of Man TT races as far back as the 1920s. He was disabled after falling off his motorbike while still a young man. His accident left him with a withered left arm. When he poured the beer he would lift his lame arm with his good one and place it on top of the tap, then as quick as a flash he'd swing a beer pot under the tap. He brought the beer to the table one glass at a time. Fritz was a bird shooter and wore the traditional clothes of the German woodsman; dark green with a felt hat complete with feathers. His shoes were like clogs and he wore them without socks or laces. He spent a lot of his time sitting in a rickety wooden chair with a filthy sheepskin thrown over it. His one-eyed sheep dog sat next to him with its tongue out and panting. He only got up when someone came in and by the 1980s this wasn't too often because the place had gone to wrack and ruin and it smelled a bit rough. Fritz was grumpy but friendly and seemed to like it when younger people came to see him. When Volker was tour managing for John Martyn in Europe, John insisted on taking the band there if they found themselves within a fifty-mile radius of the place.

From the outside the Restauration looked like a typical big house in the Bergisches Land, a mix of grey shingles and fachwerk with window frames and shutters painted mid-Brunswick green. The window frames needed attention and everything seemed a bit wonky, but if you went there between noon and eight in the evening the old door was usually open. Fritz told us that at one time the door was rarely closed. The pub had been built originally to serve the nearby Dornaper lime quarries and was filled with thirsty quarry workers washing dust down. When you walked in you came to a kind of entrance passage with a tiled floor. On the back wall was a tinplate Stollwerck chocolate vending machine from the 1880s, it was a long time since it had sold chocolate, but it was a proper antique. Not long before Fritz died some robbers came and put a broom handle between the handles of his door to lock him in and stole his machine in broad daylight.

As you turned left to go into the bar area you spiralled back in time. The tables were beech wood and scrubbed so often with beer and warm water that they had developed a patina smoother then milk. There was a blackened stove at one end that kept the place warm and a wooden bird cage hung from the ceiling. Around the walls were wooden cases filled with stuffed birds; a pair of jays, a woodcock, grouse and woodpeckers on a branch. The wallpaper was browned but you could still make out the colours of hunters on horses tearing across the fields. There was a piano with a keyboard that looked like a mouthful of missing teeth and old oil lamps with blackened glasses. When Fritz roused himself from his sheepskin chair it was like watching a ghost moving across a film set.

When he was in the mood, Fritz sometimes pulled his chair across to join us at our table. Volker translated for us, though he said it was difficult at times because Fritz spoke in an old dialect and used verbs and descriptive words that Volker hadn't even come across in German. One day the talk came round to motorbikes and Volker got Fritz to talk about his visits to the Isle of Man. I happened to mention that one of my hometown sporting heroes was a motorbike racer called 'Tripey' Dan Oldroyd.

'Tell the story Ian, I will translate,' Volker said.

I told them that Danny Oldroyd was a bit of a local rebel. He lived in Pear Tree Cottage surrounded by motorbike parts. He had been a biker all of his life. In 1926, he tried to represent the Sunbeam team in the TT races, but they told him that seeing as they already had the best riders in Europe they didn't need a tripe shop owner's son from a coal-mining town. Danny was undeterred. His mother funded him to enter as an independent rider and waved him off to Liverpool and the Isle of Man ferry with the words, 'Good luck Danny and a merry wind to your arse.' I paused to take a swig of beer and Volker started to translate. I watched Fritz nodding and smiling. Danny was successful that year, he finished fourth and beat all the other Sunbeam riders. He went back the following year and was winning, but came off his bike at speed and had to retire. Volker continued with his translation. Fritz shook his head now and started to laugh. I asked Volker to tell me why Fritz found it funny. Volker laughed now. 'Fritz says he can remember this Danny Oldroyd. He says he met him the year he fell off when he was winning. He says that Danny hit a sheep and that is what caused him to fall off.' Fritz lit his gone out pipe and leaned back in his chair, like a man remembering. Volker and I talked about that moment for years after.

Indirectly, through Volker's brother Jurgen, I ended up in a German bar with a similar timeless charm a few years later. The bar was called Brauerei zur Sonne and a tiny lady called Wilhelmina Bickel, or Brui Mina, was in charge. She was a few weeks short of her 90th birthday when I met her at the end of a chain of serendipitous moments that seem now like a surreal dream.

Jurgen, Peter the Hamburg taxi driver and I went on a Guinness drinking tour of Ireland. We set off in Cleary's bar in Dublin, went on to McDaid's, Hartigans and The Palace and more. Over breakfast next morning, Peter worked out that we had visited ten pubs. Jurgen said, 'This Guinness must be very good quality beer without chemicals, because my head doesn't feel like we saw ten pubs.' Then he had a little chuckle to himself. He said, 'We are here for ten days. If we continue at that pace, it might be possible to drink 100 pints of Guinness to celebrate our Irish adventure.' We drank our pints in Galway, in Sligo and Westport and found ourselves in a place on the Clew Bay in County Mayo.

One morning we stood looking out to sea. An old man told us

that John Lennon once owned one of the islands we could see and that hippies had lived there. This same old man said we should climb the Reek and pointed to the Croagh Patrick mountain behind us. He told us if we really wanted to do it properly we should take off our shoes and do it in our bare feet, like the pilgrims. We did climb the mountain but kept our boots firmly laced. Halfway back down we came across a young Bavarian woman who had fallen. Her ankle was swollen and she had one or two cuts and bruises, nothing serious, but she was shaken up a bit. This woman was on a solo tour of Ireland, her name was Gabriella, Gabi for short. Between us, we helped her down the stony paths and, when we reached the bottom, took her to the pub. I think the landlady found a bandage and strapped her up and she was no worse for wear. We spent the rest of the day boozing. Gabi seemed pleased to be talking in German to the lads, after struggling for a fortnight to understand what people were saying to her. There was a gypsy fortune teller in the bar and Jurgen let her read his palm. She told him that he would live a long life. Peter had just come back from a trip to the Andes, he said that wherever he went he seemed to be followed by fortune tellers and didn't want his future telling. I wasn't bothered either. The gypsy looked me in the eye and said, 'You will meet a wise old lady.'

About a month after I got back from the Irish trip, I got a postcard from Bavaria. It showed a typical Bavarian beer drinking scene on the front, with blokes in leather pants and women in blonde pigtails clanging pots together. On the back in small, neat handwriting was a note from Gabi, 'Thank you for helping me on the mountain.' With it was an invitation to visit her father's farmhouse if ever I found myself in Bavaria.

Gabi lived in a traditional town called Oettingen, a very unusual place. Half of the town was dominated by Protestants and the other half was Catholic. The dividing line ran straight down the middle of the main street. The houses on one side were baroque architecture and on the other the Protestants had built their half-timbered houses. Storks built their nests on the chimneys on both sides. The whole town seemed obsessed with low flying aircraft, what Gabi described as 'the low flighters'. There were signs up everywhere protesting. Oettingen is also home to one of the world's most automated breweries. Gabi told me that a beer pipe under the ground brings beer to the town. Like our own Sam Smith brewery, it prides itself on producing beer for the best possible price. It's a good drop of beer too, brewed to the ultra traditional *Reinheitsgebot* law of the Middle Ages which permits only malted barley, hops and water to be used in the brewing process.

I flew to Munich and Gabi picked me up and drove me to the family farm outside Oettingen. We spent the daytime swimming in the River Wornitz, a tributary of the Danube, and the evenings sitting round a huge kitchen table eating traditional food and supping strong local beers. Gabi's dad sat at the head of the table with a plastic spatula in his hand and seemed to amuse himself swatting flies. Her mother always seemed to have a pan full of stew on the go and a bread knife in her hand. I felt like I was in a fairy tale or a nursery rhyme.

On a morning I used to see an old lady going in and out of a barn chucking corn from a tin bucket to the geese. My curiosity got the better of me. I asked who the woman was. 'That is Fraulein Gertrude.' Gabi then told me that her grandfather had found Fraulein Gertrude and her sister in his cow field one morning during the war. They had been walking for days without anything to eat and were exhausted. He let them sleep in the barn and they had stayed there ever since. The older sister had died, but Gertrude still helped around the farm and preferred to carry on sleeping there. She rarely came into the house. Then almost as an afterthought, she said, 'We can ask her to play piano for us.' We did. Fraulein Gertrude came to sit at the piano. She wore traditional clothes and had cow muck splashed up the back of her bare legs. She played classical pieces for a good hour without saying anything. I never did get to know Fraulein Gertrude's story. Gabi hinted that before the war she had been to a conservatoire.

One night, Gabi drove me deep into the countryside to a

village called Obermögersheim. She said that she wanted to surprise me. She did. We walked into a pub even older than Fritz Römer's place. This was 'Brauerei zur Sonne' and they had been brewing and serving beer there since 1471. The current head brewer was like a wren. She was ninety years old and as bright as a button. This was Wilhelmina Bickel, better known as 'Brui Mina', Germany's oldest brewer. Mina looked like something out of a Bruegel painting with her black headscarf and white apron on. In her own way she was a living tourist attraction. There were no other customers in the pub that night. Mina said that we should sit with her. She went to a pantry and took down a flitch of almost black bacon and brought it to the table. She sliced pieces off it and we ate it cold with pickled gherkins and rough rye bread. She gave Gabi her homemade apple juice and fetched me glass after glass of her strong home-brewed ale. Time ticked past on an old wall clock, but the brew meister carried on talking with Gabi translating as she went. We tried three or four times to stand up and leave, but each time Mina put her little hand on my arm and insisted we just sit and listen. Over a period of about four hours she told her story.

Mina's husband Rudolph had passed away some years before, but she continued brewing with the help of some local men. Much of her time these days was spent going through her paperwork. She brought to the table piles of papers tied with string to help tell her tale. A lot of the papers had wax seals or official looking stamps on them.

Gabi listened while Mina went on an extended riff that had a sad refrain, punctuated by sighs. Then Gabi turned to translate to me. 'Brui Mina has dedicated her life to trying to sue the French government for reparation. Some officers of Napoleon's army stayed in this house and refused to pay their bill.' Mina kept her eyes fixed on me all the time Gabi was talking. When she finished, Mina waited for me to respond. I didn't know what to say back. I just said, 'I have never met anyone who was owed money by Napoleon,' and I laughed. Mina didn't laugh. She pulled out sheaves of paper, letters to various recent French presidents, de

Gaulle and Pompidou, Giscard d'Estaing, as well as older letters written by her grandfather to presidents at the time of the third republic.

In the summer of 1806, Napoleon's army were advancing through this area on their way to fight Prussian troops at the Battle of Auerstedt. Some officers requisitioned quarters at Brauerei zur Sonne in the time of Mina's great-grandparents. They supped their ale and ate the bacon over a period of weeks and then rode on without paying. One hundred-and-eighty years later, Mina was still refusing to let the matter drop. It was nearly midnight. Mina went scurrying back and forth, bringing more and more papers. There was a letter of support from Franz Josef Strauss, minister-president of Bavaria, and a medal he had awarded her. She put the medal on. I couldn't help but laugh at first, but had to turn away, so as not to upset the apple cart. To Mina, and to a certain extent to Gabi, this was serious business.

I've thought about this night a lot since and I've come to realise that I learned an important lesson about how memory works and, more specifically, how not forgetting works. My great friend Karen Babayan, a woman of Armenian heritage, once told me that her ancestors had packed their story to take with them along with their possessions. So, there we were, in a bar, two friends in their twenties with a 90-year-old woman wearing a medal on her shawl drinking beer and eating bacon, talking about how much money Napoleon still owed to the bar we were sitting in. Perhaps that is exactly what the last two centuries of European history comes to. Laughter and not forgetting, beer and bacon.

Less than a fortnight after I returned home, I got a letter from Gabi. There was a clipping from her local paper in it, an obituary notice for Brui Mina, she had died just a few days after we had sat listening to her. Mina took her responsibilities as a living tourist attraction seriously. Everybody who paid the slightest bit of interest to her was rewarded with a signed beer mat. The beer mat bore the name of the pub and the slogan 'Seit 1471'. Mina signed her name down one side, her date of birth and then put the day's date down the other side. I still have my souvenir beer mat, signed in gorgeous copper plate handwriting with an ink pen. I suspect Mina's descendants are still telling anybody who will listen that Napoleon still owes them money.

What Shall We Do With The Drunken Sailor?

The Top House, or The Featherstone Hotel to give it its Sunday name, was built as a showpiece in 1893 for a long-gone brewery called Carter's of Knottingley. The Carters were a well-to-do family with land. Nobody can remember what their beer tasted like now, but I knew an old bloke when I started drinking in the 1970s who told me that 'Once you'd tasted Carter's you didn't want owt else'. The Featherstone Hotel may be unique in that it has had less than a dozen landlords in its 120 years of history and only two in the last 63 years. Joe and Dot Cording kept it from 1955 until 1985, and Pete Green has been at the wicket since then.

The most famous landlord was a man called Thomas Jeffries Sides. Sides was landlord from 1902 until 1916 when he moved into politics and became Mayor of Pontefract. He was an entrepreneur, part-time violinist and self-proclaimed benefactor to the local poor. He regularly tossed coins and oranges to urchins in the street when he took his morning walk. He had been born in Pennsylvania in 1874 and moved to Yorkshire with his English parents as a young man to become a contractor at Featherstone Main pit. He became The Top House's second landlord and set about his task with relish. He organised fancy-dress balls, shooting matches, brass band contests and athletics events on his own track that he had built behind the pub. He even had his own rugby league team and, when cinematography came in, he bought his own equipment and filmed local matches and then charged punters a small fee to come and watch games that were projected onto a white wall in the bar. Sides was a massive self-publicist and his pub became well known.

It was in The Top House that I first met Arnold 'Sooner'

Millard. It was in the years after the miners' strike, I was in my thirties, he was in his sixties. And for the next fifteen years or so we became the unlikeliest pair of drinking buddies you could imagine. Arnold had not long since returned to our home town from Portsmouth. He told everybody that for the previous thirty years he had been at sea. The local lads whispered that the nearest to the sea he had been was when he fried onions and burgers for tourists in a van parked near the harbour. He came back during the miners' strike and was immediately chased by the bobbies after trying to steal scrap metal from a quiet pit yard. I met him one afternoon in The Top House. He saw me rolling a cigarette and said, 'Can you spare a Rizla paper for an old sailor?' I gave him a paper. He said, 'Nay lad, it's no good without a bit of bacca in.'

'Bloody hell! I'll roll it for you if you want.'

'Very kind of you young man. Roll one for Ron as well will you.'

'Ron?'

'Aye, later on!'

I liked his cheek. We puffed on our roll-ups and I stared out of the window.

'Penny for them.'

I smiled.

'I'll tell you what I always say.'

'Go on then, tell me what you always say.'

He looked crestfallen.

I felt sorry for him. 'I'm sorry, carry on.'

He came over like a Chinese philosopher. 'I always say, if you don't know where you're going, wait while it snows.' He let his statement hang like a puff of smoke.

'Go on, enlighten me.'

'Well, if you haven't made your mind up by then, at least you'll have some footsteps to follow.' He took his glasses off, breathed on them, wiped them with his hankie and put them back on. 'I can see clearly now.'

I came to know Sooner's sayings and wisdoms well over the next years. He had thousands of analects, mostly simple-minded observations, some of them profound, others ridiculous, all of them connected to the time of day, the weather, the season, to light, dark and shade and mostly to pubs and beer. We were once in a pub in Keighley. We'd had a couple of pints and Sooner was moaning that the barman was giving short measure. 'I'll fettle him,' he said, 'lend me a tenner and I'll get the next round in.' Sooner went to the bar and asked for two pints. The barman pulled two and left a big crown on them. Sooner waited for him to come back with the change. As the barman went to hand it over, he said, 'Do you think you could get a whisky on top of that beer?' The barman smiled and said, 'Yes I can do that sir.' Sooner took the change and said, 'Well put some more bloody beer in then!'

He entertained me and everyone within earshot in The Top House for three hours that day I first met him and cost me half an ounce of tobacco and five pints of bitter. It was better than going to the circus. He was a liquid acrobat, a juggler of beer glasses, a clown, a tamer of lions and a memory man all rolled into one.

Sooner Millard was what the lads on the building sites would jokingly call 'a blackguard of the finest order', but I put up with his cadging, his cheating and his double-dealing because he was great fun and I came to love him. The term incorrigible rogue might have been invented for him. We went all over together. Once I was contracted to work on an arts project near Abergavenny in Wales. I asked 'Cheesy' Davis if he would drive me there. Sooner overheard us talking and announced, 'I think I'd better come as navigator, because Cheesy gets lost when he goes beyond Doncaster.' Cheesy said to Arnold, 'Do you know where Abergavenny is?' Sooner put on a look of mock indignation. 'Do I know where Abergavenny is? I bloody ought to do. I once courted a barmaid from there.'

'When?'

'1952!'

'How do you know that?'

'Because Sir Harry Llewellyn came from that way on and I was there when he won the show-jumping gold medal at the Helsinki Olympics on a bay horse called Foxhunter.'

You could ask Sooner the simplest of questions and every time he came up with the most convoluted answer. If you challenged him on it, he would throw his hands in the air in mock indignation and say, 'It's true and I can substantiate my statement.' As catchphrases go it was a bit of a mouthful, but Sooner loved to say it and it was repeated so often that it became a Top House staple.

Cheesy said, 'Well I think the roads will have changed a bit by now.'

'Don't thee worry about that Cheesy! Abergavenny hasn't moved as far as I know, so trust your old skipper Sooner and I'll navigate us safely there.'

We set off at five o'clock in the morning to beat the rush hour traffic. We hadn't gone more than ten miles when I heard Sooner take the cap off a bottle of beer in the back seat. He supped two more before falling asleep somewhere south of Sheffield. We woke him up when we stopped for a pot of tea and a bite to eat. He went back to sleep again and only woke up as we passed Gloucester. As we approached Monmouth, Cheesy winked at me and said out loud, 'I'm going to need your help in a bit Arnold.' Sooner didn't flinch, 'Well that's not a problem, you've done very well so far Cheesy, but once you get on the outskirts of Abergavenny I'll take over.' Cheesy and I will never know to this day how he did it, but Sooner leaned over the gap in between the driver and passenger seat and said, 'Right lads, this is called Lower Castle Street, just carry on up here and after a bit it bears right, just follow it round, then look for St John Street and you want to be right again there and then up to the top of Flannel Street.' Cheesy followed Sooner's mad map. 'And then you can park up just here.' I asked him if he was sure he had brought us to the right place. He smiled, 'No! But we're not far off and in the meantime there's a pub here called the Hen & Chickens and they open at half past ten and by my watch it's just about that now.' We asked him how he knew about that pub. He told us that was where his girlfriend had worked as a barmaid in 1952. 'I wonder if she's still working here?'

Once in Beverley during Folk Festival week, we found ourselves in the White Horse, the ancient gas-lit pub known to locals as Nellie's that I'd visited with Sean and Burt after sleeping the night in Sean's car. This was in the time before Samuel Smith's brewery, in an act of social vandalism, banned music, television, radio and therefore people having fun in their pubs. Sooner, having swilled down four or five pints of hand-pulled brewery bitter in the early afternoon, was in full voice. He sang 'I'll Take You Home Again, Kathleen', 'Blaze Away', 'The Very Thought of You' and, in honour of the pub we found ourselves in, a song called 'The Soldier's Dream', or as Arnold called it, 'The White Horse'.

'See them pass by! There they go, what a show. Those guardsmen. All hearts beat high, at the sight of this grand array.'

There is a local councillor in, she may even have been a mayor. She sits at the bar in a wide-brimmed hat and a flowered satin frock, looking like she's just come back from Ascot. I go to the bar to refill our glasses and this lady taps me on the arm. 'I say! Your friend is absolutely splendid, I'm having great fun listening to him.'

'Yes, he likes a sing-song, but I have to keep an eye on him, because he's never sure when he's had enough and he can get a bit raucous.'

'Oh! Don't deter him. This is a treat. Do you think he might accept a drink from me?'

I want to say that I'm not sure that's a good idea, but before I can open my mouth, the lady spins on her stool and shouts across to Arnold, 'I say, would you like a little chaser with your beer?'

Arnold stands up to attention and salutes the lady. 'Madam, I am very happy to tell you that a drop of gold would not go amiss.'

I whisper to the lady, 'He means he'd like a whisky.' The lady turns to the barman and says, 'Pour a whisky for the gentleman in the straw benji.' The barman presses a short glass under the Famous Grouse optic. 'Would you like anything in it sir?' I know what's coming next. Arnold winks at the barman and says, 'Aye! Another one!' The lady chuckles and says, 'Better make that a double.' The barman presses again, just as the whisky flows down into the clear plastic bubble. Arnold downs the whisky in one go and then announces, 'Bloody lovely!' He then takes the froth off his pint of Sam's and announces again, 'Bloody lovely!' After this he makes his way a bit unsteadily around the table and goes to stand in front of the fireplace. He pulls out a clean handkerchief from his top pocket, flicks his wrist with a magician's flourish and wipes his chops. He calls the room to order.

'Madame Mayor and assembled company,' he says, then clears his throat. 'You have greased my clack, put lead into my pencil and released the nightingale that nests inside me. Now, beneath the light of these old gas mantles, you will be well entertained.'

He continues with his repertoire. He sings, 'The Miners Dream of Home' and wrings every last drop of pathos from it, pausing at one point to dab his eyes. He follows this with Nat King Cole's 'Mona Lisa' and then decides he'd like to yodel. The yodel is terrifying, a catarrhic growl of a sound like a wounded wolf. Sooner then announces, 'Ladies, gentlemen and assembled dignitaries, my impersonation of the marching band of the Grenadier Guards.' He tightens his lips then loosens them and lets out a breath that vibrates like a raspberry. He reckons to play the drums in imitation of a military band, lifting his hands up to the level of his nose. From somewhere deep down in his throat comes the sound of a skirl of bagpipes. He marches back and forth in front of the fireplace and ends his mad parade by saluting. There is a round of applause. Sooner bows deeply and loses his balance, knocks a table with his hip and the beer from the fullest glasses splashes over the marble surfaces of the tables.

Sooner flops into a corner seat and says, loud enough for the people in the next room to hear, 'The singer would like another glass of refreshment, I'm as dry as a cork.' The lady councillor leaves her perch at the bar and comes over to our table. 'We have been royally entertained I must say.' Arnold winks, cocks his head to one side like a thrush and takes the lady's hand. He kisses her on the knuckles. 'Madam, I am delighted to make your acquaintance. As soon as I get my wind back, I shall tell you some tales of an old sea dog.'

I know what is coming next so I try to intervene. 'Arnold, you are a very good turn, but sometimes you are on too long. I think this lady might like to enjoy her drink in peace now.'

'Nonsense!' says the woman. 'Pray do tell.'

Sooner needs no more encouragement. He picks up his empty short glass and says, 'The story I am about to tell goes well with a dram of gold.' The councillor turns to the barman, 'Another double whisky please.' I see the glint in Arnold's eye.

'I have crossed the equator many times in my career and three times passed through the Panama Canal. I have rolled along the Gut in Malta, loaded cauliflowers onto a leaking tub of a boat in Sardinia. And the prettiest girls I ever saw rolled cigars on their thighs in Venezuela.' It is a well-practised introduction and one I have heard in ale houses the length and breadth. I decide to leave him to it and go for a walk round the market.

When I get back, I see straightaway that the lady councillor is engaged in an act of diplomacy between the barman and Sooner. I put my hand on his shoulder and say, 'What's up now?'

'He's trying to stop me entertaining 'em.'

The councillor takes me to one side and says, 'He's getting a bit carried away with himself and he's been swearing very loudly. He's also been passing his hat round trying to make a collection.'

'I've told him twice now, if he doesn't knock it off, he's barred.' The barman has a look on his face that says he means it.

Arnold puts his hat back on and mutters under his breath. He says, 'Right then, I'll just finish off with a limerick that I brought back from the Bay of Bengal.' I close my eyes and try to disappear.

> There was an old man from Calcutta
> Who went for a peep through his shutter
> And all that he spied
> Were his wife's hairy thighs
> And the bollocks of the man that was up her.

The councillor nearly faints. The barman grabs Arnold by the lapels and says, 'You're barred!'

Sooner loved to have a ride out to pubs in the countryside. Whenever Jurgen and Volker came over, he'd have a bath, put some clean clothes on and wait to be invited. In this way he got nights out paid for at The Greyhound at Saxton, The Kings Arms at Heath Common and any number of trips to Leeds. We took him for a curry at Bradford one night in The Kashmir. He ate a plateful of Lamb Rogan Josh with half a dozen chapatis. Volker mentioned that he didn't think Sooner would have liked curry. Sooner winked. 'I was eating spicy food in the Middle East when you were still in short britches.'

One night we went over to The Mason's Arms at Ackworth. It happened to be quiz night and they were just giving out the papers as we got there. The first prize was £5 and a gallon of beer and, because nobody had scored the maximum for a long time, the 'snowball' had reached £50. Sooner rubbed his hands together, 'Pass one of them papers here kid, me and my young partner here like a quiz.' There were thirty questions, the usual pub fare of 'Which football team this' and 'Which TV drama that'. After twenty-nine questions I was fairly sure that I had answered every one correctly. Sooner was rubbing his hands even more vigorously now. The last question was, 'What is the capital city of Corsica?' I said to Sooner that I wasn't sure. He grinned. 'I know!' Then he paused for dramatic effect. 'Go on then spit it out.' Sooner just smiled and then said, 'It'll cost you twenty-five quid and four pints.' I said, 'Do you think that's fair? I've answered twenty-nine questions and you've got one and you want me to go halves!' Sooner folded his arms, 'Well kid, take it or leave it. It's me that's going to get you across the winning line.' I said, 'Go on then what is it?' He whispered, 'Ajaccio. We used to load up with cauliflowers there when I was in the merchant navy. It's where Napoleon came from.'

'Are you sure?'

'You could bet your bollocks on it.'

I wrote down Ajaccio on both sides of the paper. I then folded it down the middle, tore down the crease and handed one half in and kept one for marking. There was a break for sandwiches and sausage rolls. One or two of the locals sighed when they saw Sooner stuffing some into his jacket pocket. Then the answers were read out. We did have the first twenty-nine right. Sooner said loud enough for everybody in the pub to hear, 'Here we go kid, come to Daddy!' One or two people scowled across at him. 'The capital of Corsica is Ajaccio.' Sooner didn't wait for the quiz master to ask if anybody had thirty out of thirty. He held the paper aloft and said, 'Here you are kid, thirty out of thirty for the lads from Featherstone.'

There were more scowls from the locals. Some of them had been trying for three months to win the jackpot and now it was left to two interlopers, one of them a gloating old devil who had squashed half a dozen sausage rolls into his pocket and was crowing. I counted up the number of people in the taproom and worked out that we could afford to buy everyone a pint and still have change. I went to the bar to collect the winnings and said to the landlady to get everyone a drink. When I came back, Sooner said, 'I have just heard what thy has done.' I suppose I was looking pleased with myself and thought that he might say it was the diplomatic thing to do. He didn't. He said, 'You are as soft as a bag of knackers, don't speak to me anymore, you have cheated a poor old pensioner out of twenty-five quid!'

It took three days for him to come round. He never let me forget it and claimed I owed him twenty-five quid for years after.

He generally came up to our house for his lunch on Saturdays after we'd done the morning shopping. We always called into John Hill's butcher's shop because John still made brawn the old-fashioned way from the pig's head. Sooner loved brawn on hot buttered toast. We had homemade vegetable soup as well, so it was a good lunch. This particular Saturday, Sooner was bad with his insides so didn't want to eat his brawn and only managed a spoon or two of soup. He said he felt rotten. We always went to the Bradley Arms after lunch, but on this day Sooner said he wasn't sure if he could. That was unheard of. Heather offered him some herbal tea. He tried chamomile. I found a tin of Andrews Liver Salts at the back of the cupboard and he had a glass full of that.

He didn't come to the pub, he said he was feeling worse. He put the tin of Andrews in his jacket pocket. About an hour later I was in the taproom. The phone on the bar rang. Cathy the landlady answered. I watched her face. She started to frown and then said, 'Well I don't think that sort of language is necessary Arnold, but you can tell him yourself, he's standing right next to me.' She gave me the phone. 'You are nowt but a bastard! I'm fucking dying here and it's your fault! And your lass an' all. She's put a spell on me with her fucking herbs and you've tried to poison me. Them Andrews Liver Salts were three years past their sell-by date.'

Those Who Believe Their Giraffe Is On Fire

My rugby career at The Jubilee pub didn't last long. I was there for two seasons and spent most of the time sitting on the side of the field waiting to jog on as a substitute if someone got a knock. I think I probably played half a dozen full games and only then because some of the better players had Sunday morning hangovers and couldn't be bothered to turn up to get knocked about on a muddy field somewhere at the arse end of Wakefield. Then, when I was thirty-seven years old, long after I ought to have known better, I let myself be talked into giving it another go.

The Railway Hotel had become the headquarters of Featherstone Miners' Welfare rugby team. The pit had been shut down for a good ten years or more and most of the things that had been associated with it had long gone, but the Welfare, which had once been a vibrant organisation for sport, dancing, music, reading rooms, annual flower and veg shows and all sorts of social cohesion, maintained its rugby team. The lads who played there on a field at the back of the railway lines were proud of their history and refused to change their name. One or two of them were coal miners who had been moved to the handful of remaining pits, but they were mostly local lads who worked in factories or were on the dole. They were always looking to recruit new players. One night I was in The Railway when the lads came in after training. We'd had a few pints and they were teasing me. Some of them had seen a team photograph of The Jubilee. I was the only one on the picture with long hair and a beard. They said that I must have been the only hippy to have played rugby league and laughed. Paul Windmill, who played in the pack and became a good friend of mine, said, 'Why don't you come up and train with us, it'll keep you fit.' I made the excuse that I didn't have any kit. Paul's brother Chris said, 'I'll lend you a pair of my boots, they might be a bit fast for you, but you're welcome to them.'

I don't know whether it was because I wanted to be part of something that kept pride in our town, or because I was just plain daft, but I agreed to turn up the following Thursday to train. I loved it. There was great camaraderie there, the lads looked after one another and it was a very good team. One day on the bus to Dewsbury Moor, our coach Brian Kellett said, 'Do you fancy a game?' I nodded. Chris Windmill got injured in the first ten minutes, his replacement 'Boots' White nearly had a knacker pulled off at the beginning of the second half and Brian looked at me. 'Right get stripped, you're on and you'll have to play prop.' I had never been in a scrum before, never wanted to be in one and had no real idea of what to do. I packed down opposite a terrifying giant and accidentally head butted him as we bent. He reared up, bundled my shirt front up into his fist and said, 'Are we going to take it fucking steady or what?' I'm fairly sure that I took it steady after that.

I was at the Welfare for three or four years. The sport was great and the drinking sessions after the matches legendary. Sean Tomlinson once gave us a barrel of beer to sup at an end-of-season fuddle in the changing rooms. We rigged up a temporary bar with a handpump, borrowed pint pots from the pub and laid out crisps and quavers and all sorts. It was a very strong brew, I don't think many of the lads got up for work the next morning.

Paul Windmill and I and some of the other lads from the Featherstone Miners' Welfare team decided to form the Friday Teatime Club. We didn't really need an excuse to call in for a pint after work, but convinced ourselves that if we were part of a teatime club, it was somehow healthier than just going for a pint. The Teatime Club was a moveable feast. We started at The Railway in Featherstone and when that shut down for refurbishment we went to The Rock at Glass Houghton.

The Rock was a classic Victorian ale house. There was a

drinking lobby as you went in, two front rooms either side of a passage and a big back room warmed by a black-leaded Yorkshire Range. Some of the older end would tell you that a previous landlady baked rabbit pie in the oven of that range. When the beer was on form, the old men described it as being like 'a drop of rabbit gravy'. Even the lavatories in that pub were beautiful. They had porcelain hand basins on walnut legs with old-fashioned taps and mahogany doors on the stalls with brass fittings. The flush boxes bore the name of Thomas Crapper, the man who patented the floating ballcock. Thomas Crapper was born in Thorne, South Yorkshire. The beer in The Rock also came from Thorne, from Darley's, one of the great unsung breweries of Yorkshire. It was a great pint when it was on form, but like chip shop vinegar when it was on the turn.

The Rock stood at the side of a steepish little hill off the main road. It backed on to a rocky outcrop. The whole area had at one time been stone quarries. My gran told me that her brothers Edwin and Fred, who had both been killed in the war, drank in The Rock when they were Young Turks in the 1930s. I always felt good when I pondered that I probably stood in my great-uncle's footprints when queuing at that bar.

It's funny how some pubs can have their own unique culture, even though they might be only a hundred yards away from other pubs. This was the case with The Rock. It had always been different to other places nearby. For many years it had a folk music club upstairs and attracted a lot of the top musicians. It also had a famous pot-holing and caving club; some of the best pot-holers in the north were members at The Rock. The village of Glass Houghton was once a place of glass makers, hence its name, and stone quarrymen. In the middle of the Victorian times, a coal mine opened and then a brickworks. As a consequence, the little village ended up with more than its fair share of watering holes. Even today there are four pubs, a big working men's club and an allotment club. The village though has changed beyond all recognition.

After the pit shut in the 1980s, a vast area of land was freed up for development. Where once had been a coke works and slag heaps, there is now a big out-of-town shopping centre and an indoor ski slope. Glass Houghton pit shut down in 1986, within a year of the big strike ending. It's hard to imagine now what the pickets huddled round the braziers at the pit gates would have made of it all. What can you say to a bearded hipster who comes to where you once worked to buy a snowboard and a set of ski poles? How many people who sat supping Darley's in The Rock the night before a day shift down the pit could have foreseen that they'd be flogging Berghaus fleeces a few hundred yards from the pit-head baths? Strange and surreal things happened in the immediate aftermath of that strike. I knew of a bloke in South Elmsall who started making cowboy boots and there was one in my home town who opened an iguana shop. Somehow though, The Rock manages to retain its 'caught in the moment' atmosphere. A strange thing happened in the early 1990s when the company who owned The Rock decided to rip out all of the original Victorian features only to replace them with a Retro Victorian look, but the atmosphere survived.

Our Friday Teatime Club became popular, some weeks we had up to a dozen turning up and we filled the right-hand parlour as you went through the front door. It could be a bit lively. One Friday I got far more ale down me than was good for me. I didn't eat my dinner. I had the guilty man on my shoulder for a week after. The following Friday I told Windy and the lads that I was going to leave off the beer for a bit and ordered half a pint of lime and soda. Windy told me not to be so soft, but then surprised me by announcing that he too would be keeping off the beer. 'Let's see who can last longest. I'll bet you a Mars bar that you will give in before I do.' I could never drink anywhere near as much beer as Windy could, but I was fairly sure I could beat him at not drinking. I accepted the bet. Eddie Roberts, a big raw-boned lad from Sharlston who played in the pack alongside Windy, thought we were both crackers. After every sip of his beer he said, 'You don't know what you are missing, this beer is on top form today.' I had four glasses of lime juice and soda and then I gave in. Eddie was right. The beer was on top form and tasted even better after pop. Windy had another glass of Britvic before he gave in. He teased me mercilessly. 'Well, I can beat thee at drinking and I can beat thee at not drinking an' all.' He's been saying this to me ever since, every time the subject of laying off the beer comes up in conversation.

Attendance at the Friday Teatime Club dropped once the novelty wore off. We decided to form a 'Sunday Morning Surrealists Club' instead. This club's stated aim was to celebrate eccentricity. The club had two rules, the first was, you could only be in the Sunday Morning Club if you believed that your giraffe was on fire, the second was that you had to drink a glass of Dubonnet before your first pint of bitter. We ended up with some right misfits and free spirits in that club. Lenny Moxon, a retired carpenter who could drink more than a fish was one. We let him in because we liked his catchphrase: 'I know where you can get it for a pound a pint.' Llewellyn Woodfield, who didn't know if he was on this earth or Fuller's, joined us and of course there is no show without Punch, so Sooner Millard joined. When we told Sooner that one of the club rules was that you had to believe your giraffe was on fire, he didn't flinch. He stood up and started to sing.

Queen Mary, Queen Mary how oft you've been told
To stop milking bullocks before they grow old
There's galleons and stallions and things of a kind
But there's never good milk when there's bollocks behind.

We let him in on the strength of that.

The Sunday Morning Club went on occasional Saturday trips to old market towns. One such trip took us to Skipton. We nearly didn't get there after Llewellyn was almost arrested for pissing in a plant pot on Platform 2 at Wakefield Westgate station. He managed to convince the railway staff that he'd had his medication altered recently and that he'd been taken short. We had a crawl round most of the pubs in Skipton and called for a late lunch in Ye Olde Pork Pie Shoppe. Llewellyn waited outside the shop clinging to a lamppost after telling us that he didn't like to spoil his beer by eating food. We stood on the pavement dropping pork pie pastry crumbs. Llewellyn pretended to read an historic buildings sign that pointed to the castle. He actually couldn't wait for us to finish our pies and show him the way to the next pub. Windy nudged me and winked. 'Are you interested in old castles Lou?'

'Oh! Yes, I like a look round while I'm here.'

'Smashing! It's just that we generally have a cultural hour after lunch and visit a museum when we're on tour.'

Llewellyn gripped his lamppost even tighter to control his swaying. His face was a picture.

Surrealism was not out of place in The Top House. There was a man who drank in there called Joe Wynn. Joe was dry, a man of few words. In years gone by they would have called him a simple bugger, but he was very funny. He had a lot of Mickey taken out of him, but none of it was cruel and he was loved and well looked after.

Bob Sheldon took a photograph of Joe holding up a pint of Guinness. This gave landlord Pete Green an idea. At the time Guinness had a promotion that featured two pints of Guinness, one the right way up and one upside down beside the slogan, 'Pure Genius'. Greeny opened the frame round the poster and placed the photo of Joe in the middle, so that the picture featured the two pints, Joe smiling with his beer and the words 'Pure Genius' over the top. Every time the darts team were playing away they took the poster with them and explained to the landlord of the pub they were visiting what they were up to. The poster was then placed in a prominent position on a wall near the dartboard. At some point in the evening, the home landlord would pretend to recognise Joe from the poster and buy him a pint of Guinness, which Greeny settled up for. This went on for a good few weeks and the lads in the darts team and their followers started to persuade Joe that he was part of a nationwide advertising campaign and that he ought to be having something out of it. Jingo said he'd seen the poster in a club at

Flamborough, somebody else said they had seen it at Leeds, and a bloke who had just come back from his holidays in Benidorm said he had seen the poster in the bar where Sticky Vicky did her act. Joe took it all in good part, but guessed that he was being sent up. One night he asked Shenny, Pete's barman, to put a mark on the poster frame. Shenny did as he was bid, but with a non-permanent marker pen. Kenny Broxup wiped the mark off on his way to the match and put it back on again before they got back. Joe was flummoxed, but told Shenny, 'I know they're kidding me. They've got two of them pictures. One with me on and one with a bloke who looks like me. Don't say owt though, because them at Guinness have to buy me a pint every time somebody recognises me. I'm the mystery man.'

Bob showed Joe a trick one day that nearly ended up with him breaking his jaw. He wet a one penny piece and pressed it with some force onto his forehead until it stuck. Then he bent down to bar-top level and tapped his chin onto the bar so that the coin fell off, the idea being that you caught the coin in your mouth before it rolled away. Bob tried it three or four times and couldn't do it. Of course Joe wanted to have a go. Bob said that he would have to remove his false teeth because it was a dangerous trick to try with dentures. Joe took out his teeth and looked like a Cumberland gurner. Bob went through the rigmarole of wetting the coin and pressing it onto Joe's forehead, but removed it, though Joe felt as though it was still there. He whacked his chin on the bar three or four times, harder each time. The lads had to stop him when he was in danger of doing himself some damage.

Joe got locked up for three months in Armley jail for not paying his poll tax. On the day of his release, Greeny organised for him to be picked up at the prison gates in a stretch limousine. Joe was released on the same day as a good few other poll tax protestors. Two or three of the pub characters went in the limo to welcome him home. Mark Norris couldn't resist winding the window down and shouting to the ex-cons walking down the street. 'Joe owns a fleet of these cars. It's just that he doesn't agree with the principle of the poll tax.'

One afternoon Joe turned up in the taproom with a black suit and tie on. Sooner went straight into winding-up mode. 'Ooooh! I say Joe, you do look smart. Have you been for a job interview?'

Joe stated the obvious. 'I've been to a funeral.'

It transpired that Joe had been to the funeral of somebody who nobody else knew and the lads in the bar weren't sure that Joe knew him either.

Sooner carried on, 'You must like flan and Swiss rolls you Joe. It's only February and you've been to six funerals this year already. I don't know why you don't apply for a job as a professional mourner, you've got the right face for it.'

Joe ignored Sooner, he was used to being baited. He turned to Greeny and said, 'It's like this Peter. I always like to turn up for a funeral, because if you don't go to theirs, you can't expect them to turn up for yours.' Peter did a theatrical second take.

Sooner looked across. 'Do you know Joe, when I look at you, I realise that I have got a chance in this world.'

A local character called Steve Kidd ran an anarchic disco, come quiz, come cabaret, come comedy show on Sunday nights at The Top House. It was great fun while it lasted. In between songs from the seventies by Edison Lighthouse and The Doobie Brothers, Steve would keep up a continuous banter of wisecracks, dares and quiz questions.

'Well, well, well, ladies and gentlemen, that was Wild Cherry and a song called "Play That Funky Music White Boy". Now, the first man in this pub over the age of forty to come to me wearing cherry-coloured lipstick wins a Mars bar.'

As daft as it sounds, middle-aged women would rummage through their handbags to find lipstick in order to paint the lips of pot-bellied, middle-aged men and then there'd be a race to the disco unit. And because this was downtown Featherstone, this would involve a certain amount of pushing, shoving, shoulder charging and the odd rugby tackle. Pots often went flying from tables, anybody in the way would have to sidestep and false teeth were often lost in the scramble. And all for the sake of a mini Mars bar from an out-of-date selection box.

One night Steve went a bit too far. 'Girls and boys, that there was Kid Creole and The Coconuts, doing "Annie, I'm Not Your Daddy". And speaking of kids, there is a large goat chained to a post on that grass outside, the first person to bring the goat to me wins a bottle of Liebfraumilch.'

There was indeed a goat, a ram, tethered to a post on some wasteland at the bottom of Kimberley Street, with the sort of chain that you could pull a truck with. It was a huge goat with horns like a Nubian ibex. It was a vicious bugger on top of that, even the local stray dogs steered clear of it. Tony Clarkson, who everybody called High Arse, and Eddie Roberts decided to wrestle it into the pub. It took some doing, but somehow they managed it. The goat kicked, tupped and snorted its way through the front room scattering drinkers in its wake with High Arse and Eddie trying to slow it down with its chain. It stunk to high heaven as well. Sue the landlady went mad. She threatened to bar Eddie, High Arse, Steve Kidd and the goat if they didn't get out. She spent the rest of the night spraying perfume and air freshener.

Part II

Don't Get Too Much
And Spoil Your Dinner

All I'm out for is a good time – all the rest is propaganda.
Alan Sillitoe

Overleaf: In The Nook at Holmfirth. Me and Martin Oxley in full flight.

Afore The War

My grandad had a routine for every day. Monday to Friday he got up at half past four. My gran got up with him. They did it without an alarm clock. Years of regular day shifts at the pit had put them into a rhythm-spell that they couldn't break. My gran cooked breakfast while my grandad got himself ready. He put on his pit clothes and placed his clogs against the back door. In the early seventies, long after most men had given up on clogs, he still preferred them. He liked it that clogs didn't flex and you could sit on the heels of them when you knelt. He liked to eat sheep's brains with a fried egg on top for his breakfast. When it was time to leave for the bus to the pit, he'd put on his cap and scarf and wait by the open back door for my gran to come and kiss him. No matter that they might have been arguing and not talking to each other properly, they still embraced and kissed on the doorstep at half past five every weekday morning. When my grandad finally retired from the pit at the beginning of 1977, he'd had more than forty years of morning kisses. After he died, my gran liked to have half an hour talking about him most days. I asked her about the ritual of kissing him every morning before the pit.

'Your grandad got hit with a big stone when the roof came in.'
'When was that?'
'Afore the war.'
Everything in our house that was a long time ago happened 'afore the war'.

'Why does that mean you have to kiss him every morning?'
'Nay lad, you do talk bloody half-soaked for somebody who's supposed to be educated. If I don't kiss him and he doesn't come

home, I'll never get over it and besides, I've done it for that long now, if I don't do it, it might bring bad luck.'

The daily rhythms cast their spell much further than getting up with the cock's crow. On Saturdays Grandad liked to have his walk, to get, as he said, the dust off his chest. We walked to The Spread Eagle at Wragby, a pub about three miles out in the countryside. He strode out like a man measuring a distance and my little legs went like bees wings trying to keep up. At the pub I sat with a bottle of pop and a bag of crisps on a bench while he supped in the murky interior with his mates. I counted cars going by, magpies, and read my comics cover to cover. I identified clouds, the leaves on various trees and learned to recite all of the rugby league teams in alphabetical order, their home grounds and nicknames. Occasionally Grandad would come out and say, 'Don't go near that road and if anybody talks to you come and tell me. Do you want another bottle of pop? Don't get too much and have it spoil your dinner.'

'Grandad, do you know that the nickname of Oldham rugby team is the Roughyeds?'

'Aye I do. And do you know if you behave yourself, I'll buy you some pigeon milk toffee.'

Sunday morning. My grandad eats bacon, egg and Cirio tinned tomato and swills it down with a pint pot full of strong Rington's tea, with four spoonfuls of sugar in. This morning he isn't full so cuts himself a thick doorstop of bread and wipes it round the frying pan. He claims the grease puts a lining on his stomach for the beer he is about to drink in the club. My gran says, 'I'm surprised there isn't enough of a lining on your insides with the amount you supped last night. Tha was plaiting them long legs well enough at midnight last night old lad.'

He ignores her at first and carries on swigging his tea.

'And don't be swaying this afternoon. I don't want folk looking through their windows at you, it's a bloody showing up.'

He takes another swig and lights a Woodbine. 'I'm not bloody plaiting my legs and swaying when I'm coming home from that pit every day am I?'

'No! And I'm not supping bloody Tetley's when I'm cleaning this house all day and pressing them bloody shirts tha goes out in.' And on it goes, a Sunday morning chorus of twittering sarcasm, baiting banter, like two magpies fighting over a piece of rind. And Gran always has the last word. 'And when are you going to learn how to cut bread? You're like my bloody arse! Just look at this, I could put that under the door as a wedge.'

It's a nice morning. When it's sunny, Grandad likes to sit for an hour on the front doorstep glaring at the racing pages in last night's *Green Final* and wondering why every horse he has backed has failed him. He watches men coming back from the allotments with armfuls of gladioli for women like my gran who iron white shirts and starch collars. He flatters women who go by who have had their hair done the previous afternoon and shouts to kids playing cricket against a chalked gable-end wicket that they are holding their bats wrong.

At quarter past eleven he comes back in. He strips down to his vest and swills his face under the tap over the white pot sink under the kitchen window. He rubs his hands down his chops, thumb down one side and index and middle finger down the other. 'Do you think I could do with a scrape Hilda?' My gran, a foot shorter than he is, looks up and manoeuvres him into the light coming through the back window. 'I know you had one last night before we went out, but I would if I were you.' The previous evening, before he had got ready to go out, he had picked me up and said, 'Does tha want a bit of chin pie?' Before I could do anything he rubbed his whiskers on the side of my face and left a red mark on my cheek.

The shaving ritual starts. An old white pot mug with the handle missing is taken from a shelf behind a homemade curtain under the sink. Freshly boiled water from a kettle on the stove is poured into a big earthenware puncheon and then a few drops of cold water from the tap are added. Grandad then starts vigorously brushing a shaving brush on a piece of soap and dips it into his handle-less mug. The lathering is a work of art. He paints the lower part of his face from just above his ears to his Adam's apple, then works the shaving brush back and forth above his top lip and under his nose. A fresh blade is put into the razor and then the scraping starts. With every scrape he swills the razor head in the puncheon. I don't need to watch my grandad to know he's shaving, I can hear him. While he is shaving my gran cleans his shoes for him. She puts on the polish with a brush, spits on them and then buffs with rags made from a pair of her old bloomers.

By ten to twelve he is ready. Clean and freshly-ironed shirt, gold cufflinks, dark suit with twenty-two inch, turned-up trouser bottoms, a thin silk tie and sleeveless Fair Isle pullover all topped off with a raglan sleeved overcoat, whether he needs it or not. At five to twelve he ruffles my hair, goes to kiss my gran and offers his neck to her. 'Smell that!' She pushes him away and says, 'Go on with you and don't spill any!' He has a last look in the mirror, straightens his tie and licks his finger to smooth his eyebrows. 'I'll be off then.' He strides down to the Girnhill Lane Working Men's Club, which is not much more than two hundred yards from our front door. In the space of that two hundred yards he blows a kiss to my Aunt Ethel who is washing something in the kitchen window like she always is. He tackles the football off some lads at the top of the street and stands on it, 'Come and get it off me then?' When they try he rolls it back towards himself and shoves them away with his long arm. They get fed up and wait for him to give it back. He picks it up and pretends to hand it over. When one of the lads reaches for it, he throws it to the other one. My gran calls him a tormentor. Grandad's Uncle Alf is an ancient man who lives at the end of the row. He's always sat out on a stool by his front door. He says the same thing to my grandad every Sunday morning, 'Don't thee be getting too much ale and spoiling thi dinner and have one for me.'

As soon as my grandad disappears round the gable end, my gran boils a pan of milk to make herself a beaker of Camp coffee. The label on the Camp coffee bottle shows a Scottish military officer in full regalia sipping from a cup on a saucer in front of a campaign tent. His Sikh retainer stands by and a flag flying over the tent displays the words 'Ready Aye Ready'. My gran blows across the top of her milky coffee to cool it down. The smell of hot chicory essence fills the kitchen. She goes to sit in the yard. It is an earth yard. The potholes where the rain gathers are filled with broken red house bricks or ash and cinders tipped from a bucket when the fire grate is cleaned. Twelve families share this yard. On Sunday mornings the sounds from the radio waft from back doors along with the smell of dinners being readied. Doris Pyatt our next door neighbour comes out with a rug to shake, whether it needs a shake or not. The rug is just a device to come out to see what is going on. Margaret, our neighbour on the other side, comes out because she has heard voices. The 'kalling' as the neighbours in this yard like to call it, then commences. There is no agenda, just freewheeling gossip about who has been falling out with who this week, milk being turned sour by that thunderstorm on Thursday, the quality of a recent delivery of mussels at Ted Amery's shop and how idle and daft a lot of the husbands in this street are. All of this accompanied by flapping washing and the wireless, the signal drifting in and out like a tide.

A posh BBC voice announces, 'Here in London it is twelve noon, in Cologne it's one pm and now, home and away it is time for *Two-Way Family Favourites*.' This is followed by an orchestral arrangement of 'With a Song in My Heart' and a request show for people with family in the army camps of northern Germany.

By quarter past twelve my grandad orders his second pint. He'll tell my gran that he has no more than three. He actually sups three an hour. He stands at the corner of the bar wreathed in Woodbine smoke. He passes the time of day to anybody going past. If it's a man who hasn't been to the pit that week he will call them a 'glass back' or suggest that they are as soft as shit. If anybody dares to answer him back he'll say, 'There's more work in a glass of Andrews Liver Salts.' There is no compromise with Ted Fletcher. He thinks that everybody should work hard and then play hard. He believes he exists to win coal and when work is done, a man is entitled to drink a few pints. He calls it 'slaking the dust'. In the club and at rugby matches he comes across as a right hard case. The least little thing can set him off, cause him to roll his shirt sleeves up and want to fight somebody. One Sunday afternoon John Tom Hope drank a few mouthfuls from my grandad's pot. My grandad bunched John Tom's shirt front up into his fist and threatened to drop one on his chin. The following Sunday, John Tom was suspended from the club for a fortnight for stealing another member's beer and my grandad was put on a warning for threatening violence.

I sit with Doris Pyatt on a big piece of sandstone by her back door. We wait for Billy Cotton to come on and shout 'Wakey Wakey'. Once he has done that it seems like everything is right in our world. Ken Dodd has a show that seems to revolve around a catchphrase, 'Where's me shirt?' And then it's time for *The Clitheroe Kid* to come on. Jimmy Clitheroe likes to listen at keyholes at No. 33 Lilac Avenue. My gran says the same thing she does most Sundays, 'I don't want to listen to that cheeky little bugger,' then goes off to talk to her budgie. She keeps a blue budgie in a cage below the electricity meter on the wall. She has taught it to say 'bugger off'.

'Tell Jimmy Clitheroe to bugger off Mickey. Go on say "bugger off"!'

The budgie cocks its head to one side like budgies do. It looks in its mirror and bobs up and down. Then it pecks at the millet.

'Come on say "bugger off" for your mam. Come on Mickey say "bugger off". Oh, arseholes then, because you're neither use nor bloody ornament.'

As soon as she comes away from the cage the budgie says, 'Arseholes, bugger off!'

My grandad doesn't move from his perch at the end of the bar. At ten to two, he wonders whether he should have just one more pint or whether he has time for two. He doesn't want to spoil his dinner. He will square up to any man in this club without fear, but he is terrified of my gran's tongue. A few weeks earlier he got far more beer down him than was good for him. He came home drunk and late for his dinner. My gran had hers without him and put his between two plates in a cooling oven. She made him eat his dinner cold. He managed to eat a bit of potato and meat while my gran glared at him and called him all names under the sun. In the end he couldn't stand it and jumped up with his plate and scraped his dinner onto the fire back. My gran cried. He realised in that instant what he had done. He said he was ashamed of himself and went to bed to sleep off the beer. At teatime he cut a couple of cold slices off the joint and made himself a sandwich. He got ready to go out again.

At quarter past two with pans full of potatoes and cabbage bubbling on the stove and the smell of Yorkshire puddings coming out of the oven, my gran tells me to go to the top of the street to see if he is coming. It's my job now to stand on the corner to watch and wait. I see a procession of men swaying out of the front door of the club. They zigzag up the lane and sing whatever they have just heard the turn singing. They mix up the words and make up ones they can't remember. Taproom tenors and barroom baritones to a man.

> Some day I'm going to write
> The story of my life
> It's all about the night we met
> and tra lal la
> I can't forget
> the road you smiled at me eeh eeh!

As soon as I spot my grandad, I run back to my gran's kitchen to let her know. The two hundred and odd yards from the club's front door to our back door can take him anything from two minutes to a quarter of an hour, depending on how many people he stops to talk to on the way. In this time my gran mixes cornflour, hot cabbage water, meat juices and Burdall's Gravy Salt to make her gravy. She then puts out the dinner. She seems to know by instinct how close he is to reaching home and, no matter how long it takes, she has the dinner on the table just as he lurches in the door. He has two bottles of milk stout, one in each side pocket of his raglan overcoat. My gran doesn't look up. She places a dish of homemade mint sauce onto the centre of the table and still without looking up says, 'You best take your coat

117

off if you are stopping.' He takes out the milk stout and places it on the sink side. He removes his coat and jacket and hangs them on a peg behind the stairs door and then swills his hands under the tap. 'By! I'm bloody famished, pass me that salt and pepper over.'

'There's plenty of salt on it already, I should taste it first.'

'I'll just have a sprinkle.' He taps the bottom of the salt pot on the table once or twice and then shakes out far more than he should, it covers his dinner like twinkling stars.

My gran says under her breath, 'If I aren't bloody blessed.'

I have never seen anybody demolish a Sunday dinner like my grandad. We aren't even halfway through ours when he is scraping the last bits of gravy off with the edge of his knife. 'Bloody lovely! Have I to wash up?' He says this every week.

And every week my gran says, 'No, leave them, it'll give me something to do with me not being so busy.'

Grandad ignores the sarcasm, perhaps he doesn't realise that's what it is.

'Right then, I'll just have an hour.' And off he goes to bed.

My gran waits for him to get to the top of the stairs. She waits for the sound of shoes dropping onto the bedroom floor and then reaches inside his jacket pocket. She takes out his packet of Woodbines and helps herself to two. She lights one on the gas ring and goes to blow the smoke into the yard. She nips the cig halfway and puts the tab in her pinny pocket. She then starts to wash up. I dry the pots and place them onto the table. Gran then sides them. Only she knows where everything goes, a jigsaw puzzle of plates, pans, glasses and dishes that somehow fit into a sideboard that has shelves lined with old wallpaper.

Next on the wireless is *Semprini Serenade* with the introductory words, 'Old ones, new ones, loved ones, neglected ones.' Gran pours out a bottle of milk stout into her favourite glass and relights her Woodbine. She curls up on her favourite armchair with her legs underneath her and flicks through the latest *Red Star Weekly*, licking her fingers as she turns the page. By the time *Sing Something Simple* comes on she is halfway down her second Woodbine and has opened the second bottle of milk stout. Cliff

Adams and his singers run through a medley of popular songs accompanied by Jack Emblow at the accordion. These songs are thematically linked around girls' names, the moon or the weather. Sometimes the links are very tenuous, the singers can go from 'Roses of Picardy' to 'Michael, Rows the Boat Ashore' and back to 'Rose, Rose, I Love You'. Alberto Semprini plays a piano version of 'La Mer'. My gran puffs away, sips her stout and joins in. She has a Woodbine rasp rougher than Janis Joplin's. She's loud, enthusiastic and she rolls her 'R's' like Mireille Mathieu, but she really can't sing. As the show plays out, my gran joins in again.

> Sing something simple, as cares go by,
> Sing something simple, just you and I.

At tea time, my grandad wakes up, eats a sandwich of cold meat, then gets ready to go out again. At half past four the following morning he'll get up, put his clogs near the door and start all over again.

Soaking It Up In The Seventies

My father and mother hardly drank alcohol. On the second glass shelf of our china cabinet there was a bottle of VIP sherry that somebody bought us for Christmas. It sat on that shelf from one year to the next. I think my mother had a small nip out of it now and again from a thimble-sized glass that sat on the same shelf. On Sundays Mam might treat herself to a bottle of Pony, which was like a cheap cream sherry that came in a miniature bottle with a tin foil wrapper. It was sold with the slogan 'The little drink with the big kick'. Sometimes she had a Babycham from a chalice-like glass after her tea. She'd sit on the settee with her legs up beside her, plump up the cushions round her and watch *Hawaii Five-0*. She'd say 'Oooh! I do like a Babycham!' in imitation of an advert that was popular at the time and then add, 'But all t'bubbles go up your nose.'

My dad didn't like drinking. He said alcohol didn't agree with him. There was a darker reason that I didn't know for many years. He didn't talk about it, but his father had died on the way home from a drinking session when Dad was just a boy. It was probably enough to put him off for life. He once got drunk in The Junction pub after he was plied with strong ale by people who ought to have known better, and another time he came back a bit merry after he and my mother had been to see Gene Pitney at Batley Variety Club. Apart from that I can't recall my dad going to ale houses. He was much happier with his hens on the allotment or with his inner tubes in a washing-up bowl mending endless punctures.

There was a short period of time when I was about fourteen that Dad and Mam, in an attempt to stick a plaster on a failing marriage, decided to start going out on a night to try and enjoy themselves.

There was a Hofbrauhaus in town, a faux Bavarian lager house. The beer was served in litre measure steins by buxom blonde-haired wenches in pigtails and aprons made up to look like Alpine peasants. There was an oompah band who dressed in lederhosen and green hunters' hats with feathers in. At a certain time of night the band would strike up with a medley of polkas and everybody jumped onto the tables to do what they thought was a German folk dance. They'd clang their pots together, slap each other on the arse and then sit back down in all the ale they had spilled on the benches. My dad fell off the table one night whilst doing the actions to a bawdy song that was going round at the time called 'Having A Gang Bang'. At the end of the night the tenor saxophone player got his moment in the spotlight when he improvised a version of 'Yakety Sax', the Benny Hill theme tune. A cue for half-soaked blokes to chase half-pissed women around the long tables. Sometimes my mam and dad went on to a seedy nightclub called Annabelle and Tiffany's, where an incoherent DJ announced the latest hits through a muffled microphone. I knew when they had been there because I would wake up in the back bedroom to hear my dad careering down the back alley knocking tin dustbins over.

'We've got a thing they call radar love… we've got a light in the sky…'

My dad follows this with a drum solo on next door's dustbin lid.

'I've been driving all night my hands wet on the wheel.'

The sash window from next door slides up. 'Oi! Pauline, tell that barmy bastard to shut it or I'll come and shut it for him.'

'Sid, Sid! Be quiet now, you'll have all the bloody street up.'

'Brenda Lee is coming on strong.'

'I'll give you fucking Brenda Lee you soft twat.'

'Get thi bloody head back in afore I throw a rotten tomato at you.'

'I'm on a fucking day shift, I've got to be up at half past five.'

'Well get your head back in and pull your curtains.'

The back gate slams.

My dad walks into a line full of washing. 'You've left your washing out Pauline. I'll fetch it in, in case it rains.'

'No, leave it, you'll drop it all over the yard and I'll have to do it again. I said leave it! … Ohhh! Look at what you've done now, my bloody best tea towels!'

I hear a jangle of keys.

'I can't find the keyhole, have you got a torch? Here use my lighter.'

'Give them keys here, let me do it.'

'I can do it. I'm not bloody useless y'know.'

'You are!'

'I am what?'

'Bloody useless!'

The door at the bottom of our staircase creaks open. I hear muffled giggling. I count the steps: one, two, three, creak!

'Shush! You'll wake the kids up.'

I hear the bedsprings. Then the thud of one shoe off. Thud! Another shoe off. 'I say lass, give me a hand with this belt, it's tangled and I can't get it unfastened.'

'Bloody useless!'

Within minutes I hear snoring and farting. Then I hear my mother talking to herself. 'If I aren't bloody blessed.'

Ten minutes later my dad is up again. He's stumbling around the front bedroom. Then he's pissing. I hear the sound of a stream hitting the bottom of an enamel bucket, then a softer sound as the bucket fills. It seems to go on for ages, a never ending stream. My dad starts to sing again. Softly to himself this time. 'We've got a thing that's called radar love… radar loooove!'

Then he's back in bed again. 'Let me have a bit of that eiderdown love.'

My dad's flirtation with the Hofbrauhaus and Annabelle and Tiffany's didn't last long. Maybe just for the winter of 1974. After that he might have the occasional glass of Hull Brewery mild and the odd bottle of Mackeson Stout. My mam went back to her chalice of Babycham in front of the television. I never saw much drinking at home.

I may not have seen much drinking or drunkenness at home, but I didn't have to look too far to spot it. The first drunken man I saw on a regular basis was a bloke called Harry Phipps. Everybody seemed to know Harry and they put up with him when he was being a nuisance. The Girnhill Lane Working Men's Club shut for the afternoon at half past three. Harry would drink there until that time and then wait until the steward put him through the front door. Then he'd sit on a wall next to the allotments and mutter and sing to himself, only breaking off to talk to anyone who was walking past. He'd try to engage anybody who could be bothered to listen, mainly women coming home from Station Lane with bags full of shopping or kids on their way home from school. Nothing he said made much sense, he spoke in fragments, 'Always keep a straight back kid!' was one of his sayings, another was 'Prince Monolulu said to me!' whatever that meant. Harry lived up on the Coal Board estate. It took him ages to get home because he spoke to everybody along the way. My grandad told me that at one time he had been a Sergeant Major PT instructor. He said that when he was young, he had been one of the fittest men in Featherstone and he held the record for the fastest run to Pontefract and back from the bottom of Station Lane. The Girnhill Lane Club seemed to be full of men like Harry when I was a boy. Men who wore old brown suits with their tie skew-whiff, blokes who talked in surreal rhymes and riddles, old boxers, rugby players and athletes, old men who 'used to be'.

It was also the only place where my grandmother went out to have a drink. She went there every Saturday night. She had her hair done in the afternoon, a bath after her tea and put on her best dress and a dab or two of Tweed perfume before linking arms with my grandad and walking to the club. She sat on more or less the same seat every week and talked to the same people. At the end of the night Betty Wheatley would be cajoled to sing 'The Old Rugged Cross' and all the women would fetch out their hankies to dab their eyes. When she got home, my gran would kick off her shoes, roll down her stockings and sigh. 'Oooh! When Betty Wheatley sings, she breaks your bloody heart.' Grandad would reply, 'She will do, she's Welsh, they've only to open their bloody mouths and they're singing.'

The northern drinking culture came to me across the airwaves too. You would be hard pushed to find a regional dialect on television in the 1970s saying anything remotely more serious than 'Get down, Shep!' There were always one or two bit parts for workers in comedies set in factories or on dustbin rounds and in some of the grittier dramas, but even in the north you didn't get a northern voice telling you the news. Barry Hines once said to me, 'There's nothing the BBC like more than a costume drama. They love to dust off the top hats and long coats in their wardrobe department and throw in one or two parts for farm labourers in cloth caps with their comical accents.' And it was pubs that formed the backdrop for most of the tomfoolery. *Love Thy Neighbour* is now reviled as the most politically incorrect and racist programme ever transmitted on mainstream television, but back then it was the most watched sitcom. It had every stereotyped pub character going, including the old bloke in flat cap and muffler. His sole purpose seemed to be to say 'I'll have half' every time the show required cheap, canned laughter. When it came to beer, pubs and fun, there seemed to be plenty of scope for working-class people, as long as they were one-dimensional, politically neutral and daft.

The advertisers trying to sell their beer had a field day. Colin Welland, the Lancashire actor, did commercials for Younger's Tartan Bitter with a catchphrase that went, 'Tartan Bitter, worth passing a few pubs for.' Whitbread had their macho slogan, 'Whitbread, big head, Trophy bitter, the pint that thinks it's a quart.' And Webster's brewery of Halifax brewed Pennine Bitter 'For men of the North'. All of these were outdone by Tetley of Leeds who created a whole raft of commercials around a gang of mythical 'Tetley Bittermen' and coined the phrase, 'If you can't beat 'em join 'em.' They even used a real life pub, The Commercial, a back-street Leeds local as a backdrop. In the hot summers in the middle of the 1970s when lager took off, Harp promised that their lager 'Stays sharp to the bottom of the glass'.

Heineken relied on well-tried innuendo and suggested that their beer 'refreshes the parts other beers cannot reach'.

Beer drinking was of course a man's game, for blokes dressed in polyester shirts, kipper ties and Bri-Nylon trousers. These man could grow bushy sideburns and moustaches like Jason King. They could throw darts and walk into a saloon like John Wayne.

Granada Television pushed this stereotype to its limits when they created *The Wheeltappers and Shunters Social Club*. The show purported to be set in a working men's club where trays of foaming beer were handed across tables to fag-puffing ordinary people dressed in their going-out clothes. In reality it was a studio conceit presided over by middle-class regional television directors who wouldn't be seen dead in such a place. The whole thing was a charade presented by northern comedians. Bernard Manning sat at the corner of the bar with a cigar and a microphone pretending to be the club president, and Colin Crompton sat cloth capped behind a desk with a bell on it reckoning on that he was the concert secretary. The comic timing of these two meant it was funny. And the blend of entertainment of acts who were just on their way up, or usually on their way back down, made for even more fun. In this way, singers like Kathy Kirby and The Bachelors managed to keep flagging careers going. Old-time entertainers like Tessie O'Shea and Winifred Atwell got their chance to roll out the old stuff and some unexpected acts from America, who must have wondered what the hell was going on, made guest appearances. Manning rarely bothered to get up from his tall stool at the end of the bar. His main movement seemed to be to rest his half-smoked cigar on the ashtray while he muttered some witticism into a bulbous microphone about the next act. He took the mickey out of Crompton who had perfected the gormless look to a tee. It was Crompton though who had the best lines, once memorably telling punters, 'On behalf of the committee I would like to apologise. Last week's raffle prize was a divan suite, not a diving suit as previously announced.'

My mam and dad loved *Wheeltappers* and we all had to be quiet in our house when it was on. My mother was delighted when

Roy Orbison came on once to run through three or four of his big hits. Orbison had strangely become a bit of a fixture on the northern English theatre club and scampi-in-a-basket circuit. My dad was equally excited when The Three Degrees, who even more strangely had ended up on the same circuit, headlined and sang 'I Like Being a Woman'.

Yorkshire Television decided they too needed a pub-based entertainment show. They came up with a thing called *Indoor League*. The famous fast bowler 'Fiery' Fred Trueman had retired from cricket and fancied himself as a plain-speaking media celebrity. Yorkshire TV set him up as anchorman for a show that featured darts, arm-wrestling, shove ha'penny and skittles. Fred presented the programme whilst puffing on a pipe. He even had a catchphrase. At the end of each show, he would look directly into the camera, wave his lit pipe and say, 'I'll sithee.'

In the summer that the Sex Pistols sang 'God Save the Queen' I was coming up to my eighteenth birthday. There were plenty of pubs in Pontefract then that let you in if you looked vaguely old enough. One was the Ancient Borough Arms (ABA for short), which had a reputation for fighting. This reputation went back a long way to a time when the ABA and its rival The Beastfair Vaults (or Bass House for short) sold a particularly potent Bass Pale Ale. The older end used to tell us that the beer in those two places was sending everybody crazy so the police made them serve it in half pints. The Bass Pale Ale on draught was long gone, but the ABA somehow kept its reputation. The White Hart was a lot quieter, it was an old-fashioned little place with a tiny spartan taproom and a front room that looked like your auntie's lounge. The pub seemed to survive through the efforts of a handful of older blokes who divided their time between its bar and the betting shop across the road.

The White Hart had an old painted scene high up on its gable end, a picture of some hunters chasing a white deer across a rolling landscape. It was a peculiar name to give to a pub in Pontefract. The White Hart was a badge associated with Joan of Kent, the mother of Richard II. And it was this Richard who was famously hit over the head with a stick (according to Shakespeare) and murdered at the castle at Pontefract. The landlord was a tough looking little fella with Brylcreemed hair and sideburns. He always seemed to be wiping pots with a worn-out tea towel or emptying ashtrays into a tin bucket. When a group of teenagers like us walked in, he'd sigh, put his thumbs inside his braces and say 'What can I do for you young 'un?' without looking at anybody in particular. If you asked for beer, he'd ask you how old you were. Whatever you told him he'd give you a look that said 'I don't believe you!' Then he'd say, 'You'll get me shot, you can have one pint apiece and don't laugh.'

There was nothing in that taproom to distract you. No pictures on the wall, save for one handwritten sign for a meat tray raffle to be held on Saturday. No music, little conversation, just a bar, a bare floor and a few tables and chairs around a fireplace. When someone scraped a chair to stand up, everybody looked across at them. It was worse than being in a doctor's waiting room and coughing. The beer was hand-pulled Wilson's from Manchester. It kept its head all the way down the glass, which meant you could count the number of sips you'd had. And we did, in the face of not much else to do.

On the day that people are having street parties to celebrate the Queen's twenty-fifth anniversary of her reign, a gang of us decide to have a beer drinking crawl around town – well at least around the pubs that we think will let us in. I walk into The White Hart with Pete, Mick and Rasta. The landlord seems to be in one of his better moods and nearly smiles at us. Rasta is older than us and asks for the beer. The landlord looks down our line and says to me, 'How old are you young 'un?' I say, 'Nineteen.' I am a few weeks short of being eighteen, but I've managed to sprout the beginnings of a scruffy beard. He looks at Pete then at Mick. He then throws his tea towel onto the sink side and says, 'You'll get me shot! You can have one pint apiece, sit in the corner and don't laugh!' I don't know why he doesn't want us to laugh, but we obey him. In fact we hardly dare breathe.

The landlord has put on a clean, peach-coloured nylon shirt with a ruffle down the front today and a velvet-like bow tie. On the bar are two Mackeson Stout bottles with small Union Jacks on wooden sticks placed in them. The front of the bar is decorated with silver tinsel, the sort that you would wind around a Christmas tree. Above the fireplace is a picture of the Queen cut out of a newspaper and pinned to the wall with those little pins that have coloured balls on top.

We take our pints to a table in the corner near the fireplace. The landlord stares at us. 'Don't rock on them chairs!'

We talk almost in whispers and count the sip lines on our pints. An old man comes over. He carries a beer tray that has been wrapped in Bacofoil. 'Anybody want a lump of pork pie?' On the tray are pieces of pork pie cut in to quarters, the meat has fallen out of the casing and it doesn't look too appetising. We all take a piece. The old man says, 'You can have two pieces if you want, I don't think there's going to be a rush today.' We take another piece. We sit with a piece of pork pie in each hand, almost waiting for permission to eat it. 'There's some brown sauce on the bar, you can't have pork pie without brown sauce.'

Pete stands up to fetch the bottle of brown sauce. It's Daddies sauce and there is a thick dried rim of it around the neck just below the stopper. Pete drops the crust of his pie. The landlord shouts, 'Don't be dropping crumbs all over you scruffy little bastard!'

We start laughing. The landlord glares at us. We stop laughing. We start to eat our pork pie and drink our beer.

The landlord stops glaring and softens his approach, just slightly. 'Seeing as it's a special day, I might let you have another pint if you want one.' Pete goes to the bar and orders a second round. By the time we are halfway down our second pint, we are a bit more relaxed and animated.

The landlord shouts over again, 'Hey up! You four. Keep bloody still and don't put your feet on the spells of them chairs.' We move our feet back to the floor and try to keep still.

Rasta whispers under his breath, 'It's worse than being at home.'

The old bloke with the pork pies says to Pete, 'What have you got that big safety pin on your coat for?'

Pete says, 'I like punk rock.'

The landlord scowls at us again, 'Well don't be spitting in here.'

Pork Pie says, 'Aye because we've done away with the spittoons these days,' and he winks at us.

The landlord pulls himself half a pint and holds it up to the light. 'I've read about them punk rockers, scruffy little bastards. If any of 'em came in here, they'd be barred before they got through the door. I don't know what the bloody world is coming to.'

Pete blushes and looks down at the kilt pin on his lapel. He says, 'Don't you like music then?'

The landlord eyes Pete and curls his lip, 'Of course I like music, Tommy Steele, Connie Francis, Elvis, that's what you call music.'

Pete finishes his second pint and says, 'Well Elvis was like a punk rocker in his day.'

The landlord comes from behind the bar. 'Are you right in your bloody head. Elvis was a punk rocker! Was he bollocks! Elvis is the king, show some respect.'

Silence.

We sit there with empty pots with handles on in front of us.

The landlord goes back to wiping glasses. He holds them up to the light, breathes on them and polishes.

Pork Pie puts his cap on and says, 'Right, I'll be off then. Our lass has been buttering breadcakes all morning. They've put some tables and chairs out down our backs. They're having trifle and all sorts.'

We stand up to go as well. The landlord says, 'Pass them empty glasses over. I don't know, you young 'uns haven't the manners you were born with. You come in here and get proper hospitality and you can't even be bothered to pass me your empty glass back.'

When I was eighteen I started going to the Girnhill Lane Working Men's Club with my grandad. He made me a member. There was an old man called 'Shacker' Heighway who sat behind a desk to the right of the door as you came in. It seemed to be his job to ask anybody he didn't recognise, 'Is thy a member?' He said it to me every time I went there on my own. Once when I walked past him he didn't say anything. I turned and said, 'Yes, I'm a member.' He looked me up and down and said, 'Well tha wants to get thi bloody hair cut then, this is a respectable club.'

The Girnhill Lane Working Men's Club was the first licensed premises that I knew well. As a boy, I sat on a wall there to eat a bag of cheese and onion crisps and waited for my grandad to come home for his dinner, though not too often because the committee frowned on members' children waiting by the door for their dads and grandads. The locals called this club 'The Corra' and they still do. Nobody seems to remember why now, but it was probably something to do with Queen Victoria's son Edward's coronation. All of the working men's clubs in my hometown have nicknames. The Featherstone WMC is 't'Green Lane', The Progressive Club was 'Blood Tub' on account of the amount of fighting that at one time was common in its vicinity, The Featherstone Lane Club got 'Rat Trap', there is still a 'B and S' after a long defunct bus company called 'Bullock and Son', and the Old Featherstone Club rejoiced under the eccentric local moniker 'Top o' t'Knob'. You would have to know that that particular club was on the top of a hill or 'knob' to get anywhere near to understanding the etymology of that particular name. I still hear some of the older end getting on the bus and asking for 'a single to t'Top o' t'Knob please cock'. The faces on some of the younger bus drivers are a picture. A bloke I know who runs a local family bus company told me that a Polish driver he employed recently came back to the depot dumbfounded one day and wanted to know, 'Where is Normanton Cock?'

The Corra is an imposing building. When I was a boy it stood in the middle of a lively community. Opposite were long rows of terraced streets. Ted Amery and his wife Ruby kept a traditional grocers shop there. The wooden trestle tables outside were draped in that green material only green grocers use and they were laden with potatoes, carrots, turnips and cabbages. In season they sold sackfuls of mussels and seagull eggs. Mr Amery wore a brown smock and a trilby. His shop was the last place I remember that sold mantles for gas lights. I bought mantles there for Mr Hope, the last man in our street without electricity. The club was bounded on one side by two huge gasometers and on the other by allotments. Reuben Banks kept pigs in his garden right next to the club and the bloke in the next allotment grew chrysanthemums. These days the terraced rows have gone, replaced by council maisonettes, and the gas company is now a Lidl supermarket. The allotments are still there, but nobody keeps pigs anymore and I haven't seen a man with an armful of fresh cut chrysanths for ages. Like a lot of working men's clubs when the community they were built to serve goes, it sticks out like a sore thumb, yet it survives.

The club itself hasn't altered that much from the outside and it's from the outside of it where most of my memories dwell. The male voice choir practised there on Sunday mornings. I can hear the sound of 'Comrades in Arms' coming through the upstairs window still today when I walk past. I can smell the Saturday night mix of beer fumes, cigarette smoke and perfume. I can never hear the song 'Knock Three Times' without thinking about it wafting through the front door of that club. It seemed that every early seventies club turn in the north of England covered that song and brought it to our local clubs. There were turns every Saturday night, Sunday afternoon and Sunday night accompanied by the club's own resident drummer and organist. One Saturday, a young woman singer from Mansfield arrived just as they were closing for the afternoon. The club entertainment secretary, a man called Tiger, said to her, 'You're too soon love, we didn't expect you while seven.' The woman explained that she wasn't sure where she had been sent to and had set off early with the thought that it was 'better to be early'. Tiger told her that he couldn't leave her in the club as it was against committee rules and with the weather being bad he didn't want to have her walking about in the rain, so she would have to come home with him and his wife would make her some tea. When they got back to Tiger's bungalow, his wife was still out shopping. He told her to take her coat off, sit in the front room and he would make her a cup of tea. After ten minutes Tiger came in out of the kitchen and said, 'We might have to wait for our lass love, unless you know how to help me. I've filled a kettle, but I'm not sure how to turn the stove on.'

The Corra was filled with men who didn't go near ovens, blokes who would rather pick up a rattlesnake than a steam iron. My grandad got playing dominoes one afternoon and didn't come home for his dinner. My gran walked the two hundred yards from her kitchen to the games room with his dinner between two warm plates. 'If you'd rather stop in here than come home and eat a meal I've been preparing all morning, you can have it in here and don't bother coming home!' She put the dinner in front of him and took a knife and fork out of her apron pocket and said, 'And for two pins I'd ram these buggers up your arse.' The other men round the table started to laugh.

'And you lot would laugh if your arses were on fire!'

They stopped laughing. My gran stormed out.

My grandad picked up his knife and fork. 'You'd have thought she'd have brought the salt and pepper pots, I'll have to have a word with her when I get in.'

The men round the table started laughing again, like their arses were on fire.

I liked it in the Girnhill Lane Club. Becoming a member made me feel like I was a part of the history of where I am from. They had a reading room with old oak sloping desks. All the day's newspapers were laid out there with a wooden blade to turn the pages. My grandad read every paper in there, he did it he said because he wanted to know 'what the other buggers are up to'. My first membership card for that club contained a phrase on the first page that I still hold dear. It read 'For the purpose of social intercourse'.

Home From Home

In the late seventies it was all about the ale for our group of mates. Burt discovered that the only pub in the whole of Yorkshire that served cask-conditioned Boddingtons was called The Kinsley Hotel. He was even more delighted to discover that the village of Kinsley was on a direct, albeit long and winding bus route from Pontefract. None of us had been to Kinsley, but we knew of it by reputation. It was a rough little pit village with a greyhound racing track. The lads and lasses there were tough. When Burt first suggested that we go over there for a Saturday night session, one or two in our circle of mates said, 'We'll get our heads kicked in.' This was at the height of the punk-rock times and though punk fashion had made slight inroads into Pontefract, it had bypassed Kinsley completely. Our plans for a visit to The Kinsley Hotel were shelved a few times when it was pointed out that we might look a bit conspicuous. 'For a start off,' as Norman, one of our gang said, 'We aren't from Kinsley, we don't look like we're from Kinsley and on top of that, three of our number have cockatoo hairstyles, three have hair like Jesus, two like to read poetry books in public bars and four of the girls wear clothes held together with safety pins.' Burt was never deterred though. The Kinsley Hotel regularly became almost a mystical thing, a holy grail at the end of a seven-mile journey on a South Yorkshire Motors service bus.

A large gang of us got it together to pay a visit one Saturday night. We were a right raggle-taggle outfit. Pete Simpson, lead singer of our local punk band The Thrust, turned up in full punk regalia along with Ivan and Tony. Rasta came in his bell-bottom Levi's and cheese-cloth shirt with his ringlets falling on his shoulders, Burt had his usual greasy Belstaff and bike boots on and Stephanie and Sheena looked like they were auditioning for Siouxsie and The Banshees. Heather had her blue Mohawk haircut and I put on an Edwardian grandad shirt with sleeves down to my knees. The pub was heaving with a noisy, early evening gathering of drinkers. By the time we had all trooped to the bar everyone had stopped talking and stared at us. A bloke in the corner with a big hand on a one-armed bandit wolf-whistled. He thought for a second or two then said, 'Hey up, look what t'wind's blown in.' The barman came over. He was a severe looking man with the words 'Love' and 'Hate' tattooed across his eight fingers, and dyed-black hair styled like Elvis Presley. He looked at Burt and said, 'Now then Shirley Temple, what can I do for you?'

Burt cleared his throat and said, 'We've heard that the Boddingtons beer in here is first class.' It might have been something to do with his education, but Burt was a lot more confident than us in situations like this one. We were working-class kids in an unfamiliar working-class environment. All of this seemed to go straight over Burt's head.

Elvis narrowed his eyes and blew some air out of his mouth. 'Well if my beer tasted like chip 'ole vinegar, I'm sure this lot would let me know, so aye, I suppose you could say it's first class.'

'Can we have twelve pints of Boddingtons then please?'

In those days when we went out en masse we each used to chuck a couple of quid into a communal kitty.

'Yes Shirley. You can have twelve pints of Boddingtons and if them lasses prefer wine, we've got two sorts. Red and white.'

'They like beer.'

'Oh! They do, do they. I suppose they'll want pint pots an' all.'

Burt nodded.

The Elvis barman touched a button on the pump. The Kinsley Hotel didn't have handpumps then, it had diaphragm ones and you could see the beer filling through a small glass jar device on the bar.

Just as fast as everybody had stopped talking, they all started again. We took our beers from copper trays on the bar and looked for somewhere to sit. Some of the locals slid up on the bench seats to make room for us. 'Here you are love, come on, don't be shy, only don't sit on that chair, because old Jack sits there to smoke his pipe and he'll be here in about ten minutes. You can put your clock right by him.'

Old Jack did come in ten minutes later and brought his beer to the table and sat in the empty chair. He nodded at everybody but didn't speak. He was wearing a tweed flat cap with a frayed neb and a shiny jacket with elbow patches on it. His trousers were held up by a thick leather belt and braces, the ones with fastenings that you button on. He pulled a pipe and a box of Swan Vesta out of his coat pocket and lit up. He looked like a genie wreathed in smoke. He sipped steadily and puffed away for about twenty minutes, still not saying anything. He then got up to go. As an afterthought he turned round and weighed up Burt's long hair and me in my ridiculous grandad shirt and puffed his cheeks. He then beckoned us to lean towards him. Out of the side of his mouth he whispered, 'It's a very important pub is this old cocks. It's steeped in history, steeped in history.' Then he went without saying any more. We felt like we had been told a secret. One of the people who had moved up for us said, 'You can spread out a bit now, sit on that old chair if you want. He does that every Saturday.' Then he added, 'But he doesn't normally speak to anybody, so think yourselves lucky.'

We drank a lot of beer that night, though not nearly as much as most of the other people. We fed the jukebox non-stop and sang along to The Beatles, T. Rex and Slade. The Elvis barman had us put on 'The Wonder of You' again and again until even the locals told him to change his tune. As we came out into the cold night air for the last bus back to Pontefract we joined in with Jeff Beck's 'Hi Ho Silver Lining'. We made a lot of new friends and most of us acquired nicknames. Burt got Shirley Temple for his ringlets. He wasn't best pleased. I got Bob Geldof, to this day I don't know why. Stephanie was Blondie, Pete was Johnny Rotten, and Steve Tomlinson – who we called 'Rasta' for his love of reggae music – became Jesus.

The Kinsley Hotel was one of those pubs that seemed to cater for everybody. A real mix of young, middle-aged and old people, some kind and friendly and some who looked as though they'd give you a good hiding as soon as look at you. The older end seemed to take to us, the younger lads and men who were there didn't seem to know what to make of us, but by the end of the night when everyone was merry, there was a fair amount of back-slapping going on. As we came out, the Elvis barman said, 'You can come here again,' and then almost as though he was having another thought, he said, 'If you want!'

We did go again. Over a period of about two years, we visited at least once every couple of months. Unlike that first occasion when we were greeted with an intimidating silence, we were welcomed warmly, usually with a shout of, 'Hey up! They're here again look.' We got quite close to Old Jack as well. He'd tease us by asking if we had been near to soap and water recently. He'd come out with quirky sayings like, 'Get your hair cut and I'll meet you when the sun goes down.' He'd tell us to 'look both ways when you cross the road' or remind us that a plateful of dinner with plenty of rabbit gravy wouldn't do us any harm. And toward the end of the night he'd make us put our coats on and remind us to go out in plenty of time for the bus because 'the bugger is always early on a Saturday'. Jack had a lot of little blue scars down one side of his neck. Somebody once whispered to us that when he had been a young coal miner he had been buried under a roof-fall down the pit and that it had taken them hours to dig him out. W never dared to ask him if it was true.

I don't think any of us realised it at the time, but what we were doing was connecting to something quite deep down that these days gets wrapped up in the catch all phrase 'community spirit'. We went there first because we wanted to try a beer that we couldn't easily get anywhere else, and we went because we all liked the proper old-fashioned pubs where older people drank, as opposed to the false pubs with plastic beams and horse brasses that were popping up everywhere then. In the 1970s there were still people in pubs who knew about the First World War and the depression years from personal experience and we liked to talk to them. There was something else though, something that you couldn't always put your finger on. It was in the atmosphere as well as the clientele, maybe in the very fabric of the building itself that made it special. Years later we found out about the part that The Kinsley Hotel had played in the social history of that small coal mining village. It was then that we realised what Old Jack had meant when he told us that the pub was steeped in history. It was sad that Jack had passed away by the time we knew what he was on about.

In 1905, the local Fitzwilliam Coal Company claimed that due to a collapse in the market price of coal, the miners would have to accept a fifty per cent cut in their wages for digging it out. The Union brought their men out on strike and the stand-off lasted throughout the summer of that year. The colliers and their families lived in long terraced rows next to The Kinsley Hotel. These rows were owned by the colliery company. With no wages being earned and no rent being paid, the colliery owners decided to evict their tenants in an attempt to drive them back to work. The evictions were cruel and barbaric. More than seventy families were put out of their houses by policemen drafted in from other towns and had to seek shelter in tents on a field next to The Kinsley Hotel. It's not the sort of history you get to read in the official history books, which are only too keen to make sure that kind of history is swept under the carpet. Fortunately, a local amateur photographer called Mr Wales who worked in a chemist shop took his camera to observe the evictions and left an astonishing collection of photographs that bear witness to what happened. The photos show pinched-faced mothers standing outside their front doors holding their children to their hips, surrounded by mangles, bedding and rolls of linoleum. Their husbands stand defiant in lopsided caps next to burly moustached bobbies as bedsteads are handed down from upstairs windows.

The Danish artist Erik Henningsen painted one of the iconic paintings about beer drinking. In 1900, the Tuborg brewery wanted to celebrate their silver jubilee with an art poster. Henningsen came up with an image that every Danish beer drinker knows. It is called 'The Thirsty Man' and depicts a sweating man, leaning on a stick on a dusty road mopping the back of his head with a hankie. He carries his jacket over his arm and his collar and tie are undone at the neck. The road winds away in the distance as though to show he has a long way to go before his pint. It is a perfect image about beer drinking, without showing beer or pubs. Henningsen was one of the first great social realism painters. He was preoccupied with the plight of the poor and particularly the living conditions of the workers. There is a painting in the art gallery in Copenhagen that was painted in 1892, not long before the evictions in Kinsley. It is simply called 'Evicted Tenants'. The painting shows a grandmother with a tin bucket over her arm and a brush in her hand. She stares out of the picture as though looking for someone to help her. Next to her is a younger woman, perhaps her daughter. This woman clings to a bundle of possessions wrapped into a cloth and holds the hand of a little girl. They look across at a burly bobby with a notebook in his hand. The father in his shirt sleeves and waistcoat appears to be trying to reason with him. It is snowing. On the ground lie cushions, bowls, chairs and a portrait of a military figure. That image is haunting. I first saw it many years after I knew about the evictions at Kinsley, but it tells exactly the story that the photographs taken there tell.

Some of the Kinsley photos show rows of white tents lined up in the muddy fields, while others show the little children bedding down for the night in the upstairs ballroom of The Kinsley Hotel. From the beginning of the evictions in the late summer of 1905 and throughout the winter, Thomas Elstone, the landlord of The Kinsley Hotel, agreed to feed and shelter hundreds of local kids. A number of the photos show big pots of stew being ladled out into bowls set on long scrubbed tables in the backyard of the pub. I've wondered many a time since if Old Jack was one of the kids who tucked into a bowl of stew at that time. I'd bet he will have been.

All of the photos that were taken at that time are filled with emotion, but two in particular are unbearably poignant. One shows three policemen with heads bowed carrying a cradle out of a front door. Someone has captioned this picture 'Evicting The Baby'. The other shows a man called Bob Battye and his family being put out. Bob Battye was a well-known coal miner and musician. He stands below his window playing the concertina while his young son plays the harp. A newspaper report from that time tells us that Bob and his son played 'Home Sweet Home' with tears on their faces. The colliers of Kinsley were out of their homes for months. Thomas Elstone stuck to his word and managed somehow to feed and find accommodation for the children in his pub. Eventually the colliery changed ownership and new deals were struck that allowed the miners and families back to work and into their homes. Ironically, the local collieries were named for the Earls of Fitzwilliam who lived not far away at Wentworth Woodhouse, a home that is often referred to as 'Britain's largest private house'. When Kier Hardie, the great early Labour leader, came to visit the evicted families of Kinsley in October of 1905, he said, 'It's the same all over the country, the rich are doing all they can to crush the poor workers.'

The Kinsley Hotel still stands, a huge Victorian pile of a building made of solid red brick from the local colliery.

Top House Tales

I walk into The Top House with Volker one Saturday afternoon. Fred is there having a couple of pints while he waits for his pigeons to come home. Fred is eager to know who the stranger is with me. He shouts across to Volker, 'Excuse me young man, can I have a word?' Volker and I go over. Fred establishes straightaway that Volker is on a visit from Germany and now wants to know what he does for a living.

'I am a tour organiser for musicians.'

Fred looks him up and down. 'Well you've got some nice long curly hair and a beard. You don't see too many blond beards, are you a student? You look like a student with your necklace on.' Fred uses the word 'student' to mean young person who looks different to the sort of people he knows. Volker isn't sure where all of this is going. I don't think he has heard the word 'student' used in such a way.

Volker says, 'No. I'm not a student, but I organise a lot of gigs that take place at universities.'

'Do you know anything about medicinal herbs?'

Volker looks at me. Undeterred, Fred carries on, 'Only my pigeons are very excited about the big race next Saturday, they're going over the water to France.'

It is like watching two men from two different planets, neither of them appearing to have a language in common. 'They've got themselves too worked up if you ask me and I'm worried that they're not going to concentrate on getting home safely.'

Volker looks at me again. I start to explain the sport of pigeon racing.

'I could do with a bit of something to calm them down.'

'I think that he thinks that you might be able to let him have something to soothe the nerves of his pigeons,' I say to Volker.

Volker turns to Fred, 'Do you mean a herbal substance?'

Fred says, 'Aye! The last time some students came in here, they were very calm, they put it down to some buns they were eating.'

Volker smiled, 'I have a little piece of something that comes all the way from Kashmir. You could try a bit of that if you want.'

Volker broke a piece of hashish off his stash. Fred winked at him.

A fortnight later I saw Fred whistling down the lane pushing an old pram that he uses to transport his pigeon baskets. 'Tell that student, that stuff he gave me worked a treat. I got all my pigeons back in record time and they've stopped fretting.'

'Oh! Good, it worked then.'

'Worked! It didn't half work. In fact I could do with it on a regular basis. It gave me my appetite back. I went home and ate two dinners and I haven't been troubled with my knees since.'

By the late 1980s, when the pits had closed within a year or two of the miners' strike finishing, The Top House taproom became a theatre of the absurd. It was like a surreal pantomime acted out by characters who seemed to have gone half mad, drunk on redundancy money and distracted by a lack of work that meant there was not much better to do. Like all good pantomimes it was a performance that improved with audience participation. It was very funny, but heartbreaking and poignant by turns, and the humour got darker as the nights drew in.

Roy Banks walks in one afternoon, he's wearing one of his wife's dresses. He acts like it's something he does every day. Nobody takes a blind bit of notice, as though it's normal for an ex-collier with a walrus moustache to walk up and down in a Laura Ashley frock. So, Roy starts to sashay up and down like a catwalk model. Eventually Pete Green, who knows by instinct that Roy is up to something, says, 'I didn't know there were jobs for models down at that job centre.'

'No, Mr Green. It's not that, it's our lass, she's lying! I just know she's lying.'

Carol Bell who knows Roy of old, joins in with the charade. 'How do you know she's lying Roy?'

'Well she's thrown me out just because I've beaten her up again.'

There's an intake of breath all round the room and the atmosphere turns sharply. Scowls appear on faces where there had been amusement. Roy leaves it just long enough to stop the lads and lasses who have heard him from giving him a good hiding there and then.

'I mean to say, I beat her up every day. I'm always out of bed at pit time and she doesn't stir till eight o'clock.'

Sharp air breathed back out again and one or two relieved chuckles. Carol carries on, 'So why do you think she's lying?'

'Because she says she's filled two black bin liners with my clothes and put them next to the dustbin.'

'So!'

'So I know for a fact she has been lying because I've only got enough clothes to fill one bin bag.'

Roy is like a struggling music hall act crossed with a performance artist, crossed with an escaped clown. He pulls a clothes peg out of a pocket in his frock and says, 'Anyhow, I thought I'd console myself with a couple of beers and our Peg here said she'd join me, didn't you Peg?' Again he leaves a pause long enough for the assembled company to realise that he's trying to have a conversation with a clothes peg. 'Oh! Alright then, don't talk if you don't want, I'm getting used to being left out to dry.'

Roy had a mate called Gerry Roscoe. They spent a lot of their workless days riding about on a pair of rusty old bikes. They rode for miles and explained to anybody who was interested that they had been told by the government that in times of high unemployment people had to get on their bike. It must have been while they were out riding that they got their mad ideas, which they would then enact in pubs after they'd had a few beers. After one bicycle pub crawl they found themselves thrown out of the Central Working Men's Club. There was still time for one more beer and they knew that Greeny at The Top House was probably the only landlord who would put up with their shenanigans.

Pete Green is about to shout last orders. The side door to the pub is pushed open and bangs on the wall. A blast of night air blows in. Instead of coming in quickly and putting the wood in the hole behind them, Gerry and Roy embark on a bizarre sketch that is part monologue and part mime.

'That's right Gerry, now you hold that door back as far as it will go. Come on long fellow, bend at the knees, I said bend at the knees, that's it, now bow your head, steady as you go, steady… steady, hold on a minute, bow down a bit more, you can do it… now watch your neck near that jamb, steady, steady, whoah! Gerry, I said hold that door back.'

Pete and the stragglers around the bar watch like goldfish as Gerry and Roy go about their task of trying to coax an imaginary, as yet unspecified species of friend into the bar. Pete can do without two drunken loons coming in at this time of night but can't help but be intrigued. He really doesn't want to serve them with any more beer, but at the same time he is enjoying the show.

'Good evening Peter, ladies, gentlemen and Sooner. May we have two pints of your excellent bitter and a bowl of water please. Now come on fella, you just lie down over here on this carpet, that's it, you'll be alright there, everybody is friendly in here.'

Pete and the five or six customers are still slack-jawed.

'Now I know what you are all wondering,' Roy announces. 'But as Gerry is my witness, I'm sure you will lend a sympathetic ear. We were asked to leave the Central Club due to them lacking a sense of humour. On the way up the Lane we saw this shivering giraffe crying on the pavement outside the video rental shop. He was upset and a little bit miffed because they wouldn't let him borrow a film.'

Pete says, 'Well! As excuses for getting another pint whilst drunk go, it is the most convoluted I've come across.'

Gerry says, 'Ssshh Peter, you'll upset the giraffe.'

Pete plays along. 'Why wouldn't they let him borrow a film?'

Roy throws out his hands, 'Now come on Peter! You know

what they are like in there. The poor old lad had forgotten his membership card and you know what that lass behind the counter says, "No card, no film." Anyhow, we've taken pity on him and brought him in here out of the cold.'

Roy and Gerry get their pints for the audacity of it all and gradually the jaws of the regulars drop back into place. It takes longer than a tired landlord wants it to take, but gradually Pete manages to get everybody to sup their beer off and starts to corral them towards the exit. Roy and Gerry are the last two to reach the door. Pete turns and says, 'Hey you two, haven't you forgotten something? You can't leave that lying there all night.'

Roy puts his hand on Peter's arm, 'Now come come landlord. I would have expected you to know your African wildlife. It's not a lion, it's a giraffe!'

Roy and Gerry used to do a very funny sketch where they pretended to be lumberjacks. Gerry would hold both of his arms out in front of himself in imitation of a chainsaw blade. Roy, with a borrowed safety helmet from Ossie Wilkes's scrapyard next door, would then take Gerry by the shoulders and pull an imaginary starter cord on his collar. Gerry reprimanded him, 'Don't you know your health and safety? Goggles please if you would be so kind.' Roy then donned his safety glasses and took up the pulley again. The chainsaw would stutter and cough, then fail to start. Roy would scratch his head and mop sweat from his brow, while a pub full of redundant coal miners and ne'er do wells watched as two fools prepared to saw a barroom table in half. Finally, Gerry would say, 'Try the choke, then full throttle mate.' The chainsaw would come alive, Gerry making the noise of an engine warming up, then he'd drop the volume to idling speed. With Roy guiding the blade, Gerry would then start screaming on full throttle until Roy cut through the varnished table.

'Big Red' was another of the madcap characters who found his way to The Top House. He too rode about on a bicycle. He called it his horse. He also called himself a horse. Big Red was well named. He was a huge, loud man with a massive red beard. In any weather he only ever wore shorts, work boots and a moth-eaten pullover. He stunk of sweat and diesel. I don't think he ever really meant harm, but Red could intimidate an entire pub just by striding in, asking for a pint and shouting at the top of his voice, 'I am a horse.' Nobody ever knew what to say back to him. The door flew open one night, there was a strong smell of diesel, followed by Red still on his bike. It was snowing out and he came to the bar like Santa Claus in steel-toe caps. Before he could say anything, Roy winked at Gerry and said, 'Do you know, I've had a sore throat all day.' At the top of his voice Gerry said, 'Are you hoarse?' Big Red ordered a pint of Guinness and for the first time forgot his catchphrase.

The Palladium Of The Potteries

Les Dawson, the late great Manchester comic, used to relate a surreal monologue. 'I was sat at the bottom of the garden smoking a reflective cheroot whilst gazing up at the night sky. I marvelled at a myriad of stars, glistening like pieces of quicksilver strewn carelessly onto black velvet. In awe, I watched the waxen moon ride across the heavens like an amber chariot towards deeper space, where Jupiter and Mars hung, festooned in their orbital majesty. Shooting stars streaked across this wondrous formation, this purple vault filled with points of twinkling light and I thought to myself... I must put a few more slates on this lavatory roof.'

Dawson was a wordsmith straight out of the old-time music hall via the northern working men's club circuit. He didn't tell jokes in the strict sense of the term, but reflected on life in an almost situationist sort of way. Tetley Dave, the landlord at The Shoulder of Mutton, was similar and his taproom domain was his theatre of the absurd. Dave himself could conjure up a monologue or ribald ballad out of nowhere. He loved reciting 'Albert and the Lion' and did it with a face as deadpan as Buster Keaton and a voice as flat as a fart. He was a massive fan of the old music hall stars, particularly the risqué northern ones. He loved Frank Randle, who he said was the greatest comedian who ever drew breath, and he could regale you with the jokes of Al Read, Albert Modley and Robb Wilton all afternoon when he was that way out. His favourite monologue was by Billy Bennett. Dave said it was called 'The Sailor's Farewell to His Horse'. Him and Steve the pigeon man could recite every verse of it off by heart between them. Dave's wife Margaret had heard it so many times that as soon as he set off with it, she'd tut, pick up her bacca tin and go off for a smoke in the backyard.

It was the schooner Hesperus – we all lay asleep in our bunks
Bound for a cruise, where they don't have revues
With a cargo of elephant's trunks.

The sea was as smooth as a baby's top lip
Not even a policeman in sight
And the little sardines had got into their tins
And pulled down the lids for the night.

Dave became landlord of the Shoulder of Mutton after years working as a drayman and dreaming of pulling pints in his own place. One of the attractions of the pub had been that the local amateur rugby league team had their headquarters there and both they and their fans were thirsty drinkers. Unbeknownst to Dave, the club had applied successfully to the National Lottery for money to build their own clubhouse some months before. As soon as it was finished, they upped and left. Dave's takings were down by half overnight, but he was undeterred. 'Fuck 'em!' he said, 'I don't like rugby anyroad.'

Not long after, Dave made a chance discovery and it gave him an idea. He found out that George Formby had met his wife Beryl behind the mucky curtains at Castleford Theatre Royal back in the 1930s. The Theatre Royal had been knocked down for years, but the stories of acts who had played there still circulated amongst the older clientele in Tetley Dave's pub. Dave liked to tell the story of how Larry Grayson came up with his catchphrase there. 'It was in the days when the theatres were on their arses in the 1950s. They tried everything to keep open: wrestling, seals balancing bloody balls on their noses and strippers. Well, they weren't allowed to move then, so the girls just stood there naked, pretending to be a tableau from ancient Rome. One day, somebody left a side door open and the wind whistled across the stage, one of the lasses said "Ooohh! Shut that door". Larry Grayson was a young comic then, waiting in the wings to come on. When he came on he repeated that line "Shut that door" and it lasted him all his life.'

One day Dave decided that because the Theatre Royal was only two hundred yards from his pub and because George Formby liked a pint and a Woodbine, he could put two and two together and he started telling everybody that Formby liked to come to The Shoulder whenever he was in Castleford. Jim and Barry, two taproom regulars, challenged him on this and asked if he had any evidence. Dave said, 'I can feel his presence when I go into the best room and that's good enough for me.' On the strength of this he invited the local branch of the George Formby society to hold their monthly meetings there. Every last Wednesday of the month, up to thirty old blokes turned up with ukuleles to have what they called 'a plonk'. They were good drinkers too. The Formby society liked it at The Shoulder. Margaret made a fuss of them and baked meat and potato pies for the interval. Dave bought a second-hand PA system and a third-hand lighting rig. 'We'll make it look a bit more professional,' he said.

Tetley Dave loves everything about pubs and ale, he has a lot of sayings and adages and most of them are to do with pub culture. He likes to announce, 'There's no such thing as bad ale, it's just that some is better than the other.' And he'll follow this with, 'This place will never be anything other than a pub. They can do what they like once they put me in my box, but as long as I'm breathing it's a pub.'

Anything that can take place in a pub he will have a go at it. He has a selection of traditional pub games, including a fine old slate table for shove ha'penny and a dartboard that's dropping to bits. This dartboard is over the mantelpiece and there's only just enough room to mark out a throwing distance to the oche before your back touches the bar top. When it's busy, people have to duck and dive to avoid the darts. One Sunday Dave announced, 'You have to have eyes like fucking General Custer in here when they're throwing arrows.' Everybody laughed, they laughed a lot longer than Dave's quip deserved. Then for Dave the penny dropped. When he was a boy he had lost an eye. He had been lacing up a leather football with a darning needle when his mother shouted to tell him that Mother Riley was on the telly. He stopped looking at what he was doing and stuck the darning needle in his eye. He made light of it; if any of the lads were mimicking him for fun on his blindside, he'd say, 'They think I can't see what they're up to, but Tetley's brewery weren't daft when they put mirrors in pubs and my good eye is as good they come.'

There were three sets of ancient dominoes, packs of cards with more marks on them than a cheetah and even a ball and skittles game that had been donated by the lads from the travelling fair who frequented his back room. The undoubted star of his collection though is a 'Ring the Bull' game.

Ring the Bull isn't seen in too many pubs these days. It's a simple enough game, elegant in its own way. A wooden shield is fixed on a wall, sometimes with a bull's face painted on it. A metal hook is placed where the bull's nose is and the players stand a few yards back, about the same distance as a darts player does from the board. A brass ring attached to a piece of twine is then thrown towards the hook. The aim is to see how many throws it takes to get the ring onto the hook. The one who does it in the least number of throws is then declared the winner. Tetley Dave decided to make his own version. He used the wooden plaque from one of his granddaughter's gymnastics trophies and a hook off a wardrobe door. He found a brass ring in his shed and fastened some strong string to it. Some of the regulars became very adept at playing the game. Barry the long distance lorry driver and Jim the mechanic were particularly good. They graduated from 'how many goes it takes' to 'how many times in a row' you can get the ring on the hook. I think Jim had the record with six in a row. Dave's son then started showboating and could throw it on from over his shoulder. It was great fun and Dave loved to tease unsuspecting visitors. 'I'll buy you a pint if you can do it in less than three throws. And you buy me one if it takes you more.' He'd show it could be done and then he'd shorten the string when they weren't looking.

In fits and starts, The Shoulder started to rebuild its clientele. There had long been a connection between fairground workers and showmen and that pub. A lot of them had yards nearby where they stayed during the winter months. They liked a pint when they got back from working the fairs, sometimes it was nearly midnight. Dave didn't mind, so the showlads came in force. A gang of British motorbike fanatics turned up every now and again on BSAs, Royal Enfields and Ariels. Dave had a plaque made for them so they started coming regularly. Then, ever a fan of real ale, Dave put on a regular programme of beers sourced from local microbreweries. He started to attract what he called 'The Tickers'; the real ale fans who, like trainspotters, note down the beers they have tried. A woman who claimed to have sampled over two thousand different beers used to come over on the train from the other side of Barnsley. Dave made a fuss of her because she used to bring him a pork pie from Percy Turner's butcher's shop in a village called Jump. Dave declared that Percy Turner's pork pies were the finest in the land.

The taproom was a weekly pantomime filled with outrageous storytellers, ne'er do wells and downright liars. Alf Varley, self-styled 'Lord of the Potteries', frightened everybody with gruesome tales of when he worked in a slaughterhouse. Brian Hood would argue with anybody and everybody and, if he couldn't find someone to have a go at, he'd argue with himself. Hoody was one of them who had lost his purpose after he retired. He lived on his own and work had been his world. As soon as he didn't have work to go to he went to the pub; he was rattling the door knob at eleven o'clock every morning. He didn't look after himself properly and didn't eat right. Many a time I have heard Tetley Dave say to him, 'What's for dinner Brian?' Only to be told the same thing each time. 'A tin of stewed steak, a tin of new potatoes and a tin of marrow fat peas.' Jim and Barry were two likely lads who liked to wind Hoody up. It was taproom banter that went a bit too far sometimes but they were genuinely fond of him and were the first to help him when he fell ill. The famous pools winner Viv Nicholson used to call in for a glass of white wine. Viv had been famous in the media at one time for her catchphrase, 'I'm going to spend spend spend.' And spend she did, even after all the money had gone. Viv was good-hearted and generous. One day she asked Tetley Dave to fill everybody's glass and said that she would be paying. Dave looked round the room and saw a dozen thirsty drinkers and his eye lit up. When he had finished pulling he said, 'Including myself Viv, that'll be £31 for cash.' Viv pulled a credit card out of an ancient snakeskin purse. Dave said, 'Now come on Viv, you know I haven't got facilities for plastic cards.' Viv didn't bat an eyelid. 'Well I'm sorry Dave, it's either that or put the beer back into the pump.' Dave nearly fainted on the spot.

In his own way Dave was a glorious storyteller with an half-soaked style and anarchic presentation. He was also a good musician in his own right and played everything from the blues harp to the penny whistle and the African djembele to the bagpipes. He loved dressing up and seemed to have an outfit for most occasions. He had what he referred to as his James Bond outfit, it comprised a clean white shirt, faux silk dickie bow with a cream-coloured sports jacket. He generally wore it with a flower in his button hole. When the George Formby Society came for their 'plonking' he pulled out all sorts of fancy dress. They did a song called 'The Left Hand Side of Egypt'. For this he would don his Arabian gear. This was a striped candlewick dressing gown topped off with a plain tea towel held onto his head with a frayed snake belt. He'd come onto the stage like a poor man's Wilson Kepple and Betty doing a sand dance. Even in his ordinary daywear he was eccentric. He often wore a red top hat that he'd bought off a hawker on the harbour side at Whitby during Folk Week. When he wasn't wearing that, he wore a checked trilby with a peacock feather in it. He had a collection of way-out waistcoats and held his shirt sleeves up with elasticated silver sleeve garters like a honky-tonk pianist.

We found ourselves in a pub at Filey one evening. He shambled through the door like a fairground barker. Within minutes he had the assembled company spellbound with his ditties and parodies. The landlady had a lively Jack Russell and it jumped up and tried to bite Dave. It took a piece out of his trousers. Dave was mid-stream telling a tale and hardly paused to take stock. He just winked across at the landlady and said, 'That'll cost you three more pints!' On the way back from Filey we stopped off at the Howden Arms in

Tadcaster. We knew 'Tozzer' the landlord there. Dave started singing on the way in. Sam Smith's had not long before brought in their ban on singing and music in their pubs. Tozzer said, 'You'll get me bloody shot.' Dave kept a miniature harmonica, only about as big as a cufflink, in the back of his wallet. As soon as Tozzer's back was turned, Dave took out his harmonica and hid it between his lips. He then strolled round the bar blowing 'John Brown's body lies a-mouldering in the grave'.

The problem Tetley Dave had was that his pub – while being a proper old-fashioned backstreet local, the sort of pub that everybody claims to love – just didn't have enough customers for it to make him and his family a living. All the customers knew each other by their first name, they all had their habits and drinking times and only so much money to spend. The company that rented the place to Dave were ruthless and unsympathetic and their rep told him that things couldn't go on like this. In the middle of a monthly meeting, the rep told Dave, 'We can make more money off this place if it was a car park.'

The Shoulder of Mutton started life as a toll house on the road out of Castleford towards Leeds in the middle of the eighteenth century. Castleford at one time was famous for its potteries and some of the old family firms like Clokies and Hartley's had their works near the pub. Even though the last of the works had closed down in the 1960s, the people who lived in the terraced rows still liked to say that they came from the potteries. Castleford also had a glass and engineering industry and these factories too were just over the way from The Shoulder. In its heyday the pub catered for thirsty workers and was a goldmine. Tetley Dave used to talk about a legendary barman called Tommy Whatshisname who would start pulling pints at half past eleven on a Sunday morning and not stop till time was called at two. 'He had a right arm like Popeye,' Dave would say. The Shoulder was noted for the quality of its Tetley bitter, one of those pubs that aficionados would visit because it kept a good drop.

Dave had longed to own his own place, but could never afford it so he had to rent. When the holding company started talking about making more money from the land as a car park, it upset Dave. He was adamant that he could turn the place around. When the rep asked him how, he said, 'I've got some ideas.' The rep said, 'Have you got a business plan?' Dave shook his head and told the rep that he didn't know what a business plan was and anyhow he wasn't a very good speller. The rep shook his head this time. He said, 'I'll give you a month and then we need to look at your books.'

Dave needed a guardian angel. He ended up with two of the unlikeliest angels he could have wished for. First came 'Professor' Peter a graduate of Lampeter University. Peter had recently been working in Manchester for an examination board but had come home to Castleford to look after an elderly mother. Pete was a kind and intelligent man, but he did like the odd sherbet or two and one night knocked his head on a lamppost outside Dave's pub as he meandered home. Dave went out to help him. They became mates. Pete became Dave's unofficial scribe and started to put Dave's paperwork and correspondence in order. Next came Nick Strutt, a musician who looked like an old-time western preacher. Nick was an enthusiastic imbiber of drink and marijuana and down on his luck. He knocked on Dave's door one afternoon with an old suitcase in hand and the clothes he stood up in and asked if he might have a room for a few nights. He stayed for three years and became as familiar in the taproom as Dave's dartboard. It was partly through Nick's ideas that Dave started to build a new clientele. Nick had studied at the University of Leeds in the 1960s. While there he became one of the first people in the city to be arrested for growing his own cannabis. After he graduated in 1970 he formed a band called Natchez Trace along with Roger Knowles. For a while they were a highly regarded country band and had a certain amount of success, they even managed a support slot with Willie Nelson when he toured Britain. According to Dave, Nick Strutt had a bigger entry in *The Encyclopaedia of Country Music* than Willie Nelson did. Nick was a brilliant multi-instrumentalist. He played banjo, guitar, autoharp, bass and, most notably, mandolin. He had an idiosyncratic style and played whatever he heard that he liked. He joined Bob and Carole Pegg in the folk-rock group Mr Fox. They won folk album of the year in a *Melody Maker* poll and were adored by the critics but never made a go of it commercially. By the 1980s Nick was on the old-time country music circuit. He also ran huge jam sessions and encouraged musicians of all backgrounds to turn up and play. He was a great teacher as well and helped a lot of young people who were looking to play rootsier music styles.

Dave played hell up about Nick at times, but usually forgot what he had been annoyed about by the following morning. 'I don't think I've ever eaten so well,' Dave told me one day. 'He cooks with herbs that he's growing in two old pot sinks round the back.' It wasn't just culinary herbs that Nick was growing either. 'He keeps bloody funny hours though. He's like a bloody vampire. He sleeps most of the day and he only seems to come alive once it's dark. Last night I'd called last orders and I was putting some glasses to soak in the sink when he came down in his paisley dressing gown and silk cravat and said "Anybody for gaming?" We ended up playing dominoes till three in the morning and he only went to bed when he'd finished a bottle of vodka.'

It was Nick who helped Dave to turn the pub into a venue for great live music. They pulled some old fitted seats out of one end of the lounge and they built a little stage with some recycled timber. Dave rechristened his lounge 'The Palladium of the Potteries' and decorated his walls with photographs of musicians and worn-out instruments. He even had an antique lit-up revolving sign over the stage that had been in the foyer of a local cinema and had once pointed people to the upper circle. Nick organised regular Sunday lunchtime sessions and managed to persuade some able players to turn up and play in exchange for beer. Brian Golbey, the country guitar picker came, as did the fiddlers Graham Hall and Walter Fairburn who had played with the lads from Lindisfarne and Jack the Lad. There was an Estonian accordion player called Tyvo who came, and Stevie Mac, a talented guitarist and singer of Irish folk music, was always there. They all blended seamlessly with musicians from up the road and sometimes there would be as many as two-dozen playing away on 'Meet Me on the Corner' and 'Blowin' in the Wind'. The beer flowed and The Shoulder became a secret venue for musicians who wanted to enjoy a no frills, no fuss pub. I took my friend, the jazz musician Mark Witty in there one evening. He brought his saxophone in with him. Dave was straight over, 'I don't think we've had a saxophone in here before, does thy know "Baker Street"?'

The company who owned the pub still wanted Dave out, but put him on a peppercorn rent for two months as a sop. In the meantime they started sending men with clipboards round to measure up, note down and survey the land at the back. Caravan Gary, who lived in an old caravan in the garden, panicked when he saw these men and so did Dave. Nick was wiser, he said to Dave, 'Just play them at your own game David, act simple!' Dave smiled and then did a double-take like James Finlayson does in the Laurel and Hardy films. Nick said, 'You know what I mean, slow time them.' The next time the surveyors came Dave went out into the yard with a rusting telescope and put it to his good eye. The surveyors noticed him and wondered what this man in a red top hat and waistcoat was doing looking at the eaves of a pub through a telescope. Curiosity got the better of them and they asked what he was looking at. 'Oh I'm just looking at a hole where the bats come in and out. I like to know about wildlife, don't you? There's a bloke from the council estate over the way who says that I've got a very rare colony of horseshoe bats living here, but I'm not sure. I say, you wouldn't happen to know anything about bats would you?' He offered the telescope to the surveyor. The surveyor shook his head and declined.

'Only I've heard that they're not to be disturbed, but you know what these wildlife conservation people are like don't you? Always protesting about summat or other. That bloke on the council estate goes walking round ponds looking for great crested newts. He's even been up my garden to the beck that runs along that fence. He says he's seen water voles in there.' Three weeks earlier

Dave had been prowling his grounds with an air rifle. I came to the pub with something for him early one morning and he was crouched behind a dustbin taking aim at rats.

As the surveyors got back into their car, Dave said, 'Do you want to see my chipmunks before you go?' The men in suits couldn't wait to escape. Dave opened a flap in the wooden side of his garage and made a squeaking noise to encourage his pet chipmunks to come to the bars of their cage. The surveyors jumped into their car and roared out of the yard, never to return.

Tetley Dave was the master of slow timing and could fix his expression into the mask of a man befuddled with the world around him. He could push his bottom lip up over his top one, narrow his eyes and, with the slightest shake of his head, make you believe that although he was trying his best, he had no idea what on earth was going on. Of course he knew very well what was up, he was as sharp as a tack, as wily as the coyote. The pub company rep came to tell him that even with the peppercorn rent and despite his own efforts, the pub wasn't working. He said Dave's lease would end in the near future and the pub would shut down.

Dave threw himself into a mock rage. 'Well you thick-skinned enamel bastards! You'd throw a hard-working man to the streets would you? What century are you living in?'

The rep started to apologise for the inconvenience and mentioned that the eviction would be made as smooth as possible.

'Inconvenience! It's not inconvenient, it's bloody inhumane! Anyhow, you can't do anything for at least two years can you?'

'I'm sorry Dave, we need to start on this straightaway.'

Dave pulled his bottom lip up, thought for a bit and then said, 'Hold your horses lad. I don't see how you can. After you came here last time and put me on that peppercorn rent, I went straight up to the bank and paid two years up front. Seeing as I haven't heard anything back and your company accepted my money, I thought everything was in order.'

The rep never came back. The company got in touch with Dave and asked him if he wanted to buy the pub. Dave told them that, 'Aye I'll take it off your hands.' And within a few months he owned the place lock, stock and barrel. He set about building his little empire with glee.

At the drop of his trilby hat Dave could conjure up a story to publicise himself and his pub. He was constantly on the telephone to the local radio station spinning them a yarn to let them know he had won some award or another. Dave had certificates for all sorts of awards, nobody seemed to know where they came from. I was in the taproom one afternoon when Dave came out of the cellar with beer barrel tap in his hand. He said, 'Just look at this plastic shit, it's not worth a toss, it's split and there's beer running all over my floor. I'm going to have to buy some proper steel ones.' He discovered that an old-fashioned firm of beer cellar suppliers in Birmingham were still making steel taps. He nearly fainted when they quoted him £100 apiece, but bought two anyway and then set about trying to recoup his outlay.

He decided he would celebrate Yorkshire Day by ceremonially whacking the two steel taps into firkins with a well-worn mallet and then give a lecture on the ancient art of cellarmanship. The beer came from Denzil's, a little brewery at Great Heck. Dave arranged for it to be transported by various forms of traditional vehicle. Denzil knew a bloke with a horse and cart. The week before Yorkshire Day, Dave turned up at the brewery wearing a white rose tucked into the band of his hat. He loaded the two casks onto the cart. He then took the reins of the horse, said 'Walk on Silver' and clip-clopped his way down to the Aire and Calder Canal a couple of miles down the road. Les Bowkett had a small boat waiting on the canal and the beer was loaded onto that for a five mile an hour journey down to Castleford. At the basin the beer was transferred to a 1940s Land Rover to be brought to the pub. Dave had arranged for the whole process to be filmed by Bob from the local CAMRA branch and this caught the attention of many passers-by who followed Dave like he was a pied piper down to The Shoulder of Mutton. With a captive audience, Dave was in his element and spun more and more bizarre yarns. He ended up with a full pub that afternoon and the following week when he ceremonially tapped his casks. He more than paid for his new taps.

For a few years on a Sunday afternoon we had a regular domino school at The Shoulder of Mutton. Dave used to put platefuls of dripping on bread and sliced black pudding on the bar top and by ten past twelve you could hear the sound of dominoes being shuffled on a polished table. Amongst the players was a bloke called 'Plant Pot', a lovely man who was famous for the quality of his tomatoes. He shared them with us as soon as they came in season. Barnsley Brian enjoyed a game and there was a smart old lad called Sonny who had flown in Lancaster bombers during the war. Then there was Don. Don loved to play Fives and Threes and liked to smoke Benson and Hedges, one after another while he played. When the smoking ban came in, Don moved the domino table nearer to the fireplace so that he could blow his smoke up the chimney. Tetley Dave was a bit relaxed at first about the smoking ban. He didn't encourage people to carry on, but turned his blind eye away most of the time. On weekend evenings when the pub had a nice few in, Dave called time at eleven, but kept open until the last person had had enough. By half past eleven, the curtains were pulled tight and the ashtrays were on the tables. One day he told us that the council had sent someone with a tobacco smoke detector and they had given him an official warning. The next time Don lit up Dave went across and told him, 'I'm sorry Don old lad, but I'm under strict orders from the government not to let anybody smoke from now on.' The domino table nearly went up in the air. 'If you think the bloody government is in its rights to make an old pensioner stand outside in the wind and rain to have a cig, then you've another think coming.' Dave didn't know what to say, so he went back to the bar shaking his head and muttering under his breath. We didn't see Don after that and Sundays weren't the same. We tried to carry on but losing Don upset the rhythm and Plant Pot lost his partner. Then Plant Pot stopped coming in as well and the game was up.

For months after, Dave told his tale of woe to anybody who stopped to listen for long enough. The Shoulder used to get occasional visits from rugby league fans from Lancashire whenever they were playing Castleford at Wheldon Lane. Dave would say,

'If you think it's quiet in here, you can blame the government. I haven't heard a domino on that table since the fucking smoking ban and as for that pub down the road that does Sunday dinners, I don't think they've peeled a potato this year. Give it three months and that place will be a car park.' He was referring to a rival pub called The Fourways. It didn't become a car park when it got knocked down, but it might as well have done. Some young Lithuanian lads brought wash leathers and an old, hand-turned wringing machine and now run the wasteland as a car wash place.

Enter Martin Stage Left

Tetley Dave surveys his whole world from behind the bar in his taproom at The Shoulder of Mutton. This afternoon his world is troubled. For the past few days he hasn't been able to sit down properly owing to a swelling on his backside. This morning he'd yelped like a pup in pain when he went to the cellar to tap a new barrel.

There's just me, Brian Hood, Brian Jones and Old Pete the retired brickie in. Old Pete's reading the obituary notices in the *Pontefract and Castleford Express* and he's not to be disturbed. Steve the pigeon fancier comes in like a gust of wind for his early half of mild. He upsets Tetley Dave straightaway by suggesting that he's been given short measure. 'Hey up,' he says, 'Is the vicar in?' He points to his glass with a good inch of froth on it, 'Because there's a bigger white collar on that than there is on the vicar up at St Paul's Church.' Tetley Dave lifts the glass and holds it up to the light like he's examining a specimen, grips the handpump like he's about to swing a club and squirts a few more drops into it. 'Here! Don't drink it too fast. I don't want you tumbling down in this taproom and putting a claim in.'

Now they stand either side of the bar waiting for the other to say something, it's like watching two chess players without a board. Tetley Dave winces every time he picks a glass up to wipe.

'What's up with thee Vicar?'

'Not that it's owt to do with thee, but there's something on my arse and it's as sore as a boil.'

'It might be a boil.'

'Aye. It might be a boil.'

Steve thinks for a bit. 'Well you know what you want don't

you?' He doesn't wait to be asked what Dave wants. 'You want a poultice.'

'A what?'

'A poultice. My grandmother swore by bread poultices when she got a boil and at that time she was riddled with boils.'

Old Pete looks up from his paper, sighs, shakes his head, then licks his finger and turns a page.

'Just break a bit of stale bread up, slice an onion and put some warm milk on it, then mix it into a paste. Then what you do is hold it on with a clean rag.'

Tetley Dave starts to hum the melody to 'Tell Me The Old, Old Story' and winces again.

'They say that cabbage poultice is good as well. I can fetch a couple of cabbage leaves up when I come back from my allotment if you want. You need them dark green 'uns from the outside.'

Dave is getting irritated now. 'To speak frankly Steve lad, I don't think I want to rub the cheeks of my arse with one of your cabbages, but thank you for the offer all the same.'

Brian Hood has been sitting on his stool in the corner listening. Hoody doesn't say much, but when he does, it's usually a dry rejoinder. His comments range from pearls of true wisdom to simple-minded fool's play. 'Bacon rind! They say bacon rind is good for fetching puss out.'

Tetley Dave spins round and winces again. 'Now look here Hoody, I don't know who's rattled your cage, but if I was you, I would keep that out!' He points to his nose.

'Of course!' Steve chimes in again. 'If you want a really old-fashioned remedy that draws puss out and works every time, there's nothing finer than the hot bottle.'

Old Pete looks up from the paper again and nudges Brian Jones. They both shake their heads.

'It's simple Dave, all you have to do is swill one of them bottles out that you've got in that empties crate and stand it in red-hot water for twenty minutes. When it's ready, drop thi trousers, empty the water out of your bottle and press the rim of it over your boil. That'll fetch everything out. You might have to ask your Margaret to do it for you, cos it'll make thee jump.'

Dave has had enough now. 'If thy thinks I'm going to let my wife hold a red-hot beer bottle anywhere near my arse, thy's got another think coming.'

Laughter erupts from the beer bellies of everyone in the room. Dave thinks he is being laughed at. He is. As soon as the penny drops, he shows he doesn't like it. He jabs Steve the pigeon man in the chest with a huge finger. 'Look here thee. Across that road,' now he jabs his finger towards the window, 'there's a surgery and in that surgery there is a Pakistani doctor, he's called Dr Hussein. He's a very able young man, an expert in most matters medical. When I want advice or treatment regarding my health, whether it's stomach ache, headache, ball ache or a boil on my arse, I think I'll go and seek it from him. And when I want advice from a bloke with mucky hands who spends half of his life in a fucking allotment and the other half in an ale house I'll let thee know.'

There is a pregnant pause. Steve the pigeon man looks crestfallen. Tetley Dave glances down at Steve's near empty glass. 'And don't thee worry old lad, if ever I get a poorly pigeon, you can bet your knackers that your allotment will be my first port of call. Now do you want another half in there?'

Steve swigs the last few dregs of his beer. He doesn't say anything, but pushes his glass towards the handpump. Tetley Dave refills it. Still, nobody says anything, so Dave starts skat singing, 'Shoo da be doo ba, shooby doo.' Nobody takes a blind bit of notice of him, so he raises the volume and starts to sing a George Formby song.

> Up the west end, that's the best end
> Where the night clubs thrive.
> There's a jazz queen, she's a has-been
> Has been Lord knows what.

Old Pete looks up from his newspaper, folds it and throws it onto the windowsill behind him. 'My early new potatoes are about ready for digging up. I'll fetch a boiling in tomorrow, all you will need is some fresh mint to go with them.'

'Bloody lovely!' Dave says and smacks his lips at the thought. The conversation moves on to home produce from the garden and all talk of boils and arses dissipates into the smoke-filled air of the little taproom.

The door swings open. Martin Oxley strides in like a whirlwind. 'Fill us a tankard of rough, landlord, my stomach thinks my throat is cut. I've been standing at that bus stop for nearly half an hour. That bus service is like my bloody arse!'

We all look at Martin and try not to laugh.

He says, 'What?'

Nobody says anything.

'Have I to go out and come back in again?'

Martin makes a big to-do of going out and coming back in again. When he comes back he goes straight to the Ring the Bull game and says, 'First pint on thee landlord if I get it on first time.' Dave rushes from the back of the bar. Martin takes hold of the ring. 'And before you can get your cheating fingers on this string...' He throws the ring and it goes straight onto the hook.

One time Martin and I were in Cambridgeshire at a grand old pub called The Blue Ball in Grantchester. The Blue Ball has a very good example of Ring the Bull. We sat on our own in the corner and listened to the locals telling the tale. There were more than enough rugger union chaps in and some of their talk made us shudder. I don't think I've seen so many blokes with the sleeves of argyle sweaters draped over their shoulders. They were teasing each other, boasting and telling lies. Two of them challenged each other to a game of Ring the Bull and had a couple of practise swings like Sunday morning golfers. Martin and I watched them and tried not to laugh. They were no great shakes. Eventually one of the blokes got the ring on and claimed victory. They went back to the bar. Martin winked at me and went over to the blokes at the bar. 'Is it all right if we have a go? We've never seen that game before and it looks like a lot of fun.'

'Of course lads, be our guests. Show them how it works, Giles.'

'I think we'll see what they are made of first, Miles.' I saw him wink at his mate.

Martin and I took it in turns. He'd already told me under his breath not to try too hard. It was hardly Minnesota Fats and Fast Eddie, but I knew Miles and Giles were hustling. So was Martin. The throwing distance was just a bit longer than in Tetley Dave's taproom but the ring and hook were much bigger. Martin got it on by the third go. 'You lucky bugger! How did you do that?' Martin winked again, 'Watch and learn brother, watch and learn!' Then he deliberately missed the next dozen goes before giving up. I could hear Giles and Miles sniggering into their beer behind us. I turned to them. 'There must be a technique that you can show us?' Miles pulled his jumper off his shoulders and took hold of the ring.

'You need to pull back until the string is taught, then eye up the target and swing in a gentle arc.' He did it and missed by a good three inches.

'Oh! Bad luck, Miles.'

Miles handed the ring to me and said, 'Here, have a go.'

I swung and got it on. 'Hey I think I've got the hang of it Martin. Me and you ought to have a match.' We played best of ten throws each and made a pig's ear of it and drew one apiece.

Giles said, 'We normally play for a pint, do you two fancy a game of doubles against us?'

I said, 'I'm not sure we are ready for that yet.' Martin said, 'Go on Ian, it's only for a pint and it'll be a bit of fun.' I saw the eyes of Miles and Giles light up.

We beat them hands down and suggested it might have been beginner's luck, so offered double or quits. We beat them again in the return fixture and when Martin suggested a third game for luck, they both decided it was time they went home for dinner. The landlord pulled two pints into our pots and said, 'And these are on me lads, that's the best laugh I've had for ages.'

One afternoon not long after, I was stood with Martin at the bar in Tetley Dave's and we told him about the Ring the Bull at

Grantchester. Dave studied for a bit and then said, 'We ought to start an English Ring the Bull Championships and play that pub home and away.' Then he got distracted. Pete who worked at the Malt Kilns was playing darts with his brother. One of them said, 'I wonder why the numbers on the board are in the sequence that they're in?' Martin decided that there must be some sort of mathematical formula to it. He ripped the front off a couple of beer mats and sat in the corner, adding, subtracting and dividing. Tetley Dave kept saying to him that he was wasting his time because the sequence was completely random. 'Nobody knows why it's that way or who came up with it.' Martin ignored him and carried on. 'There must be a reason Dave, there's a reason for everything.' Dave blew air though his lips. Dave thought there was neither rhyme nor reason for most things that happened. 'I'm telling thee Martin, it's a mystery, let it be. And stop ripping my fucking beer mats up, they were clean out today.' Martin wouldn't be said and carried on with his scribbling. In the end Dave said, 'I'll tell you what, I've got Dennis Priestley's mobile phone number, I'll phone him, he'll know if anybody does.'

'Who's Dennis Priestley?'

Dave went as a red as a Tetley beer mat. 'Who's Dennis Priestley? Who's bloody Dennis Priestley? I thought you were supposed to be educated. He's only the finest dart thrower ever to come out of South Yorkshire. That's who Dennis Priestley is. He beat Bristow six-nowt in the final. He's got a newspaper shop in Mexborough. What he doesn't know about darts you could put on a Rizla. He's a mate of mine, in fact he's thrown darts at that board over that fireplace.'

'Phone him then.'

'I will.'

'Go on then!'

Dave held the contacts directory of his mobile up to his good eye. Dennis Priestly answered. Dave asked about the sequence while pointing at the numbers on the board in front of us. We heard him say, 'Right then Dennis, thank you very much, I'll let them know.'

Martin looked up from his scribbling. He was still trying to work it out even as Dave talked on the phone. He said, 'Go on then, what did he say?'

Dave said, 'He doesn't know.'

Martin chucked his pen across the room.

Martin Oxley is a living and breathing pub character of the finest order. He is also at times the master of mistiming. We were at the Cambridge Folk Festival sitting in a circle on fold-up chairs. We all had a pint of Wells bitter: Joop from Amsterdam, Ian from County Durham, Vernon up from Cornwall with his wife Dot, Jane and Colin from Kent, Martin, Heather and me. Martin can't sit still for more than two minutes, even when he's got a pint in his hand, so he was standing up for a look round, talking for the sake of it and generally getting on everybody's wick. We were trying to listen to Nanci Griffith singing her gentle country songs. 'It's a bit slow for me I'm afraid,' Martin announced, 'I'm going to find something a bit livelier, I've heard that there's some Shetland Island fiddlers on the other stage.' He went stomping across the field. We were relieved to see the back of him. We listened to Nanci Griffith's set hardly breathing. Martin came storming back after half an hour. His return coincided with Nanci Griffith exhaling the last few bars of a beautiful rendition of the Julie Gold song 'From a Distance'. There was a silent second or two while everybody let out the breath they had been holding and you could almost hear hearts beating. Then applause and when the clapping died down, Martin stood in the middle of our circle and announced, 'Well I don't know what you lot have been listening to, but them Shetland fiddlers were the dog's bollocks.' Not just us, but everybody within earshot looked at him.

I first met Martin when we were boys. He lived next door but two to my Aunt Alice on South View near the railway line. Martin liked to sit under my aunt's laburnum tree and write down the numbers of the trains that passed by. After he left school Martin got a job as an engineer at Ackton Hall pit and studied for his papers at night school. His real passion was for amateur dramatics and singing. He had a natural singing voice that could slide between tenor and light baritone. There is a lovely story about Featherstone Amateur Dramatics becoming the first amateur company to get the rights to do *Jesus Christ Superstar*. In 1983, the week after Featherstone Rovers won the cup at Wembley, the secretary of the local am drams wrote to ask permission to perform the musical. They got a letter back granting them permission with a note attached congratulating the local team for their fine cup win. Whoever was dishing out the permissions had seen the cup final. They said they were impressed by the fact that a pit town, not much bigger than a village, could put on such a show at Wembley. Martin landed the role of Jesus. He grew his hair and beard and looked liked Jesus. At least he looked like Robert Powell looking like Jesus. After that, Martin established himself in the lead role in everything the am drams did. In *Seven Brides for Seven Brothers* you could almost see and hear Howard Keel when he sang 'Bless Your Beautiful Hide'. That's if Howard Keel had ever come from a pit village in West Yorkshire. When they performed that show at Wakefield Theatre Royal and Opera House, Martin was in his glory. He managed to get me some tickets for a box and I sat there flabbergasted. He slapped his buckskin thigh just like they did in the MGM musicals.

Martin had more hobbies than any man I've ever known. He retained a life-long passion for steam trains and trained first to be a fireman and then a driver on the North York Moors railway. He had a model railway in his attic with scaled down villages and woods for the trains to go past. He had a collection of Paul Robeson records second to none, as well as recordings by the Red Army Choir. He had fly fishing tackle, guns for shooting game birds, military memorabilia, stamps, coins, four pairs of clogs for dancing in and more outfits than Mr Benn. He joined the English Civil War Society and thought nothing of walking about on the public roads in full costume. One Saturday morning I was preparing a cooked breakfast when I realised I had run out of bread. I nipped into Station Lane to buy a loaf. I was jogging back up the Lane when I dropped on Martin who was going off for the weekend to recreate the Battle of Adwalton Moor. He had the full Cavalier gear on, complete with thigh-length boots and a wide-brimmed hat. He shouted across the road to me at the top of his voice, 'Good morrow kind sir, I see that you have the staff of life beneath your arm.' I shouted back, 'Good morning comrade.' If anybody passing had seen or heard us they would have thought the pair of us wanted certifying.

Most of all Martin liked to sup ale. When he was on his jaunts fighting the Roundheads, he supped out of a pewter tankard that he kept fastened to his belt with a piece of leather. He had a collection of glasses that he bought at every folk festival he went to and at Tetley Dave's pub he had his own glass with the insignia of the Royal Naval Association on it.

Martin could spend time in the company of anyone or anybody and within five minutes he'd be joining in with tales, regaling them with anecdotes that connected to their culture. Ask him something about native American Indians and he'd pull out an obscure fact that you'd struggle to believe, but he'd assure you, 'It's true.' Probe him on the love poetry of Persia, he'd give you a recitation. Martin seemed to know something about everything, but was especially passionate about the vernacular folk traditions of England.

It's Saturday afternoon and the Holmfirth Folk Festival is in full swing. In the cobbled yard outside The Nook, The Britannia Coconut Dancers of Bacup are coming to the end of their performance. The dancers, all men, have blacked-up faces and dress mainly in black clothes, apart from their skirts which have a red and white stripe on them. They have wooden bobbins strapped to the inside of their palms and kneecaps and they carry floral hoops. To accompany their dance they have a drummer, a fiddler and an accordion player. It is one of the strangest things I think I've seen on the way into a pub. Martin has relished every moment from start to finish and as they take their bows he cheers them and pats every one of them on their back. He gives me a fiver and says, 'Here, go and get the ale in, I'm just going to have a word with this chap here.' Before I get across the yard, I hear Martin address his new mate by his first name and ask about the history of the dance group.

Five minutes later Martin bounces into the little room at the side of the bar with a white turban on decorated with flowers. 'I've made myself a member!' He then launches into a lecture on the entire history of the Britannia Coconut Dancers. 'I've been wanting to see them for ages. I've read a lot about them and that chap I spoke to just then has confirmed a lot of what I'd thought. Do you know that dance they were doing goes back to the seventeenth century when Moorish sailors landed in Cornwall and then moved up to Lancashire to work in the quarries and mills?' I know what is coming next, so under my breath I say, 'No I didn't know that the dance went back to Moorish sailors who washed up in Cornwall and then made their way to Lancashire.'

Martin has the uncanny ability to give a loud, lucid and entertaining lecture on any subject you can mention, even if he's just digested the information he wants to recycle. We were in the Bradley Arms when he told me he was house hunting. I happened to mention that there was an old stone cottage opposite where I live for sale. I said that I'd heard that it was an old saddlemaker's workshop. Ten minutes later, I heard him tell Max Morley, 'I'm thinking of buying the old saddlemaker's cottage on Ackton Lane. Do you know Max, it goes back well into the 1600s and that oak beam across the front is the original wood from when it was a workshop.'

Today, Martin says, 'The trouble with a lot of folk these days, is that they have turned their backs on their own traditions. There's nothing wrong with a bloke in a beard dancing with a flower garland.'

I suggest to him, between mouthfuls of Taylor's Golden Best, that the dance we have seen seems a bit anachronistic these days. 'It borders on the mildly racist as well.'

Martin spits out a mouthful of beer. 'Fucking racist! Don't you tell me that you have joined the fucking politically correct brigade. How can that be racist?'

'Well they black their faces up.'

Martin studies my expression. 'It's not the chuffing Black and White Minstrel Show. That's muck on their faces. Working man's muck!'

'I thought you said the dance was brought over by Moorish sailors.'

'Aye, well that black face you see now represents the pits they worked in. Fuck me! You come from Featherstone and you don't know what a coal miner looks like before his bath. Thi grandad would be spinning in his grave. Fucking racist! I mean to say, it's coming to something when a man can't put a bit of black on his face and dance in a pair of clogs without getting accused of summat or other.'

We drink our Taylor's and Martin says, 'It's your turn.' In the opposite corner of the room, we hear three musicians speaking in French. Two of them are fiddle players and one has a concertina. They start to play a little two-step. Martin takes his cue and shouts over to them. 'Laissez le bon temps roulez!' They smile and strike up with the old Louisiana waltz tune 'Jolie Blon'. From somewhere Martin remembers fragments of lyrics from the song and starts to sing.

'Jolie blond, jolie fille, tu m'a quitte pour t'en aller.'

When he forgets the next line, one of the fiddlers feeds it to him and Martin immediately picks up on it, hardly missing a beat. It's very entertaining and by the end of the song everybody in the bar is cheering and clapping. Martin stands up, bows deeply and then turns to me. 'You can't beat a bit of the old Cajun.' Then he turns to the musicians and asks, 'Where are you from lads… Baton Rouge?' The concertina player says, 'Well actually, us two are from Huddersfield, but our friend here is from Rouen, so we try to speak in French for him.' The French fiddle player from Rouen nods and smiles.

Martin sits back down. He lights up a cigarette and blows the smoke up into the air like an engine. 'Rouen, eh? Well you'll know that Joan of Arc was burned at the stake there, won't you?' And here we go again.

We drank half a dozen pints in The Nook that afternoon. As we came away, the lads from Rouen and Huddersfield were playing 'My Old Man's a Dustman' accompanied by a guitar player, who Martin had established came from Norfolk. Martin had already told him that Woodforde's beers Norfolk Nog and Wherry were his favourites from down there and that he had supped many a pint of them whenever he was in Norwich.

Outside in the yard, another impromptu session had broken out. Half a dozen guitarists, two banjo players, an Irish whistler and three violinists were going at it full pelt. In the corner of the yard there was an old plastic washing-up bowl full of leaves and rainwater. Martin picked it up, chucked the water out and joined the session, playing the washing-up bowl like a bodhrán with his fingers.

Saturday Afternoon Society

Martin decided he wanted to go to see the Haxey Hood game. This is an ancient form of village pub folklore that takes place every January on the twelfth day of Christmas, or as Martin would have it, old Christmas day. Haxey Hood is a kind of rugby match that involves hundreds of villagers from Haxey and nearby Westwoodside struggling across open fields with a leather-coated cylinder, trying to get it back to their favourite pub. Once the landlord or landlady of the pub touches the cylinder the game is over. It can take up to four hours to complete the game and by that time there is mud all over, more than a few cuts and bruises and the odd broken bone. Local folklore says that the game has been taking place since the middle ages. In 1359, so the story goes, Lady de Mowbray, the wife of the John de Mowbray, Baron of Axholme, was out riding when her silk hood blew off as she came over the brow of the hill between the two villages. Some field labourers chased the hood as it blew on the wind, until one lad caught it and returned it to the lady. So charmed was the lady by the kindness of the lads, that she is said to have donated a piece of land on condition that the chasing of the hood was re-enacted every year on the same date. It could be true, except that their are no written records to take the game back much further than Victorian times, but there certainly was a Baron and Lady de Mowbray back in the middle of the 14th century.

The year that Martin, his partner Hazel, our mate Paul and I went, the Hood was held on a Saturday. If the twelfth day of Christmas falls on a Sunday, they hold the game the day before. These days, the Hood is played between four pubs: Kings Arms, The Loco, Duke William and Carpenters Arms at Westwoodside.

The idea being that the hood is delivered into the hands of the proprietor of one of those four pubs. Before the game starts there is a great procession like something out of *The Wicker Man*. A 'fool' dressed in brightly coloured strips of cloth is followed by 'boggins' dressed in red hunting coats and bowler hats with flowers on them. The fool then stands on a stone in front of the church and makes a speech. At the end of the speech some damp straw is set alight around him in a ritual known as 'Smoking the Fool' and then he encourages the crowd in a chant 'Hoose agen hoose, toon agen toon, if a man meet a man, nok 'im doon, but doant 'ot 'im.' After that everybody heads up to a field above the village and the game starts when the hood is thrown into the air. Before all of that though, a lot of singing and supping happens in the Duke William.

The singing is loud and raucous. The pub is overflowing. It takes Martin nearly half an hour to come back from the bar with the ale and he prides himself on his ability to catch a barmaid's eye. We spill more beer than we sup trying to find a place to stand amongst the elbows knees and sweating bodies. The gathered crowd sing 'John Barleycorn' and 'Drink England Dry' and at least three versions of 'The Farmer's Boy'. Martin joins in with glee.

And when the lad becomes a man
The good old farmer died
And left the lad the farm he had
And his daughter for a bride
The lad that was, the farm now has
Oft smiles and thinks with joy
Of the lucky day he came that way
To be a farmer's boy

On the last line everybody chucks what is remaining in their glasses into the air. I don't know who gives the signal, but as one, everybody leaves the pub and makes their way up to the field beyond the church. The chief boggin throws the hood into the air and what the locals call 'the sway' forms. It's like a rugby scrum involving robust men, women, boys and girls of all ages. The scrum collapses, they all stop then stand up again and off it goes once more. It's exhausting work and very muddy. A lot of the players wear sports wear, overalls and boiler suits, but we see teenage girls in jeans and t-shirts getting stuck in as well. Of course there's no show without punch so Martin joins in with the shoving and decides he's on the Westwoodside team and tries to help their lads push the sway over the brow of the hill and down to the Carpenters Arms. The sway is like a whale thrashing about in the shallows, but once it gets onto the road between the two villages it gathers momentum.

On the day we were there the sway lasted over four hours, it was dark before the landlady at the Kings Arms at the other end of Haxey managed to get a grip of the hood. We enjoyed taking part in the game, it's something that is a special part of village and pub folklore. More than that, there's a lot of dressing up involved, a lot of singing and storytelling and, most of all, a lot of ale drinking. Martin was in his glory that day.

The pubs in Haxey are used to the mess and prepare for it days before. They move anything that might get broken out of the way and line the carpets and walls of their pubs with thick sheets of plastic. On the street outside everybody moves their parked cars. One of the locals told me that a visitor who didn't know the routine once left his car in the way of the action. He found it the following day in a field, hundreds of yards away from where he'd parked it.

Martin decided that we should form the Saturday Afternoon Society. It was a very exclusive club consisting of two members, him and me. Somehow he managed to persuade his partner Hazel to join us and drive the car. The Saturday Afternoon Society involved paying a visit to an unusual place of interest and then having a few pints in a pub nearby. On our first Saturday out and about we went to see a wallpaper shop in Hunslet on the south side of Leeds. Stephenson's wallpaper shop is a great incongruity. It has a window display of rolls and rolls of wallpaper that looks like something from the 1950s. At one time it wouldn't have been out of place because Hunslet was a teeming and vibrant community with streets full of smoking chimneys, a shop on every corner and kids playing hopscotch on chalked flags. These days the community is knocked down and warehouses and industrial units have taken over. Somehow the wallpaper shop survives, stuck out like a sore thumb amongst the breeze-block barns with brightly-painted plastic facades. I don't know whether it was through a genuine interest or because there was still an hour to opening time, but Martin showed a great enthusiasm for the various wallpapers on display. He had the woman behind the counter, who probably thought she had seen everything in her time, bringing out all sorts of patterns.

'Oh! Yes, I do like a nice, red flock wallpaper. it reminds me of the inside of Tetley pubs and curry houses we used to go to back in the 1970s.'

The woman suspected he was slow timing her, which he was, but she didn't bat an eyelid. The only time she flickered slightly was when Martin said, 'We thought we better come to see you, because we didn't know how much longer this shop would be here for.'

The lady gave him a look that said, 'Why, do you know something I don't know?'

At opening time we sauntered across to The Garden Gate, another of Hunslet's beautiful sore thumbs. Back in the early seventies, Leeds City Council embarked on a slum clearance programme. This involved knocking down hundreds of red-brick terraced rows and replacing them with concrete maisonettes. The Garden Gate, a jewel in the crown of the Tetley brewery estate, was smack bang in the middle of this redevelopment. The council in an act of extreme ignorance decided that the ale house had to go as well. In more enlightened times we might wonder what the hell possessed these people and ask 'What were you thinking?' Back then the dodgy architect Poulson of Pontefract was on the prowl and T. Dan Smith of Newcastle was signing all sorts of deals that would send working-class people out of proper streets to live in the sky. The great Geordie songwriter Alan Hull wrote about this in his song 'Dan the Plan'.

175

Oh Dan. You're a terrible man
You killed me old man
You turned his house into a caravan.
What went wrong with your city, the Brazilia of the north?
Isn't it a pity that no one knew its worth.

The Garden Gate is a glorious example of late Victorian/early Edwardian pub architecture. It was built in 1902 in the middle of a huge area of working-class housing. It is still like a palace now and must have been very special then. It has a glazed tile facade and its name in art nouveau lettering over the front window. Inside is a corridor leading to a vaults and a number of small parlours. The etched glass, wood in walnut and mahogany and brass work are all original as is the ceramic work in the taproom. All the work was done by craftsmen from Leeds firms. At one time women could drink ha'porths of gin here and their men folk supped pints of bitter with huge fluffy heads, served from a unique bank of five handpumps.

It took a group of long-haired students to realise the worth of this pub. At the time of the compulsory demolition order, Paul Shearsmith was studying at Leeds School of Architecture. He lived in the Leek Street flats with three fellow students. He told me that when he heard the old building was about to be pulled down he called in for a pint one night just to see it. He was gobsmacked by how beautiful it was. That night he said to his mates Graham and Chris that they ought to mount a campaign to try and save the pub. Paul ended up forming 'The Friends of The Garden Gate'. He managed to get a feature in the *Sunday Times* and also contacted the Victorian Society and English Heritage. Tetley's brewery showed little interest in their own history at the time but said they would consider 'reusing' some of the original internal screens in a new pub.

The Friends of The Garden Gate agreed that though redevelopment was necessary to revitalise what had become a rundown area, some buildings, owing to strong social and architectural focal points, should be saved. They argued that The Garden Gate was an important landmark and one that, at a time when garish fake Victoriana was all the rage, provided a rare example of the real thing. It was also a place that truly served the community by being both traditional and familiar.

The *Yorkshire Post* sent a reporter to the pub. He spoke to elderly men in flat caps, welded to chairs in the taproom. They said, 'We are all good friends in here and we don't want to drink in another pub. We want to drink here.' The landlord, Bill Priestly, who had been there for years himself, came out with a soundbite almost as decorative as his pub. He said, 'This pub is like finding a swan at the bottom of a quarry.'

For a change, a local community campaign prevailed. The pub was Grade II listed and saved from the wrecker's ball.

For all of its association with being a beer for the working man, Tetley brewery did make some appalling decisions. They could have got behind the campaign to save The Garden Gate, but didn't. Some years after, they made a terrible decision at The Junction pub near where I live. The taproom there was a classic. It was filled with retired coal miners most days who played cards and dominoes and supped a lot of beer. The pub was given a makeover and turned into a 'Sports Bar' with televisions all along the walls and loud rock music blasting out. The only sports and games were on the screens and the dominoes disappeared. It didn't attract many new customers. It did lose its regulars. The old coal miners who once played and told stories there were as important to the fabric of that building as the bricks and mortar. They're gone now.

With The Garden Gate saved for future generations, you would expect that the brewery who owned it would look after it. On the day Martin, Hazel and I went there, it felt as though it was on its last legs again. The pub is still very lovely to look at of course, but the beer wasn't too good and there was a disconcerting smell of shit in the passage. The young lass behind the bar apologised if we could smell something bad, but admitted they had a problem with a sewage pipe. After just one pint we decided to move on. We stood on the pavement outside to admire the Edwardian elegance of it all. Under our feet on the pavement and roadside there was broken glass everywhere. A young lad came up on his bike and said, 'I'll guard your car for you Mister for fifty pence.' Martin said, 'It's all right cock. We best be off.' The young lad said, 'Well fuck off then,' and rode off at speed.

Since then The Garden Gate is on its way back up. It's being treasured by the local community as the special jewel that it is. The locals have even had another fight on their hands when the council announced plans for a trolley bus scheme. Having once wanted to knock it down, they now planned to attach brackets for power lines to it.

Martin read about Britain's longest-serving pub landlord. This landlord was coming up to his sixtieth year as a licensee. We had a ride over to Stalybridge to a pub called The Wharf. Dick Grainger, the landlord, sat at his bar. He was a big old boy with the waistband of his trousers all the way up to just below his chest. His braces were twisted, but he didn't seem to be bothered. We'd only just got through the front door when he said to Martin, 'Have you come to visit me, love?' We said that we had. He smiled at his barmaid and said, 'I know you have because you are strangers and all the strangers come to see me.' He was sat like a Public House Emperor on his high stool. We almost felt that we should kowtow. Before we even got served, he went into a well-rehearsed mantra. 'I took my first pub just after the war. I came here in 1949, the locals moaned when I put the beer up to one and a tanner, they're still bloody moaning now. That'll be two pounds seventy-five apiece and don't bloody moan, it's the cheapest beer you'll find round here. I've seen that canal outside busy with boats, then I've seen it filled in and now they've dug it out again and they're using it for tourists. Can you believe that? Bloody tourists in Stalybridge! And I'll tell you something else, they don't piss and moan like these buggers round here. Because round here all they bloody do is piss and moan.' He paused for a breath. 'Now, what else do you want to know?'

We didn't know what to say. Eventually Martin muttered, 'I suppose you will have seen a lot of changes in the time you have been a landlord.'

'They all say that.'

Martin looked a bit crestfallen.

'But the truth is this, love. Governments come and go. I've seen every prime minister from bloody Churchill to bloody Blair and nowt changes much. Folk come in here for their beer, they moan about the price, then they come in the next day, sup some more and then moan again. Now and again we get some likely lads who can't handle their beer. They get out of hand and I throw them through that front door, straight onto the pavement. No! Nowt changes, except I'm less vigorous than I used to be. I'm eighty-odd now, but I'll still throw you onto that street if you get too much ale.'

Martin looked at his pint.

'Can you see that dint on the front door?'

We looked at the inside of the front door.

'I was chucking a bloke out one night and the door blew shut before I could get him through. He whacked his head on that door. He came in a bit after and started to apologise. I told him he'd have to pay for the door. I've never seen him since and that door has stopped like that for years now. I was six feet one in my stocking feet and eighteen stone two when I was in my prime.'

We ordered another round.

'Will you be having another after this? Only this barrel is about to run off and I like to have half an hour on the sofa in the afternoon.'

We drank our beer and excused ourselves. We crossed town and called for a couple more in the buffet bar on Stalybridge station. We got talking to an old bloke in there about where we had been.

The old bloke said, 'Did he tell you about that mark on his front door?' We told him that he had.

'Aye, he will do. He tells everybody that tale.'

'Is it true?'

'Well it depends what he told you.'

At that moment it occurred to me that local characters like Dick Grainger are every bit as much history as buildings and monuments are. Dick wasn't so much a long-serving landlord as a local landmark.

Martin said to me one day that we ought to think about taking the Saturday Afternoon Society to somewhere that didn't involve ale drinking. This was a surprise. 'Only it's not fair to keep asking Hazel to drive us about when we've been supping ale all day.' I told him that I had heard about an ancient temperance bar, a place in Rawtenstall in Lancashire that had been open since Victorian times and they only sold soft drinks. Martin soon changed his tune. 'Don't talk so bloody daft! We can't go to a pub that doesn't serve ale.'

I convinced him that we could combine a visit to Rawtenstall with a scenic drive through the Pennines and a visit to the local market. Hazel liked the idea. So we went.

On the way there we reminisced about an old lass called Lil who used to drink in the Lancs and Yorks pub on Aketon Road in Cutsyke. She drank bottles of stout in great quantity. When she'd had five or six bottles, she'd light up a Woodbine and say, 'Anybody for a sing-song?' Peter Sterling would do one or two country and western songs, 'Nobody's Child' was one, 'I Never Promised You a Rose Garden' another. Sooner would sing a parody from the music halls. Lil would then nip her Woodbine, put it behind her ear, take out her top set of dentures and stand on a chair. She sang every verse of 'Rawtenstall Annual Fair'. It was glorious.

'Down behind the gas works, down in Rawtenstall…'

As we went over the Pennines that Saturday afternoon Martin and I remembered fragments of the lyrics and belted them out. Hazel laughed her head off.

'Oh roll up roll up, come and see the mermaid
See the lovely lady, half a woman, half a fish'
In went the lads, to see it were no swank
And little Tommy Higgins put some whisky in the tank.

'Oh, roll up, roll up, see the tattooed lady
See the lovely lady with the pictures on her skin'
In went the lads and they began to cheer
For tattooed on her skin was all the towns of Lancashire

We had a walk round town and bought some black pudding off a stall and the biggest Eccles cakes any of us had seen. Then we went in search of Fitzpatrick's Temperance Bar.

The Fitzpatricks were an Irish family of herbalists who came over to Lancashire in the 1880s, just as the Temperance movement was in full swing. The drink of choice at the time was Vimto and it was popular and moreish, so the Methodists were having a decent amount of success at getting people to sign the pledge and abstain. This early success didn't last and, in the years leading up to the First World War, most of the Temperance bars shut down. Somehow Fitzpatrick's survived, probably because they made their own root and herb drinks to original recipes and they are delicious. The family ran their bar for going on a hundred years and it's still there to this day, like a museum piece offering recipes for a healthy modern lifestyle.

We got to the front door. Martin held his foot in the air above the threshold. 'I can't do it!' he said. 'My leg will not allow me to step into such a place.' Hazel told him not to be so bloody daft and pushed him in.

Nothing has altered here since it opened. They even have the original copper hot water boiler. There is a good range of drinks: Cream Soda, Black Beer and Raisin, Ginger Beer, and Sarsaparilla. Hazel and I had a Sarsaparilla and Martin had a Black Beer and Raisin, probably because it had beer in its name. He screwed his nose up, but then after a few sips announced that it was 'champion'. We ended up trying halves of some of the different flavours. I've no idea what the chap behind the bar made of us.

On the way back we took the scenic route through Todmordon and Hebden Bridge. Martin said, 'I'll tell you what Hazel, follow this road here, it takes you up to Heptonstall, I'll show you where Sylvia Plath is buried.'

Hazel purred and said, 'It's been lovely today, there's nobody stinking of beer and now we're going on a cultural visit.'

We went up the hill and paid our respects at the grave of Sylvia Plath. As we walked back to the car, Martin said, 'The Cross Inn is open, it would be a shame to pass by and not call in for one, it's a lovely pint of Tim Taylor's in there.'

Hazel just went, 'Martin!'

We just had two or three.

Martin had a pair of clogs made for himself. Mick the Clogger had a little workshop at the back of his house in Glass Houghton. Mick was a great one for folk music and Morris dancing and made the most beautiful bespoke clogs with effortless ease. He put down a piece of newspaper, drew round your feet with a biro and a few weeks later phoned to say your clogs were ready. Martin wanted his clogs to wear at folk festivals. He had a full outfit: clogs, moleskin trousers, baggy white shirt, Edwardian waistcoat, red neckerchief and Breton cap.

We went to the Moonraking Festival at Slaithwaite. Martin drove there in his stocking feet after realising that clogs weren't the most ideal footwear for the pedals of an Audi Quatro. Slaithwaite is an old West Riding village on the Huddersfield narrow canal. This is an amazing stretch of water that, by means of 74 locks and a three-mile-long tunnel, manages to climb over the Pennines. Back in the day, the canal was a handy route for smugglers. The story goes that one night when the water was reflecting a big full moon, the local militia came across some likely lads dangling big wooden rakes into the canal. When the militia asked them what they were up to, the lads reckoned they were trying to pull the moon out of the water before it drowned. These days, the moonraking is recreated every couple of years. On the night we went there the village was lit up with hundreds of paper lanterns. A huge illuminated moon was being dragged out of the canal by a gang of laughing teenagers. We joined a procession around the village and sidestepped into The Commercial. Martin had the chair within minutes. He was singing and telling the tale even before he'd got halfway down his first pint of Moonrakers Mild.

A woman sitting on the other side of our table asked Martin if he'd ever been to the Marsden Cuckoo Festival. When he said he hadn't, the woman told us that the people of Marsden liked cuckoos because it meant that spring was here. One year they decided to build a wall around the cuckoo to keep spring in all year round and so now they have a Cuckoo Festival.

Martin burst out laughing, 'Any excuse for a piss up eh?' Then he said, 'I've got one better than that.' The woman's face dropped a bit. 'Near where we live there's two villages, one called Kippax and the other called Allerton Bywater. On the boundary there was a tree and every year the cuckoo came to cuckoo in that tree. The people in Kippax said that the cuckoo was their cuckoo and the ones in Allerton Bywater claimed the cuckoo for their village. The cuckoo debate went on for years. Eventually an agreement was reached. The people in Kippax could call it their cuckoo, as long as them in Allerton Bywater could call it their tree.' Martin stopped for a swig of beer. Then he looked at the woman, 'What about that then?' The woman smiled and walked over to the bar to join her friends.

Martin started to sing an old song. 'The cuckoo is a pretty bird, she warbles when she flies.'

On the way back from Slaithwaite we decided that we couldn't drive through Linthwaite without nipping up the hill to see Ron Crabtree at the Sair. We hadn't been for a couple of years. As soon as we got through the door, Ron said, 'I've got something for you.' He came back two minutes later with a figure of a man sculpted out of scrap iron. It was about three feet tall and very rusty. He gave it to Martin. 'The last time you were here you left it behind. It's been sat in the back garden waiting in the rain.'

We sat near the window. Martin propped his statue up against the table leg.

'Where did you get that from then?'

Martin looked flummoxed. 'I'm not sure really. The last time I came here, I had a good session on the Old Eli. I seem to remember an artist being in. I might have bought this off him.' He then took off his Breton cap and put it onto the head of the sculpture and said, 'What do you think of it so far?'

By the time Ron called last orders we were all singing 'Hey Jude' when it came on the jukebox and someone had put a cigarette behind the scrap-iron man's ear.

Time Gentlemen Please

It's just after eleven o'clock on a Monday evening in The Top House. Time has been called and there's not many left in the taproom. Fred Perry is entertaining the stragglers with a bass-baritone version of 'Strangers in the Night'. He sets off at talking pace, but quickly catches the melody.

'Wond'ring in the night, what were the chances.' Halfway through this line he realises what is coming next, so he looks across at the barmaid. 'We'd be sharing love, before the night was through?' Fred winks, Elizabeth turns to remove some glasses from the glass washing machine, then places them onto the shelf. Fred raise the volume, 'Something in your eyes was so inviting.' Elizabeth raises her eyes and tuts. 'Something in your smile was so exciting.' Elizabeth sets her lips into a straight line and shakes her head slightly like her neck is itching. 'Something in my heart, told me I must have yoooou!' Fred holds the last syllable and throws out his arms to reveal the tattered cuffs of his sports jacket. He continues, improvising with words that aren't in the song, speeding up and slowing down until he gets to 'Love was just a glance away, a warm embracing dance away... and...'

'Every night alike, come on now lads. Drink your beer and get yourselves off home. I don't want to have to tell you again.'

'Ever since that night, we've been together.'

'Come on now, am I wasting my breath? If that beer isn't supped in two minutes, it's going down the sink.'

'Dooby dooby doo, do do do dooby.' Sooner, who has been dozing off until now, joins in, while Fred removes his cap and pretends to ask for donations.

Elizabeth slams the bar flap down with a purpose and walks over to the table. She starts to place empty glasses onto a tin tray. She hovers her hand over Fred's pot. Fred places a huge paw gently onto her arm. 'Now sweet lady of my dreams, you wouldn't deprive a man of his last few sips would you?'

Elizabeth smiles, 'I'm ready for bed, now come on.'

'I'm ready for bed an' all. Shall I walk you home?'

Elizabeth pulls away. 'Come on now. I don't want to have to say it again. Beer off and bugger off.'

Fred Perry is a roll-up smoking, bitter swilling, bear of a man with a voice as deep as a Volga boatman, he loves a sing-song and the company of mates who he has known for most of his life. He knows every crack in the pavement between his house and the side door of the ale house. He has an allotment where he grows potatoes and cabbages for his own table and he keeps his racing pigeons. He wheels the pigeons about in a wicker basket that balances on the chassis of an old Silver Cross pram, and he carries his pigeon clock like it's a precious relic.

Fred replaces his flat cap. 'Is there time for a night cap? I think a drop of whisky would keep out that cold night air. Whisky all round Liz.' He reaches into his pocket and drops the contents onto the middle of the table; a packet of Rizla cigarette papers, three tab ends, a shirt button, two dirty polo mints, a distressed bus ticket and about £1.50 in small change. 'Whisky all round and take it out of that.'

Elizabeth starts to turn off the lights and drapes beer towels over the handpumps. She empties ashtrays into a tin bucket. She then wipes the ashtrays over with a grey dishcloth. 'And you as well Sooner, don't you dare drop back to sleep in that chair.'

Fred leans back in his chair and closes his eyes. He starts to sing softly to himself now. 'A man without a woman, is like a ship without a sail. There's only one thing worse in the universe and that's a woman without a man.'

'Come on bloody Bobby Darin, let's have you now.'

'Elizabeth!'

'Yes, Frederick.'

'As a silver dollar goes from hand to hand, a woman goes from man to man.'

'Charming! Now sup that ale. Get your coat on and let's have you home. It's free beer tomorrow.'

'You said that to me yesterday.'

Fred downs his beer in one, stands up, sways, puts a hand out to steady himself and knocks a chair over. He straightens himself up as though to say, 'It wasn't me!' Then he reaches the coat rack. He takes a moth-eaten, woollen scarf down, ties it round his neck like a man tying a bag of corn and makes for the door. He turns round to say goodnight, forgets that he is holding the door open and when he turns back again he bangs his head on the jamb. Quick as a flash, he shakes himself and announces, 'Whoever designed this door frame wants horse-whipping.' Then he staggers out into the night. Sooner follows him and they weave down the footpath with their arms over each other's shoulders. 'Gee it's great after staying out late, walking my baby back home.'

Part III

I Raise A Glass To Them Still

The piano has been drinking, not me.
Tom Waits

Overleaf: My landlord hero Roy Edmond at his ancient pump in The Eagle at Sterne, one of England's lost treasures.

Close Enough For Jazz

I've stumbled out of a fair few pubs in my time. I've also stumbled across a lot of my favourite pubs by accident. There was one at Peterborough called The Still. I think it's gone now, but for a few years in the 1980s it was a sort of talisman that I had to visit whenever I was in that city. I was in that city a lot too, mainly to change trains. When I went to visit Volker and Jurgen in Germany, I went by boat from Harwich or Felixstowe and caught my train to there from Peterborough. I also started going to the North Sea Jazz Festival every year at the Congresgebouw in The Hague. I saw some of the most exciting music I think I've ever seen there: I saw Van Morrison on a night when he seemed to be enjoying himself; the great pianist Jay McShann, who had once played in bands with Charlie Parker and Ben Webster; James Brown; Billy Eckstine; the breathy Bossa Nova of Astrud Gilberto; and I saw the Texas blues guitarist and fiddle player Clarence 'Gatemouth' Brown rip the place apart with a red-hot set of blues and jazz standards. Roy Herrington loved to tell the story of how one night when he was looking for the lavatory, he opened a door to find himself in a rehearsal room with Ray Charles. Those were heady days of music and beer.

We used to travel over by train and boat. We took the Friday lunchtime train from Doncaster and changed at Peterborough for the train down to Harwich for the overnight ferry to Hook of Holland, then another train after breakfast up to The Hague. In Peterborough we had to wait over an hour for our connection so I asked a porter if there was a good pub nearby. He told me that the best pub in Peterborough was in the middle of a shopping centre across the road. I thought he was winding me up. 'No!

It's true,' he said when he saw me pull a face. 'There's an ancient pub in a cobbled courtyard. They weren't allowed to knock it down, so they built the shopping centre around it.' We followed his finger for directions. We crossed a footbridge, passed a load of indoor shops, the sort you find in every town, and looked for a gold-coloured door. Once through the door it was like climbing out of the back of the wardrobe into Narnia. It was true what the railway porter said, there was a lovely courtyard with real trees in it and a pub down one side. It seemed to be a secret that only the locals knew about, an oasis away from the hustle and bustle of twentieth-century shopping, where everybody sipped pints of Elgood's, McMullens and Adnams. The atmosphere there was as right as ninepence. I came to look forward to my occasional visits. I was always sorry when I had to sup off my pint and sprint back through the shopping centre for the train down to the coast. If ever there was a mystical pub that weary and thirsty travellers find at the end of a mirage, The Still was it.

Another pub I stumbled across was one called The Angel near Shaftsbury Avenue in London. It served a lovely pint of Courage Best. I found that one because I was an avid fan of Ray's Jazz record shop. Ray's became a London landmark for me, I never went to work down there without paying a visit. Near the counter in that shop was a large cardboard box that had a handwritten sign on it, 'Rare as hen's teeth'. I could never afford any of the 78s or LPs that were in that box, but I liked looking. From the 1980s up to the early 2000s I had a certain ritual that I couldn't break. I'd spend a few hours rooting through the bookshops on Cecil Court. This little street had once been London's 'Flicker Alley' for all the film companies that were based there. Now, it was home to rows of antiquarian bookshops. I became such a regular that the poet Jeremy Reed, who whiled away time looking after the Red Snapper bookstore, would lift his beret whenever he heard the doorbell ring and saw my outline in the doorway. He'd say, 'I see you are down from the frozen north again.' I bought books by Jeff Nuttall and early editions of *The Wild Party* by Joseph Moncure March there, as well as the collections that

Jeremy published. After that I'd do my rounds to Ray's and Doug Dobell's place on Charing Cross Road. I started a collection of Blue Note LPs at Ray's and it was Ray Smith himself who put me on to Ike Quebec. Ike was A&R man for Blue Note and a tender sax player in his own right; I have collected just about everything he ever recorded. At Dobell's I bought all sorts of obscure folk and blues stuff on the then hard to find American independent labels like Folkways, Yazoo and Arhoolie, and the famous English folk label Topic. In between I would call for a couple of pints in The Angel, sporting a carrier bag with a black cat logo on it from Ray's. Whenever you had a carrier bag from Ray's to drop down by your side at the bar there, you felt very cool and it was always something that would get you into a conversation.

The Angel was a quiet pub mid-afternoon, plenty of room to spread out and pore over your vinyl purchases. I've often filled an entire table top in there with records, just to look at them, with the excitement of a trainspotter poring over his notebook after a day on a chilly platform. It was in The Angel that I started to appreciate southern beer, or what my friend Burt would call 'flat ale'. There was never a head on the beer, save a few bubbles, in The Angel. You just got a straight glass filled to the brim with clear amber liquid. It looked unappetising at first, but I soon got used to it and it always tasted good after a trawl round the book and record shops. I can't call southern beer in a way that a lot of northerners do. I like some pints that I've had in London every bit as much as the ones I've had in backstreet ale house in Leeds, where the froth gives you a tache like Mr Pastry.

My final ritual before heading to Kings Cross station is a bit embarrassing, but I'll tell it. I became entranced by a film called *84 Charing Cross Road*, a film featuring Anne Bancroft and Anthony Hopkins. It's based on a book by Helene Hanff and tells the story of a New York writer who falls in love with a London bookshop called Marks & Co. The writer only ever corresponds by letter and parcels with the shop and doesn't actually visit until it's too late. 84 Charing Cross Road stopped being a bookshop in the late 1960s, but the building is still there. I like to visit the building and stand on the pavement outside. I look through the window and try to imagine when it was a dusty old antiquarian place with leather-bound volumes, stepladders and ladies in twinsets and pearls. When I first went there it was a CD shop, then a café, and now I think it's a McDonald's. I don't know why, but when I stand there I feel as though I'm connected to something, I don't know what it is, but it's a pleasant sensation. I do miss the feel of the carrier bag from Ray's Jazz Shop though, the weight of half-dozen vinyl records and the notion that I was once part of something quite cool.

Just before Ray's shut down due to extortionate rents, I decided to buy something from the 'hen's teeth' box. I bought a Freddie Slack 78 on the Capitol label, a 1942 recording featuring T-Bone Walker on guitar. I treasure that record like a memory of every antiquarian bookshop or old-fashioned taproom I've been in. Nearly all of the independent specialist jazz, folk and blues record shops have gone now. So have a lot of the quirky pubs in the arse ends of towns I once loved. It makes me sad. That feeling that makes you feel part of something starts to dissipate and you set off to wonder if you can replace it. In my case I carry on stumbling and hoping to find.

We all love a country pub. It's where we take our visitors when we want to show them what it used to be like. We want the pubs to have roses chasing each other around a front door that barely shuts. Sad to say, a lot of these have long gone. I read somewhere that Britain has lost a quarter of its pubs in the last thirty years and a lot of them were in the countryside. There are two not far from me that I have being going to for over forty years and they haven't changed much in that time. My cousin Angela took me to the pictures at Leeds to see *Jaws*. On the way back she said, 'I know a village pub.' She introduced me to the Chequers Inn. It's a pub in a Yorkshire stone village in a dip in the landscape. It goes back to the 1600s and has all of the features you would expect in an old village inn: low beams, roaring open fires and meat and potato pie on the menu. It's full of middle-class people of course, who drink their halves and talk business. There aren't any working-class country pubs these days. Even Betjeman observed that when he said, 'Oh, that old pot-house isn't there, it wasn't worth our while, you'll find we have rebuilt the "Bear" in Early Georgian style.'

The Chequers has a spectacular garden and I'd go there just to sit in it. In recent years the pub has sourced its beer from The Brown Cow brewery just up the road. It's one of those pubs that make you believe all is well in the world when you sit in that garden with a pint of local beer and a plateful of dinner. For many years the pub only had a six-day licence and has only recently started opening on a Sunday. The story goes that the local Lady of the Manor was on her way home from church when a gang of local ruffians threw mud and stones at her carriage as she passed by the pub. She forbade it to open on the sabbath after that and for nearly two hundred years it didn't. I like a pub defined by a story, whether it's true or not.

My favourite country pub of all lies a few miles further towards York. This is The Greyhound at Saxton. It was Burt who first took me there. At that time it was run by a very old lady called Eileen who served beer from wooden barrels racked up on a gantry at the back of the bar. Eileen could be grumpy and you had to watch your Ps and Qs with her or else you were barred. You could be barred for many things in that pub at that time. 'Getting too cocky at dominoes' was one, or 'Looking at her the wrong way' was another. The beer was Tetley's. At some point in the early 1980s the pub was taken over by Sam Smith's and as Sam's always do when they get their hands on an ancient property, they look after it with great care. The Greyhound is a beautiful example of what tiny rural pubs must have been like when our forefather and foremother farm labourers supped there. Within its whitewashed walls The Greyhound manages to cram three tiny downstairs rooms: a bar that seats about seven people, a middle room decorated with plates and knick-knacks and a parlour at the far end that has an old piano in it. I like the end room. It's decorated a bit eccentrically. I know of no other pub that has badminton rackets and sword fighters' body protection pinned to the roof beams. There are some lovely photos in there too. One shows the village cricket team from 1923 and an even older one shows farm labourers standing by a haystack with beer pots in their hands. I visit it once in a blue moon and I'm always reassured to see that nothing alters. The lavatory is outside in the yard. Swallows nest on a beam in there. Those swallows come back every year. If ever there was a symbol of continuity in my life, it is the swallows that nest in the lavatories in the yard at The Greyhound at Saxton.

Saxton is a quiet village now, save for the odd tractor, rook and sports utility vehicle. Near here on Palm Sunday in the midst of a snow storm in 1461 up to 30,000 men were slain in the bloodiest battle ever fought on English soil. The Battle of Towton saw Edward, Duke of York, defeat the Lancastrians with arrows carried on a strong wind and allowed him to claim the throne as Edward IV. A lot of men are buried in and around the All Saints church that overlooks The Greyhound, including the Lancastrain leader Lord Dacre, who was buried on his horse. Local farmers used to tell stories that a peculiar rose flowered near the battlefield. It had white petals spattered with red.

I am a fan of the surrealist photography of the young American artist Francesca Woodman. In a series of self portraits in old houses Francesca gets beneath the wallpaper to inhabit a space inside the walls, as though she is listening to the ghosts that once lived there. When I sit in The Greyhound I feel as though I want to put my ear to the walls to listen to what the ghosts are whispering about.

In the 1990s, Yorkshire Television asked me to present a series of short documentary films about traditional pubs. I couldn't have landed a better job if I'd tried. One day we drove down to the Lincolnshire Wolds, to a tiny village called Swinhope that was miles from anywhere. There's a pub there called Click'em Inn. It's a pub that is steeped in history and it's won a lot of awards for the quality of its beer. That part of Lincolnshire still has a lot of squires, who these days play a ceremonial role around the little churches. The Squire of Swinhope was in the pub having a few pints before his dinner. He sat on a stool at the bar looking well refreshed. He was like a little wizard with a goatee beard and quick eyes. I asked him if we might do a short interview with him about the pub and about beer in general. 'My dear boy,' he said, 'You can ask away, I have taken much pleasure from the pursuit of beer over many years.' Our cameraman Jim and sound recorder Sam started to set up. I sat at the bar and chatted away with the squire, his eyes were all over the shop and he seemed to lose his thread every time he spoke. As we were about to start filming he slid from his stool and staggered across the room. 'I think I may have to go home,' he said. He had two or three goes at getting on his coat and put his cap on skew-whiffed and plaited his legs towards the door. 'But I will say this before I bid you good day. All beer is perfection my dear.' Then he toddled out of the door. The landlord winked and smiled at us. 'He does that most days,' he said.

It was on this series that I met the only other pub landlord who came close to Tetley Dave for eccentricity, a bloke called Trevor Wallis who kept The Bowling Green pub in Otley. Trevor described himself as 'a frustrated actor'. We sat at his bar and he insisted on wearing various outfits for the interview. He first came downstairs in a Viking helmet and swapped this for a tam-o'-shanter when he put his Highlander outfit on. My mate Mark Witty who directed the programme, never one to miss an opportunity for a bit of fun, then suggested that Trevor and I ought to both dress up and have a stroll around town. Trevor jumped at the chance and brought out his homemade spacesuit and loaned me what he called 'one of my three wise men outfits', complete with Arab headdress and fly-whisk. He suggested we ought to try to find two more wise men, but added that it would be difficult in Otley market place. The strange thing was, very few people in that busy little town's market place bothered to turn their heads. They were either used to Trevor's antics or that kind of behaviour was normal for Otley.

Trevor's ale house looked like a cross between Albert Steptoe's backyard and an alchemist's laboratory. Adorning every wall, alcove and cubby hole was a collection of objects the like of which I'd never seen: a ten-foot stuffed crocodile, a coffin complete with plastic skeleton, a boar's head, a stuffed badger bearing its teeth, a barn owl in a glass case, gas masks and enough bric-a-brac to run a car boot sale every Sunday of the year. The bar top was a coffin lid and Trevor called time by means of a hand-cranked World War Two siren. He called his pub a monument to chaos, a visual representation of what went on in his head. I suggested that he might just be crackers, he thought for a bit and said, 'You might be right,' but added, 'I can't see the point of being normal.'

I asked him how he got started with his collection. He lifted off his space helmet and reminisced about Dave the DJ who ran a 'bizarre objects' competition in the middle of his disco. 'He started to bring in things like broken dolls heads, old caps, barometers, stuff like that, and always left them in a box after he'd finished making up a story about them. Eventually we had boxes and bags of his junk stored all over the place. I thought about throwing it all out, but Dave the DJ said, "Why don't you display them on the walls?" That's how it started.'

In a rare thoughtful moment, Trevor told me the history of the pub. 'It's been a pub since the 1860s, but it started as a chapel for dissenters, then it was a courthouse and for a while it was a theatre.' Then he got bored with his lucidity and asked me if I might like to see his collection of unusual drinks. 'You see, when the collection started growing, customers started to bring their own curiosities and one of the themes was unusual drinks from far-off lands.' He blew the dust off a series of bottles and took great delight in telling me what was in them. There was snake wine from Vietnam, fermented mare's milk from Kazakhstan, a vodka with a scorpion in it, a drink from Iran called 'Lion's Milk' and a rice-based drink from Korea that might as well have been horse piss, because that's what it looked like. Then he shook a bottle that he said came from China. It contained baby mice. I asked him if anybody had tried to drink any of it.

'One of the locals had a go at the Chinese one,' Trevor said.

'And?'

'Well to be frank, I'm not sure we've seen him since,' and then he winked.

Trevor retired and auctioned off his crocodile and boar's head. The pub was boarded up for a while after, they tell me it's a Wetherspoons now. I'll bet it's not half as much fun.

Mark Witty called me one day to say he had found a pub in rural East Yorkshire that was almost unchanged since the day it opened in 1823 and it still didn't have a bar. The Eagle at Skerne, a village of a few hundred souls on the Yorkshire Wolds, was on some sort of inventory of unchanged pubs. So exclusive was this list that all of the pubs on it fitted on a folded sheet of A4 paper. It took me as near to pub heaven as I have ever been. Skerne is the sort of village where you could still see a dead crow hanging from a fence. The pub's landlord was a grand old chap called Roy Edmond. Roy had taken on the pub I think in the 1950s, with his wife Sylvia. He was still there in the early 2000s, though Sylvia had passed away a couple of years before and he slept downstairs with his memories in a little room to the right of the central corridor.

The earliest rural public houses were farmhouses that opened up a couple of downstairs rooms and served beer from a back kitchen to the table in jugs. Over time the public part of the house became a pub and a counter or bar was added for serving. And as more time went by all of the other decorations and additions came along, so that the original place no longer looked like someone's house, it became what we know as a pub. Except nobody told the landlords at The Eagle at Skerne and it stayed just as it was. To walk into the front door of that pub was to walk back two centuries. It was like touching old leather or opening an old photo album you thought you'd lost.

The pub really was unaltered. It stood round the corner from Saint Leonard's, a Norman church. It was whitewashed on the outside and had a yard with an outside toilet at the back. As you went in there was a red-tiled passageway with a room off to the right and another to the left. The room on the right was very plain, with plank walls and wooden stools around a couple of tables. The left-hand room – Roy called it his lounge – was wallpapered and had cushioned seat covers. There was no bar. The beer was fetched to you at the table in jugs and then poured into pint pots. Roy filled these jugs from an old pump attached to a barrel that settled at the bottom of three or four stone steps off to the left of the passage. The pump looked like none I've seen before or since. It was like a wooden Victorian cash till. I believe it's in a museum now. There was no wines or lagers, no piped music, flashing lights, no television. I once asked Roy if there was anything to eat. He said, 'I might be able to find a packet of crisps if I have a look round.'

I liked Roy as soon as I met him. He looked you straight in the eye when he talked to you and was never distracted when you talked back to him. He'd stand there with an empty glass in his hand or a dishcloth and wait until you finished. He was like some sort of wise relative that you went to see for advice. The word 'avuncular' might have been coined for him. Roy seemed completely tuned in to the pub and though he was elderly and slow by the time I met him, he seemed to glide around the inside of that old place like it was his dance floor. In his younger years he had been a great country man, he liked shooting and fishing and foraging in hedgerows. He knew every blackthorn bush in the vicinity and every autumn collected sloes to make sloe gin. Roy made the best sloe gin I ever tasted. He was the one who taught me how to make it. I said to him that I'd been looking for a recipe for ages, but everybody I talked to said it was a secret. Roy said, 'Take no notice of that. All you need is an old sweet jar. Fill it half full with sloes that have been pricked by a thorn from the bush you pick them from, pour plenty of gin over them and chuck some sugar in. It's ready when it goes deep red.'

'How much gin and sugar shall I put in?'

Roy said he didn't know. 'I just leave a gap at the top of my jar and I measure the sugar into my hand. The trick is to turn your jar upside down and give it a good shake now and again.'

We made a lovely little film with Roy. He managed to find

some old cine camera footage of people enjoying themselves in his pub when it was his wife's birthday. I think the footage dated from the sixties. They were all dancing in his lounge and flicking ash from their cigs.

I went back to Skerne a good few times. Once I saw a local Morris dancing team hopping up and down with their hankies outside. Another time I took Sooner Millard with me. Sooner loved it, especially when Roy fetched his bottle of homemade sloe gin out to chase the beer down.

Roy sold Camerons Strongarm beer. If you went there the week after it had been delivered it was bang on. The problem was, before Roy finally closed his door to move to an old folk's home, he didn't get much custom. On these occasions, the beer could be a bit vinegary. I supped it anyhow. It was enough to sit in Roy's parlour and listen to his soft East Riding accent as he told about walking through a local wood. I loved Roy and The Eagle at Skerne. It's gone now. The building still stands, but it won't be a pub again. Of all the thousands of pubs that have closed in this century in Britain, that pub is one of our greatest losses. Of all the images I fix into my mind of things I've seen in pubs, the picture of Roy Edmond coming up the stone steps with an enamelled jug full to the brim with frothing ale is the strongest.

Some Pubs You Might Want To Make A Journey To

A lot of beer and pub books are lists. I wanted to write a book of stories, but I can't resist listing some of my favourite pubs. I have only included pubs I go to a lot, so I make no excuse for most of them being not that far from where I live.

North Riding Hotel – Scarborough
Stuart and Karen Neilson run this hotel near Scarborough's Peasholm Park and North Bay. One of the least pretentious pubs I know. Stuart the landlord brews his own beer and offers a big selection of other beers that he likes. The taproom is lively with more barroom banter and characters than you could shake a stick at. The best room is full of conversation. Heather says that the Mosaic Pale is probably the best beer she has ever tasted.

Crown Posada – Newcastle
A little gem full of polished wood and stained glass. I love the old pubs of Newcastle, but this is one I always go back to. If you're lucky enough to get a seat in the little snug on the left as you go in, you can watch the world go by in an afternoon. They say that the 'Posada' part of the name comes from a Spanish sea captain who kept a mistress in Newcastle and set her up in the pub.

The Blue Bell – York
This pub is a national treasure. It was refurbished in 1903 and it hasn't been touched much since. It has a public bar at the front and a little lounge at the back linked by a stand-up drinking corridor. It retains most of its Edwardian fixtures and fittings. As you might expect in the middle of York, it caters for a procession of tourists,

but it's too small to be overrun by them and feels like the sort of local you wish was at the end of your street.

The Greyhound – Saxton near Tadcaster
I first came here forty years ago and fell in love with its timelessness. The public bar is full if there are seven in it and if you are tall you have to watch your head. If you had to draw a picture of a rural pub, this is what you would draw. They don't go in for modern stuff like guest beers here. It's owned by Sam Smith's brewery and the handpump just has their Old Brewery Bitter on it. It's as good a pint as you will find anywhere.

Wakefield Labour Club (The Red Shed) – Wakefield
It's not a pub strictly speaking, but qualifies in my book as a beer drinking establishment. They serve a bewildering array of guest beers sourced locally and nationally. It's a members club, but guests are welcome, especially if they are on the left-hand side of the political spectrum. The building is a wooden shed painted red overlooked by a shopping centre. A vernacular throwback if ever there was one. There is a television on a shelf in the corner, functional furniture, a room for acoustic turns and meetings, and a small bar run by volunteers. The beer is well kept and the clientele is friendly. The only licensed premises I have been to that has a notice in the entrance that says 'Refugees Welcome'.

White Horse Inn (Nellie's) – Beverley
Like an old market town should be, Beverley is full of great pubs. There's a smashing pop-up pub here called The Chequers, but Nellie's takes some beating. It has open fires, gas lights, scrubbed tables and a unique atmosphere. It's a place full of friendship and conversation, but there are spaces around the spoken words that suggest something special. It's like when you whisper in a church to show reverence for the building. Nellie's truly is that special.

The Junction – Castleford
This pub was boarded up and rotting. Landlord Neil Midgley had

a vision that involved stripping it back to the way it once was. In many respects it's still a work in progress, Neil is just as likely to be seen with a saw or a plane in his hand as a bar towel, but it has become a well-loved local again. The beer exclusively from wooden casks is fantastic.

Birch Hall Inn – Beck Hole near Goathland

The present landlady told me that when she moved here, she promised the former landlady, who'd been there for half a century, that she wouldn't alter anything. She has kept to her word. This is a beautifully looked-after and lovingly-preserved ale house. There is a tiny taproom to the right, a slightly bigger room on the left as you look at it and, squeezed in between, is a small village shop. Popular with walkers, it offers lovely beer, including its own 'Beck Watter' to those who have had a good hike over the moors.

The Black Horse – Whitby

One of Tetley's original 'Heritage' inns. The front bar if you can get a table – there are just two! – is somewhere you could sit all afternoon to watch people come and go. You are spoiled for choice in this town. I love The Fleece, especially its balcony overlooking the harbour, and the little pop-up bar in an old waiting room at the station is well worth a visit.

Featherstone Hotel (The Top House) – Featherstone

I can't make a list of my favourite pubs without including one that's just down the road. It's a big old, no frills boozer, probably unique in that it's only had three landlords since the end of the Second World War. The food is homemade and there's always a guest beer or two. It can get lively at times, but I've found a lot of friendship here over the years.

Angel Inn – Leeds

Leeds has some great pubs hidden away up snickets off Briggate. The most famous one is Whitelocks, a superb Edwardian luncheon bar. I prefer the Angel, a basic, straight up and down ale house with a utilitarian taproom and the best priced beer you will find in a city that gets dearer by the month.

Sheffield Tap – Sheffield

An old waiting room on Platform One at Sheffield railway station that was given a new lease of life as a real ale bar and a brewery. The restoration is first class. The tiled walls particularly noteworthy. It just shows what can be done with a bit of imagination to take bars and boozing on a notch or two. If you like pubs on railway stations, the ones at Stalybridge and Bridlington are grand examples too.

The Fat Cat – Sheffield

A Victorian gem in the Kelham Island district. It was the first pub in the city to realise there was life outside of big-brewery-owned ale houses. From the start it offered beer from the smaller independents and for the last couple of decades has brewed its own Kelham Island beers. The Pale Rider is a great beer.

The Robin Hood – Pontefract

People who drink in Pontefract delight in telling folk that at one time the town had more ale houses per head of population than any other. The other thing they'll tell you is that Robin Hood came from just down the road. The historian John Holmes once published a lyric poem that connected the names of at least forty of the town-centre pubs, twenty five of which are no longer with us. It starts, 'One day Robin Hood and his merry men set off from The New Inn to visit their companions at The Ancient Borough.' I've always had a lot of time for The Robin Hood. Back in the 1970s it had a left-field jukebox and a landlord who would tell you that he kept the cleanest lines in town. By luck and good management it has kept its original old-fashioned layout and the tap room is one of the best you will ever see. In recent times it has brewed its own beer in some outbuildings in the yard. This year, new life has been breathed into the old rebel. Dean and Sally Smith have given it a dignified makeover and our mate Paul

Windmill is going to be brewing in the backyard. A national pub of the year in waiting if there was one.

The Corner – Huddersfield

In a town blessed with any number of great pubs and lashings of top-notch ale to choose from, you are hard pressed to name a favourite pub here. The Corner, actually Mallinsons Brewery Taphouse, is one of the town's newest pubs, but one you shouldn't miss. It's a gem tucked away in an alley just five minutes walk from the railway station. There is a bewildering variety on offer in a clean, light space at the top of a staircase. It feels more like a modern Nordic drinking room than one based in a gritty northern town, but as they say round here, 'Nowt wrong with that.'

The Blue Bell – Old Ellerby, East Yorkshire

My old mate Sooner used to say, 'When you don't know where you are going, there's always a good pub round the next bend.' This pub is one of them. It's in a little village in the remote flatlands beyond Hull, an oasis for lost and thirsty travellers. Dave and Shirley, who have run the place forever, offer a warm traditional welcome. It's got darts, dominoes, a bowling green out the back and beautiful beer. A proper ale house serving its local community but also greeting strangers like old friends.

The Green Shoots Of Recovery

Monday afternoons had always been a good time for boozing in The Top House. Even before the miners' strike when the pits were still open, there could be a good gathering of colliers who were supposed to have been on days or preparing for afternoon shifts. They called these sessions 'Miners' Monday'. These usually coincided with a win for Featherstone Rovers over a big town club, somebody taking the bookies to the cleaners after a race at Doncaster or a top turn being on at the Green Lane Club the night before; all shorthand for having had too much beer over the weekend. After the strike a lot of the likely lads sat in the bay window that overlooked Station Lane. They wiled away time reminiscing, winding each other up and telling lies to outdo each other. The popular saying at the time was that 'More coal had been dug out in that bar than ever was hewed from Ackton Hall Colliery'.

It's a few years on from the strike. It's only midday, but the bay window gang are already gathered. Fred Perry is there, as is Sooner and Don Howarth. Don is a creature of habit. He comes in the pub at twelve on the dot, gets his pint and then starts to read the *Daily Mirror*. When he gets his second pint he swaps the *Mirror* for the local paper. Then he has another pint and looks for something else to read. They joke that he'd read the side of a cornflake packet if one was left out. They notice through the window a group of college kids and their tutors walking about with clipboards, pens and ordnance survey maps. Fred Perry taps hard on the glass and beckons the group to come in. Led by their tutors they cross over the road and do as they're bid. Fred winks at Sooner and Don. The party reach the door and push it open but seem nervous to step inside. Fred stands up, 'Welcome friends and strangers. We can see that you are doing some kind of survey and we wondered if a group of retired old coal miners might be able to assist in any way.'

The eyes of the tutors light up. 'Well this is a group of sociology students and we are looking at change in the former coal-mining communities.'

Fred looks the tutors up and down and scans the row of students who stand like ducks in a fairground shooting gallery. 'Aaah yes! I was just saying to my colleagues here, that those ladies and gentlemen look like they might be doing a survey of change in the former coal-mining communities. Well it's your lucky day, because assembled here are some of the finest minds and most knowledgeable men on that subject that you could wish to meet. Take a seat, sharpen your pencils and ask any question you like.'

The tutors and students find themselves seats amongst their newfound friends. Fred places his bacca tin on the table, shapes a worm of tobacco and licks a paper. 'Nay, take your coats off kids, if you're stopping, you won't feel the benefit when you go back out.' The party remove their coats. Fred says, 'Just excuse me while I replenish my glass then we can make a start.'

One of the tutors says, 'Can I get that?'

'Oh! There's no need for that young man... well only if you're sure. I say Peter, would you mind filling this glass and I was about to get one for Don and Sooner, so see to theirs while you're there and what about you Bob, are you joining us? This young man is kindly paying.'

Before he can catch his breath the tutor finds himself paying for half a dozen pints. Fred lights his roll-up, rubs his hands together and says, 'Right then, what do you want to know?'

For the next hour the sociology students are entranced, cajoled, astonished and howl with laughter at the stream of lies, made-up facts and figures, parody songs and slow timing witticisms that the old men round that table come out with.

At one point Fred says, 'So I said to Joe Gormley at the

delegates meeting back in the early 1970s, "Look Joe, nobody likes to work on a Friday because they like to prepare for the weekend and Tuesday can be difficult because we need recovery time after Miners' Monday, so how about if we just work Wednesday and Thursday?'"

By now the kids are completely in Fred's thrall. They gaze up at him like they would a stone Buddha. Don is on his third newspaper. 'What do you reckon Don? If we were to just work Wednesday and Thursday?' Don looks over his paper. 'What! *Every* Wednesday and Thursday?'

The tutors snort with laughter. It's taken them a while to cotton on, but now they are enjoying themselves, even though it's cost them three rounds so far.

Don chucks his paper down and looks for something else to read. Russ Banks walks in wearing a pair of shorts and a sleeveless shirt, showing most of his tattoos. He waits at the bar until his pint is pulled, then takes it to the other side of the room. Quick as a flash Don says, 'Hold still a minute Russ, I haven't finished reading thee yet.'

More laughter. This is punctured by the arrival of Don's wife. She holds open the front door with a heavy shopping bag. 'You're here again with your stupid mates are you? I've just come to let you know that before I came out to do this shopping I spent nearly two hours shovelling coal into a wheelbarrow and chucking it into a bunker. I'm now going home to put the dinner on. But don't you worry. You just sit there and sup your ale.' She then picks her bag up and lets the door slam behind her.

There is a silent pause. Don takes a swig from his pot and places it back onto the table. He looks at it as though measuring how much he has got left. 'Two hours eh! I've been meaning to get a bigger shovel.'

More howls of laughter. One of the tutors says to Pete, 'Is it like this every day in here?' He thanks everybody for the entertainment and leaves enough money for another round. Before they leave, one of the more serious students says, 'Excuse me, but I have one last question. Has anything changed for the better?'

Fred jumps straight in, 'Oh! Yes lad. We've got the makings of a forest now.'

The student looks at Fred. 'A forest.'

'The green shoots of recovery are here.' He points through the window at half a dozen saplings fastened to lengths of timber on some grass in front of the new-build doctor's surgery over the road. Two of these saplings are already bent and broken with kids swinging on them and another has a plastic carrier bag blowing in its branches like a white flag.

Progress vs Vandalism

I ponder on the notion of localness a lot. Is there something about where we are from that both shapes us and protects us? These days we hear a lot about 'community', it's a much used and abused term which gets held to ransom. I don't think community is the same as local. I heard the term 'Premiership Football Community' and I blanched to hear it. I once worked at Wakefield prison as a night school tutor. One of the other teachers in the education block talked to me about how we were improving relationships within the 'prison community'. I must have been that way out so I said to him, 'There's no such thing.' He said, 'How do you mean, no such thing?' I explained that I thought there was no such thing as a 'prison community'. That it was just an abstract notion dreamed up by people in positions of power who like to pretend if they attach the word 'community' to something then it's all right.

'I don't see prisoners in here having friendships with officers, I don't see cleaners planning holidays with senior staff or anyone talking to visitors in any other way than to tell them to sit down or showing them where to go, so how is that community?'

The teacher looked at me as though to say 'What's got your goat?' He scratched his beard and said, 'Why do you come here then?' I told him that I came here because it was my local prison, that I wanted to help people improve their writing skills and because I was interested in meeting different types of people. 'But the prisoners here are not my mates and if you were to be honest with yourself, they're not your mates either.' He didn't talk to me after that.

I have noticed in recent times the fashion for calling a pub a 'community hub' rather than a local pub. Local pub means something. It's about where you are from. Community hub doesn't mean anything, it's just a made up thing, a device to suggest togetherness, a politically romantic idea that we can all be the same simply by being in the same place. I have had a lot of local pubs. I go there first because they are handy, but also to find friendship and to have fun. I have also had more fights and arguments in local pubs than anywhere else I have spent time in. We shouldn't pretend then that local means the same thing as community. I do meet mates in my local, but I also know that standing not too far away are people I can't stand. I wouldn't want to change that, I'm for localness wherever it comes from, but I struggle to embrace a community I can't get on with. Local is about where you are from, but also about where you want to be. I have come to the thought over a number of years that community is as much about falling out as it is about coming together, and localness is about feeling at home wherever you are. In this way I have noticed that there are pubs no more than twenty miles from where I live that I wouldn't go in, even for a piss. Likewise I have found camaraderie in ale houses thousands of miles away.

If I had to pin a medal on a landlord, it would go to Andy Pickering at The Concertina Band Club in Mexborough. Andy has a well-thumbed copy of the first ever Campaign for Real Ale *Good Beer Guide* at the back of his bar. He is the only person I know who has one. I once asked him how he first became involved with real ale. He told me that his dad had been a fan of the original Barnsley Bitter, a legendary beer that was brewed at Oakwell Brewery near the football ground. They were bought out by John Smith's and the beer was never the same after that. So, Andy and his dad set out on a quest to find proper beer at a time when South Yorkshire was becoming a bit of a desert for cask-conditioned ales.

In the Victorian and Edwardian era, concertina bands were very popular in working-class communities and a lot of small northern towns had one. The town of Mexborough – a pit, pottery and railway town halfway between Barnsley and Doncaster – had one of the best. In 1906, the Mexborough Concertina Band, playing a repertoire more akin to a brass band, lit up the Alexandra Palace in London with a dazzling show of virtuosity and came away with a thousand guinea prize. After the First World War was over, the band decided that they ought to have their own clubhouse and bought an old joinery premises on the Dolcliffe Road. They added a concert room not long after and when most concertina bands faded away when pop music and teddy boys arrived, the Mexborough band club kept going. By the 1970s their numbers dwindled as the original members grew old and passed away. They struggled on until the 1980s, but shut down before the miners' strike owing money to Tetley's brewery. Andy's dad had been a steel fabricator, but found work harder and harder to come by with the decline in coal mining, so he went to his love of beer and bought the club. Andy built a brewery in the cellar. One day he asked me if I'd like a brewery tour. I followed him down a steel ladder that drops through a trap door in his stock room. 'Mind your head down here,' he said, 'it's a bit low.' I've never been in a brewery like that one. Andy brews eight barrels a time while stooping to avoid the roof. Yet he brews exceptional beer; The Bengal Tiger, an IPA that has a right bite to it. He once fetched a firkin to our house when we were having a Christmas fuddle.

Andy Pickering is one of the unsung heroes of real ale. He labours in a cellar less than his own height, to make a product that he himself sells behind a well-stocked bar. When he's not in his club he's out on the road picking up malt from Fawcett's at Castleford or delivering to the handful of places that he allows to sell his beer as a guest. He loves his local history and he still displays photographs of old blokes with their concertinas.

Mexborough is a tough town, not yet recovered from the years of neglect that Thatcher's Tories brought down on many towns like it. Even the rain seems muckier in Mexborough. It's not the sort of town you might look to when setting up a microbrewery. Andy did and carries on stoically. He brews good beer. He also gets support from a handful of creative souls who come together every year for an annual poetry festival in the name of the former poet laureate Ted Hughes, who was educated at Mexborough Grammar School. I went there to read with the poets Ian McMillan and Ian Parkes one time and we supped Andy's beers during the interval. Mexborough has a proud tradition of poetry. Harold Massingham, the poet son of a local collier, went to Mexborough Grammar School just after Ted Hughes, he wrote 'Old Miners' and nailed the atmosphere of work and ale house.

> Caged, their manhood dropped a mile,
> Their stomachs like up-ended beehives.
>
> Over cool dinner, the sour hoppy breath,
> Plates to be dashed quicker than discuses,
> And a household on tenterhooks.

At the Concertina Club they run a poetry night every month under the banner 'Pitmen Poets'. It's a rough and barely ready event. An anarchic, ale-soaked cabaret run by a tattooed, flat-capped ball of energy and confusion called Tony. They have a microphone like the one Norman Collier used, a floor space lit by a strip light with a wonky starter, and plenty of willing volunteers. One by one a procession of men and women of all age groups walk to the mic, tap it, say 'Can you hear me?' and then blast through poems at breakneck speed that are about politicians they don't like, unemployment and the benefit system, cheap supermarkets and what they've seen on the television. I was invited to be a guest there. I read from a book that I'd written about my dad. As I read, Tony walked round the room with a box full of crisps that were out of date. He threw bags of these crisps onto each table and repeated a mantra, 'Don't say I never fucking give you owt.' The audience walked in and out to smoke roll-ups by the front door and some shouted for pints of Tiger to be brought to the table. The old music hall turns who moaned about having to perform at the Glasgow Empire can never have been to the Concertina Club at Mexborough. I finished my reading. Tony was on his way to the bar. He shouted, 'Do you want a pint, kid? I'm buying one for that lass, otherwise she says she won't let me shag her tonight, so I might as well get yours while I'm here.'

Andy Pickering seems to take it all in his stride. He knows his town. He gets on with it. He brews and serves fine ale. He will never get the recognition he would get if his brewery was in a more fashionable leafy town, he's not bothered. He knows that those who know about beer, know. Roger Protz, who edits the *Good Beer Guide*, knows. He once listed Bengal Tiger as one of the '100 beers you should try before you die'. He was right.

Working men's clubs with good ale are the exception rather than the rule. When I started drinking in the 1970s they had mostly switched to cold, filtered, dead beer that was delivered not in barrels, but in tankers. And it was horrible. I could never understand how men of my grandad's generation, who had been brought up with quality real ale from great local breweries like Bentley's, Darley's and Beverleys, allowed themselves to be conned into drinking gassy pasteurised beer served from a Day-Glo electric pump. My introduction to beer drinking more or less coincided with the revival in real ale and having tasted the lovely cask beers that were coming back, I couldn't drink the beer in working men's clubs.

There are some clubs where the beer is good, but many of them seem to have refused to change with the times. I like one at Alverthorpe near Wakefield. They embraced real ale and made a grand fist of rotating locally brewed guest beers. It still feels like a club for ordinary working men and they still have turns on Saturday nights, but the beer is good too. These places though are still few and far between and it's a crying shame to see working men's clubs with steel shutters at their windows, prior to being knocked down, for want of visionary committee men who are prepared to change their habits. I shudder when I go to a club and I'm confronted with brightly-lit, plastic beer pumps advertising 'Ice Cool', 'Creamflow' and whatever else the marketing men dream up to sell fizzy chemicals masquerading as beer.

For a while before they knocked it down and replaced it with bungalows with garages, I was a member of the splendidly named 'Top o' t'Knob' club. The committee thought that second-rate turns singing to backing tracks, bingo and subsidised, keg-fizz beer was still the way to go. They had a local clientele that just about kept the place going, but a lot of them were getting older and poorly and they were dying off one by one. I challenged a committee man one day to try something different and said that I'd be prepared to sit down with him and come up with some new ideas. He turned on me and said, 'Look here young man, thy has been a member here for two minutes and you are trying to alter the way we do things with highfaluting ideas. It doesn't work like that kid, now I'd be obliged if tha would keep thi bloody neb out.'

I suppose I ought to have given more thought to the way I approached him, they had always done things in the way that worked for them and it was true, I had only been a member for a moment compared to most of the others who went there. I kept my 'neb out' after that, not because I didn't want to upset the apple cart, but mainly because I had a lot of affection for the old place and the steward Tony and his wife Tina were lovely people who went out of their road to make people welcome. I loved going in there on Monday afternoons just to sit, listen and learn. The old colliers congregated to 'sup a gallon' and eat sausage rolls and lumps of pork pie. To a man they all could tell you who would win the 3 o'clock at Market Rasen, they'd all caught a bigger fish than the day before and they had more catchphrases than Bruce Forsyth. It was there one Monday afternoon that Sooner challenged Arthur Blakestone to a press-up competition. They were both in their mid-seventies and they had been drinking since opening time. Sooner claimed the title with three very shaky press-ups but, not to be outdone, Arthur completed a neat forward roll before cracking his forehead on a table leg. Sooner made everyone laugh like drains when he pretended to come to Arthur's aid with a borrowed bucket and sponge, like a rugby league trainer with a Woodbine in the side of his mouth.

I played dominoes in there on Sunday afternoons with a

handful of elderly members, all with great stories to tell. These old men were dry and funny, but sat in that club like they were waiting to see a doctor. I used to think they deserved something better. One by one they started to pass away. Sometimes we were lucky to have four of us who wanted to play Fives and Threes. I drank Guinness because the bitter was tasteless and I watched out of the corner of my eye as various committee men huddled, whispered and shook their heads The club sold its car park to property developers. The drummer and organist retired and the turns sang to their backing tapes, just a slight notch up from karaoke. Eventually the breweries were demanding cash on delivery. One day the club was boarded up with wood. Tetley Dave used to say, 'While there is wood at the window, you still have a chance, but when they come with the steel shutters, you know it's lost.' Two weeks later, some workers came and removed the wood and put up steel. A few weeks after that the old club was set on fire and then knocked down.

Just before the demolition team came, I went up there with Tetley Dave to see if there was anything worth saving. We prised back one of the steel sheets and went in for a look round. A working men's club that is about to be knocked down is a sad place. We crunched broken glass beneath our feet and listened to dripping taps and pigeons fluttering. The electric had been disconnected, so we lit a rolled-up piece of the club's headed notepaper to see where we were going. Some chairs were still stacked on the tables where the cleaner had put them and a pack of cards had been thrown across the floor by the local kids who had been making a den in there. I cracked my knee on something. It was a bench. Dave and I dragged the bench onto the pavement. This was the bench where Gilbert and Sam had once sat to put the world to rights. At the age of sixteen, when he had been a farm labourer, Gilbert had attempted to rescue some Canadian airmen from a burning plane that had crashed into a field where he was working. Six times he went into the burning plane and carried the crew out on his back. His mate Sam had lost both legs in a tank during the war. They both held the British Empire medal for bravery. The bench was their favourite seat and no one else sat there when they were in the club. Dave organised for one of the fairground lads to pick up the bench and he took it to his own pub and made a little plaque for it.

Tetley Dave suited his name to a T. He acquired it in the days when he worked for the brewery as a drayman. This was at a time when draymen were treated to drinks at every pub they called at. This is when he developed what he called his 'gallon bladder'; he reckoned he could do a gallon before he needed to make water.

In Yorkshire in the 1970s the county was awash with Tetley beer and the recipe seemed just right. The brewery advertising was in full swing and the mythological 'Tetley Bittermen', a kind of no-nonsense, down-to-earth, gang of homespun superheroes who went down to the pub every night, were all over the TV. The poet Seething Wells created a satirical paean to them in his poem 'Godzilla vs The Tetley Bittermen'.

The real Tetley Bittermen knew where to go for their pints. The Market House, a semi-legendary pub in Dewsbury, run by an ex-rugby league player kept a great pint of Tetley. The Black Rock at Wakefield was another, then there was The Black Bull at Otley, the Gaping Goose at Garforth and amongst this company was The Shoulder of Mutton in the potteries at Castleford.

Another of Tetley's advertising slogans was 'A man can get attached to a Tetley's'. I don't know of any man who was as attached to that beer as Dave was. When they knocked the old brewery down in Leeds, Dave shed tears, he was almost inconsolable. He called it the biggest crime in the history of beer brewing and he said that he hoped whoever was responsible for the decision would fester and be haunted for evermore.

Not long before then, Dave had been called to a meeting along with other well-known landlords in the boardroom at the brewery. They were there to brainstorm ideas and to discuss the new look livery and design that the brewery had come up with. It became clear to Dave after an hour of what he called 'fancy talk' that the landlords had been called there to agree with everything the 'creative thinkers' had come up with. Dave interrupted the meeting and said, 'Excuse me, but I've come here to speak my mind, not to answer a lot of bullshit questions. I'll just say this. I've come to Leeds on the train this morning. At one time there used to be a big metal sign on a fence as the train came into the station. It said "Welcome to Leeds, Home of Tetley Brewery". I don't know whose idea it was to take that sign away but it wasn't there this morning. Now, I have noticed that the Tetley huntsman logo has been redesigned and you have taken away his monocle. You will call this progress. I call it vandalism. The Tetley huntsman with his nice smiling face and his monocle is what reassures people. When you start interfering with things like that you're asking for trouble. Not only that but you are denying history and tradition and where you are from. If you don't see where you are from, how the bloody hell are you expected to see where you are going? And I'll leave you with one more thing, because I'm going back to the station now. There are fourteen people in this room this morning and I am the only one with the manners to wear a Tetley tie. I bid you good day.'

When Dave got back from his meeting, he repeated his speech that many times that everybody in the taproom learned it by heart. Dave's vision was spot on though. He predicted that the brewery would be closed down in his lifetime. Everybody laughed, 'They couldn't possibly close down the most famous brewery in Yorkshire could they?' But they did. When Dave heard the news he said, 'I fucking told yer.' A few weeks after the demolition Dave got one of his mates to drive over to Leeds. They chucked a load of bricks from the demolished building into the back of a pickup. Dave used the bricks to make a wall for his front porch. He had a brass plaque made which read, 'These bricks were rescued from Tetley's brewery Leeds 1822-2012. Rest in Peace.'

On Dave's own gravestone there is a vintage Tetley hand-pump clip featuring the famous huntsman logo complete with monocle. On the day of his funeral, Dave lay in state in an open coffin. We turned up at the Shoulder at ten o'clock in the morning. The curtains were drawn. Margaret said, 'If anybody wants to pay their last respects, he's in the best room next to the bar where he belongs.' I went in to pay my respect with some of the fairground lads. Dave lay in his trilby with his Tetley tie on. The fairground lads touched him on the forehead and made a sign of the cross with their thumbnails. I just said, 'Ta ra old lad.' At St Paul's they played 'Ernie (The Fastest Milkman in the West)' as we trooped into the church. On the way out it was 'When I'm Cleaning Windows'.

Clubbing Together

At the beginning of 2016, the author Barry Hines died after a struggle with Alzheimer's disease. *Kes*, the film of his best known book, has been a favourite round here since it first came out in 1969. I once talked to Paul, a trade union mate of mine. He declared that the best three films ever made were filmed not more than a ten-mile radius of where we were standing. I said, 'Go on then.' He said, '*Kes*, *This Sporting Life* and *Brassed Off*.' Ken's DVD shop in Pontefract still sell an average of half a dozen copies a week. There is a whole generation who weren't even at infant school at the time it came out, who can now quote whole chunks of the dialogue almost verbatim.

'Right, we're Manchester United. Who are you?'

'We'll be Spurs sir then there's no clash of colours.'

'Right... it's the fair, slightly balding Bobby Charlton to kick off.'

The Tap & Barrel, a pub opposite the old court house on the edge of the town centre in Pontefract, decided to form a film club and put on movies. They called it 'The Cosy Cinema'. This was in honour of an old flea-pit picture house down the road. The original Cosy Cinema had once incongruously played host to the blues singer Big Bill Broonzy. He played a short set in front of the curtain to a gang of startled local urchins before *Flash Gordon* came on. This was sometime in the late fifties. This tiny footnote in local history lie dormant for years. Then, when everything was being shut down or boarded up, there came a revival of interest in intangible local culture. The Cozy Cinema, at the end of a terraced street in Glass Houghton, had long since stopped being a picture house. For years it was a clothing factory and then, after that, a car park. When the Tap & Barrel started its film club, the name came alive again.

The Cozy Cinema decided to kick off with *Kes*. They sold tickets for the event at the back of the bar, all proceeds to go to the Alzheimer's Society. It was a sell-out. Fifty-odd people turned up and sat behind a velvet curtain. We had the back of our hands stamped with an inky stamp like the ones they have in nightclubs, for when we went to the bar or the lavatory, so that we could get back in again. The audience was a mixture of middle-aged film buffs, local culture vultures and younger people who had heard of *Kes* while they were on their media courses.

There were sighs of recognition from the older end when the lads got the cane for smoking in the lavatory, nervous laughter at the casual brutality of Casper's older brother Jud, and knowing chuckles at the use of local dialect.

The landlord at the Tap & Barrel, Dean Smith, had form for bringing entertainment into the pub. Previously, Dean had run a cracking two-hundred-year-old village pub called the Bradley Arms. The Brads had struggled for a few years, but through the efforts of a few locals and couples who came out on a Saturday night it managed to keep going, just! During the week it was like sitting in a waiting room on a branch line waiting for something to come. That all changed when Dean and his wife Sally arrived. They sprinkled magic, put candles and fresh flowers on the tables, made sure the log fires were roaring and put on plenty of events. Quiz night filled the place, acoustic music brought them in and eccentric charm and old-fashioned hospitality made it a place to go to.

For a few years in the 1970s, the Bradley Arms had held an annual pub Olympics competition. A lot of the events took place in the beer garden round the back. There was throwing the horseshoe, beer crate stacking, tug o' war and the inevitable yard of ale drinking event. Indoors they played darts, crib and Fives and Threes. The blue-ribbon event was the bale of hay tossing competition. The idea was to see how high you could chuck a standard bale of hay with a pitchfork. Two sticks with a bar across stood in two buckets filled with soil to form a kind of pole vault apparatus. The undisputed champion was a big, raw-boned lad called Jack Rayner. He won it year after year. One year he faced a serious challenge from Liza Barker. Liza stood six feet four in his stocking feet and weighed about eighteen stone. Liza thought he had won it with his final throw, but on his last attempt Jack went at it like a Hungarian hammer thrower and nearly chucked the bale onto a barn roof. He retained his title and his undisputed ownership of the strong man event.

By the time Dean and Sally took over the Bradley Arms at the turn of the millennium, the pub Olympics was a distant memory. One or two middle-aged blokes talked nostalgically about it over Sunday lunchtime games of dominoes, but nobody ever got up enough enthusiasm to start it off again. Dean decided that he would bring pub games back. He marked out a quoits throwing pit in the garden. The game caught on for a few weekends over the summer, but chucking horseshoes over a steel bar driven into the ground was seen as a bit old-fashioned by that time. Undeterred, Dean decided to form a pub darts team. Somebody told him that the best darts thrower in the district was a bloke called 'Dodgy Dennis' from Pontefract. Dennis, as far as anyone knew, hadn't thrown a dart for a fair few years. That was only half of the problem. Dennis was notoriously unreliable and was drunk a lot of the time. He was also prone to putting money on himself to lose, when he had been backed heavily as a favourite. There had been a scandal some time in the past when a lot of people had lost a lot of money on the outcome of a final, a lot of people apart from Dennis. He'd been thrown out of the league and banned sine die.

I knew Dennis of old. He could get contraband tobacco from Belgium. In fact Dennis could get contraband most things, from Levi jeans to Tommy Hilfiger shirts. Dean asked me to bring him over to the Bradley Arms. I went to see Dennis in the working men's club where he spent most of his afternoons playing snooker. He said, 'Who will pay for the beer and bus fares?'

We got him there one quiet midweek morning. He turned

up in a calf-length, faux-leather overcoat, with gold sovereign rings on most of his fingers and his trademark jam-jar bottom spectacles. He looked like an all-in wrestling promoter. Dennis thought he looked like George Best. Sooner said he looked like a pox doctor's clerk.

Dean came straight out with it. 'I'm forming a darts team Dennis and I wondered whether you might be interested in playing for us.'

Dennis sighed. 'I've had a kipper for my breakfast this morning and it hasn't half made me thirsty.'

Dean pulled him a pint and watched him as he swallowed half of it in one go with a shaky hand. 'Aaahhh! that's better, I was as dry as a witches tit.'

'So. What do you think Dennis. Will you give it a go?'

Dodgy Dennis laughed and took his beer over to a stool by the fireplace. He picked up a poker and turned one of the logs over. The log caught a flame. 'It's grand to see an open fire in a pub on a cold morning like this.' Then he stared into the fire like a man trying to remember something that wouldn't come back to him.

Dean looked across to me and whispered, 'Can he really still throw darts? He's shaking like a wet dog.'

I was fairly sure that Dennis could still throw darts, but asked him anyhow. 'What are you studying Dennis? Can't you throw darts anymore?'

Dennis shook his head slightly and spat onto the fire. 'Now, you wouldn't ask Lester Piggott if he can still ride his horse would you?'

Dean said, 'Let's see you then.'

Dennis drained his pot. 'I'm always better when I've had a couple of beers. Did you ever see Bill Werbeniuk playing snooker? I'm a bit like him. A couple of beers settles my nerves.'

Dean said, 'I'll tell you what Dennis. I'll give you three darts. If you can get a bull's-eye with any of them three, I'll buy your beer all afternoon.'

Dennis didn't say anything. He poked the fire again and watched the flames lick up from under the logs. Then he took his long coat off and folded it over the back of a chair. He flexed his wrist, a thick bracelet jangled against his watch. He reached into the inside pocket of his jacket and pulled out a set of darts. He weighed the darts across the palm of his hand and made a fuss of adjusting the flights. You could have cut through the atmosphere.

Sooner piped up. 'Even money he does it.' Nobody took his bet.

Dennis made a big to-do looking at the board and adjusted his glasses like Eric Morecambe. 'What do you think of it so far?' And he laughed loud. Then he turned on his heel and launched his first dart. His wrist jangled and for effect he left his hand still in mid-air like a teapot spout. The dart landed in the outer ring, just above the bull. 'I'm a bit rusty, but it's not a bad sightline.' He threw the second arrow, this one landed in the outer ring as well, just below the bull. He tutted to himself. 'Oooh! I need a bit of practise.' He then took off his jacket and turned the cuff of his shirt sleeve, looked across at Sooner and said, 'What do you say Sooner? My pound against your fiver?' Sooner shook his head. Dennis threw his third dart. It landed straight in the centre of the bull's-eye. He didn't say anything. He swaggered to the board like Errol Flynn when he played Robin Hood. He retrieved his darts by gently turning them anti-clockwise as he pulled them out. He put them back into his leather case and slipped the case back into his inside pocket. He patted his jacket and sat back on the stool by the fire.

Dean was flabbergasted. He looked across at me and Sooner and mouthed, 'Bloody hell! How did he do that?'

Dennis turned the logs over again. 'Landlord, I think you need to fetch your axe in and chop a few more of these. And if I were you I'd fetch a bucket full of coal in. It might be a long session!' With that he drained his second pint and slammed it hard onto the table. He then muttered something about blacklists and playing under an assumed name. He had a good afternoon on the beer and went home plaiting his legs, but he never once turned up on match night.

About seven years ago, our mate Kevin heard a radio documentary about a record listening club in London. The idea for it had sprouted from the rediscovery of the pleasure to be had from listening to a thirty-three-and-a-third rpm LP record. The premise of the club was simple; get a few mates together, listen to a record and discuss it. Kevin phoned round half a dozen of us after he listened to the documentary and asked if we'd like to form a similar club. We could meet in his garage every second Tuesday. Kevin had a garage that he'd converted into a workspace. One of our gang, Wayne, found some nice fold-up wooden chairs that an old church hall was throwing out, so we had something to sit on. Kevin said that we could use his 1960s Hacker Grenadier portable record player. The Rolls-Royce, he said, of portables.

We called our meetings 'gatherings' and we gathered on that first Tuesday to listen to *Sgt. Pepper* and an introduction from Kevin. He said, 'Well, this might not be the greatest LP ever made, it might not even be the best LP The Beatles made, but it is a classic and it might just be the first LP that can be called a classic. My mother and father bought it for my birthday the week it came out. The copy we are going to listen to is my original mono copy.' It was a grand introduction. There was a familiar smell of old valves warming up. The even more familiar sound of a needle being dropped into a groove and the crackle as it worked its way through dust. Then 'It was twenty years ago today...' And for the next thirty-nine minutes and fifty-two seconds we sat still and listened. The only sounds came from four lads from Liverpool in 1967, the creaking of wooden fold-up church hall chairs and the occasional burp as we sipped from cans of Stella, John Smith's Smooth and bottles of cider.

As the record came to its run-out groove and the famous gibberish sounds captured there, Kevin said, 'Right! We'll have a fag break and then a short discussion.' Ian, Johnny, Gary and I smoked roll-ups at the garage door while Dick, Terry and Neil opened the cheese Quavers and Doritos. We then sat for another three-quarters of an hour supping off-licence beer, chomping crisps and chewing the fat about the merits of what we had just listened to. Neil said, 'I'll go first. I think it's dated. To tell the truth I'm not sure that I was too keen on it when it came out. I once took it to a party and got my leg over with a bird who liked George Harrison.'

Kevin took a sip of Jack Daniels. 'I'm not sure we need to know what you got up to at parties in the sixties thank you Neil. I'd just like to say that some people say Ringo is a shit drummer, but I think his drumming on this album is magnificent. And "She's Leaving Home" is one of the finest songs ever written.'

I think I mentioned that I still had my original *Sgt. Pepper* cardboard cut-out moustache and stripes at home and that I remember the day I bought my copy from a long-gone record shop on the corner of Finkle Street called The Kiosk Record Bar. We all agreed that what we had done was an enjoyable experience. We enjoyed the music, we got half pissed and then we argued about what record we should pick next. We decided to take it in turns and Gary had first pick. We reconvened a fortnight later to listen to *Pet Sounds* by The Beach Boys. Gary gave his introduction and started by saying, 'Brian Wilson is my favourite musician. I like the way he writes about love, hope and fear. Most of all I like the way he fuses emotion to studio production and uplifting harmonies.' Gary obviously put a lot of thought into his presentation. On only our second gathering, he raised the bar for how we might say something about the music we liked. He also managed to down four cans of Stella and smoke two joints before 'Wouldn't It Be Nice' finished and 'Caroline, No' started.

By the time of our third gathering to sup alcohol and listen to records in the garage, Kevin was producing a newsletter, notes about the record we were about to hear, and an agenda. Terry was elected treasurer and collected subs in an old bacca tin. And we named ourselves The CAT Club, 'Classic Album Tuesdays'. Kevin took it on himself to produce a logo and came up with a cat on its hind legs playing a trombone in the moonlight. A gang of middle-aged mates, swigging ale out of cans and reliving moments from youth became a thing. We even had the local newspaper do a feature on us.

When it came to my turn, I didn't know whether to pick a Van Morrison, a Bob Dylan or a Billie Holiday. I even considered The Watersons *For Pence and Spicy Ale*. It's a record I have treasured since I found it in a box on a trestle table outside of a long-gone record shop called Shakespeare Bros. which was on the forecourt of Hull railway station. In the end I thought that three-quarters of an hour of old English folk song in the confines of a garage bedecked with Jerry Lee Lewis posters might be pushing it a bit. I settled for *Dusty in Memphis*. My mother was a big Dusty Springfield fan. She played her singles on an old Dansette at home. Dusty's music has been in my life for most of my life. There are songs on the *Memphis* album that I never tire of; 'Breakfast in Bed,' 'Just a Little Lovin'' and of course 'Son of a Preacher Man'. Sad to say, on the night we played that record, the stylus was playing up, so we didn't get the full benefit of the music, but we all agreed that Dusty is nothing short of a musical goddess.

The meetings at Kevin's garage became something to look forward to, as much for the friendship as the supping and music. We kept it going well for the first couple of years and non-attendance was frowned upon. Then we started to look at ways of keeping the momentum going. We decided to invite a series of guest presenters. We drew up a list of people who we thought might come. I had known Graham Oliver, lead guitar player with Saxon, for a number of years. We asked him to be our first guest. He only lives at Mexborough, so he didn't have to come far. He picked Jimi Hendrix's album *Axis: Bold as Love*.

On the night that Graham came we picked up a new member called Stuart. Stuart told us that he'd seen Hendrix play at the infamous concert at The Giro Club in the gentile market town of Ilkley back in 1967. He fetched his membership card of the club to show us and regaled us with tales of that night when Hendrix managed to get through one song and a mighty amount of feedback, before Sergeant Tommy Chapman of the West Riding Constabulary shut the place down for overcrowding.

Stuart became a CAT Club regular. He brought another dynamic to our garage nights. He liked The Animals, The Troggs,

The Who and Buddy Holly but not much else. Our post record discussions, which up to that point had been mildly drunken rambles about the merits of various LPs, started to become shouting matches. Stuart would announce, 'Well I didn't like that at all, in fact it's fucking shit.' When pressed to develop his argument about why it might be 'fucking shit' Stuart would lean forward on his church-hall chair and say, 'Because it is fucking shit, that's why!' It was funny at first and then it became irritating. We had found a way to put up with Neil spinning tall tales about how many young women he had shagged at parties in the 60s and 70s, but we never really got a handle on Stuart and his 'fucking shit' refrain. It all came to an head after three consecutive meetings where voices were raised. Stuart really didn't like *Never Mind the Bollocks*, he said it was truly 'bollocks'. He couldn't make head nor tail of Love's *Forever Changes* album and suspected that we might be all communists because of our affection for it. Then it came to Ian Daley's choice of *Clandestino* by Manu Chao. It was all too much for Stuart. He said, 'If that's what I've got to put up with I'm not coming anymore.' He didn't come anymore. That was a shame, because despite his outbursts, Stuart was very funny at times. He gave me the best laugh I ever had at that club. During the playing of *The Indestructible Beat of Soweto* Stuart broke the strict club rule of not talking while the record was playing. After one track that had him going redder and redder in the face, he burst out, 'What the fuck was that?' I whispered, 'It's a track called "Emthonjeni Womculo" by a singer called Mahlathini.' Quick as a flash Stuart said, 'It fucking sounds like it.'

We carried on with our occasional guest presenters. Gary who worked on the guest list and doors at Back to Basics nightclub in Leeds told us that he often talked to Howard Marks, the author of *Mr Nice*, when he came clubbing. Howard was agreeable and said he would come for a bottle of brandy and a bag of home-grown weed. He picked Frank Zappa's doo-wop album, *Cruising with Ruben & the Jets*. He told us in the after-album discussion that he had listened to a lot of doo-wop on a tinny transistor radio back home in Wales when he was a teenager.

Ian was working with Tom Hingley of Inspiral Carpets on a memoir. He invited Tom and he came along with a copy of Dr. Feelgood's *Down by the Jetty* LP. Tom gave us perhaps the best introduction to an album we'd had up to then and afterwards played some of his own songs on an acoustic guitar. It felt special to be sat supping ale in a backyard garage with mates while listening to a stripped-down version of 'This Is How It Feels'.

One time Terry, our tobacco tin treasurer, mentioned that he had a mate called Mick who had once coached the Congolese national football team. This Mick was friends with the legendary bass player Danny Thompson and from time to time when Danny was in the north he stayed with Mick. Terry said he would mention The CAT Club to Mick and ask him if Danny might consider coming. The night we played John Martyn's *Solid Air* we had a nice surprise. An email came to us from Danny Thompson. It said, 'Wotcha! I hope you enjoy *Solid Air* and the wonderful poetry of my curly-haired mate John. A lot of rhubarb has been written about our antics, but his songs are the finest indication of the real man, one I miss every day. It would be a treat to enjoy one of your evenings, hopefully you will allow me as a passing guest some time. All the best to you at the club. Danny Thompson.'

A few months after that, Danny Thompson did come as a guest. It was one of the few CAT Clubs that I missed. I was on my holidays. The lads told me of course that it was the best CAT Club ever! In honour of the great man they dispensed with the usual one album rule and played loads of selections from various albums that Danny had played on. Everything from Pentangle, to Marc Bolan and Donovan, to the soundtrack for *Kes*. Then Danny regaled the lads with tales all night.

I think we had over one hundred gatherings in the garage and some great evenings of camaraderie and beer. We also took The CAT Club on tour. Over time the money we put into the bacca tin mounted up. We bought the occasional new stylus and a few times we bought new records if we didn't have one in our collections, but we still ended up with a fair bit of money saved up. In the finest tradition of clubs, we decided that we should have day trips out.

One of the trips was to The Brudenell Social Club at Leeds to see The Pretty Things, with most of their original line up still intact. The Brudenell is a former working men's club, in what was once a working-class district of Leeds called Hyde Park. In many respects the club should be past its sell-by date, but a change in the culture of that area of Leeds meant that it not only survived, but thrived. The mill and engineering factory workers who had traditionally lived in that part of Leeds started to move away in the 1980s. The ever expanding student population at the two universities moved in. The student population created a demand for live entertainment and so The Brudenell morphed into a gig venue. It's a grand gig venue as well, probably the best example you could find of a new use for a tired working men's club. And the best bit of all is the fact that they still manage to cater for the original members. I went to see the American troubadour Ryley Walker there. While he was doing his John Martyn/Bert Jansch inspired ballads on stage in the concert room, some old lads were laiking dominoes in the other side. The club also serves good real ale from microbreweries from all over the north. A far cry from the days of working men's club tank beer that tastes of nothing and makes you piss like a horse.

The Glossop Labour Club in Derbyshire is another club that has managed to embrace the now. We discovered that they too had a record listening club when we were invited to visit them. They meet on regular Wednesdays. The invitation came to me, so The CAT Club decided I should choose the record. I picked *Songs for Distingué Lovers* by Billie Holiday. Kevin thought that my choice might be a bit too mellow and tried to get me to alter it to something livelier. He suggested Jerry Lee Lewis *Live at the Star Club, Hamburg*. He said that it was more representative of The CAT Club's taste. It was also his own personal favourite. I stuck to my guns and explained that Billie's album was a late-career highpoint and in Ben Webster, Harry 'Sweets' Edison and Barney Kessel, it featured some of the finest jazz musicians of the 1950s.

It also features a splendid version of 'One for My Baby (And One More for the Road)' which I thought was entirely appropriate for a record club of boozers on tour. We had a cracking night at Glossop Labour Club and Billie Holiday went down well. As did the beer. The town's football team, Glossop North End, had qualified for the semi-final of the FA Vase. In their honour, a local farm brewery had produced a commemorative ale called 'North End Bitter'. We supped a good few. Dick got a bit rowdy and had to be told off by Kevin for talking while the record was on. Kevin said he was bringing shame on our club with his bad manners. He was half joking.

There are a couple of photographs from that night. They show a bleary eyed gang of Pontefract revellers on tour. Kevin couldn't resist bringing his copy of *Live at the Star Club, Hamburg* and holds it up prominently in the middle of the photo like a trophy. A couple of days after our visit, Glossop North End went all the way down to St Austell in Cornwall to play their semi-final. They won. Not long after that they went to Wembley to play South Shields in the final. They lost 2-1 in extra time. I imagine some sorrows were drowned on North End Bitter in the Labour club that night. The Labour club is a beauty. One of the oldest Labour club's in the country, it's a real asset to the town. They have a people's kitchen, a sewing circle, acoustic music evenings, as well as the very vibrant and well-run record club. One of the club regulars has a part share in the minibus that the North End footballers use for away games. As we were leaving that cold November night, they mentioned that they might borrow the bus to pay us a return visit.

At Christmas we had a fuddle and a quiz and invited friends and family to join us. A mate of ours called Samantha Smith opened a little bistro in the upstairs room of a long shut down Pontefract pub called The Pineapple and we started to meet there. The Pineapple had shut some time in the early 1960s. Local legend has it that the jukebox there was attracting too many 'rockers' and pioneering users of substances. Its licence was taken away. The building stayed, more or less whole. It has a very ornate facade, topped off with a sculpture of a pineapple. Over the years the building has been converted into all sorts of uses. There was a record shop called Rock Ola there for a while and for the last few years a games shop called Console Yourself has occupied the downstairs area where the bar was. Upstairs in a front room overlooking the street is a hairdressing salon. There was an empty room at the back, so Sam opened her little bistro there. She gave it a vintage theme and hired it out to private parties. She cooked delicious food and always had a barrel of good ale on handpump. There will be very few buildings that have held licences to sell alcohol with a fifty year gap between licences. At one time Sam had been the youngest landlady in town, when at the age of nineteen she had taken on a rough and ready ale house called The Turk's Head. The pub was known for its rowdiness, it attracted long-distance lorry drivers who stayed overnight on a car park nearby and blokes who wanted to fight them. Sam soon sorted them out with a no-nonsense approach and turned the place round. She became known for the quality of her real ale and moved on to run the famous Huddersfield pub, The Sportsman. When she came back to open her bistro, she sourced some lovely beers. The CAT Club had marvellous nights there. One time Andy Pickering from the Concertina Brewery gave us a barrel of Bengal Tiger. In between our homemade tapas, a devilish pop quiz and plenty of banter, we managed to finish the barrel down to its last dregs.

Dean Smith had been an on-and-off member of The CAT Club for a while and when he took over the licence at the Tap & Barrel he suggested we should hold our gatherings there. It was a pub that had had its ups and downs over the years. A lot of regular drinkers remembered it as The Greyhound, a pub that had reinvented itself as a live music venue for a while. After that it became a real ale venue with plenty of guest beers, but it started to fade. It was boarded up for a bit, then it was bought at auction by a company that wanted to turn it into a craft beer and artisan coffee place. That failed after just a couple of months because everybody said it was too dear. It seemed that Pontefract wasn't yet ready for pubs with tiled floors, espresso machines and framed vintage prints. It was boarded up again. Dean was now ready to work the same magic on the Tap & Barrel that he'd applied to The Brads. He called us all to a meeting to suggest that we move from the garage to the pub. We all agreed that it was a good idea. After five years of supping out of cans in the garage we went public.

We tried at first to retain the same ethos: play a record, listen to it in silence and then discuss it over a few pints. It didn't work. What might be right for a handful of mates who know each other's ways isn't the same in a public bar. We'd also by then started to run out of ideas for what records to bring. The first couple of meetings in the pub were retreads of what we'd done before. Next we attempted to attract some younger people. We asked a young local band called Allusondrugs to pick their favourite record and play a short gig. They picked *Nevermind* by Nirvana. Their fans turned up en masse and struggled to catch on to what was happening. A lot of them got bored and after a couple of tracks went off to the yard to smoke and play with their iPhones. The short gig turned into a bit of a mosh pit. I came home a bit crestfallen that night. It seemed to me that the writing was on the wall. What had started out as an intimate little club for a group of mates who liked a drink and music didn't really work when it opened its door.

Nowadays, The CAT Club carries on as a commercial event that is part of the pub's wider entertainment programme. The tobacco tin is no more. It's fine I suppose for what it is and there have been some smashing evenings; Clinton Heylin, Bob Dylan's biographer, launched his book *JUDAS!* at a CAT Club event. Iain Matthews came and did a brilliant gig after choosing Gene Clark's *No Other* as his record and Andy Kershaw came to talk about his passion for Dylan's *Highway 61 Revisited* and how that passion had led him to make a radio documentary about it. It's not the same for me though. When we were in the garage I never thought for once that 'I've been here before'. Since the move to the pub, it's like 'Here we go again'. I think a lot about things like this. I like things to be what they are, not what they might be. I think I'm with the old folk singer Pete Seeger, who once said, 'I want to turn the clock back to when people lived in villages and looked after one another.' People who like pubs like to talk about 'their local' but when does the pub you call your local stop being your local? In over forty years of trying to have a local, I've had a few, but not just because they're at the top of the street, but because I feel at home there.

Localism

There is a singer who I always wanted to see live. More than that I wanted to see her live in Paris and preferably at L'Olympia Music Hall. I don't know how the tune first came into my head, but 'Sous Le Ciel de Paris' has always been my go-to melody whenever I'm feeling a bit down, or I'm distracted or a million other reasons for a tune worming its way into your ear and coming out as a hum. For many years I didn't know who sang that song. Through reading about Miles Davis's love affair with her, I discovered it was Juliette Greco. I became a fan. I liked the way she looked, her voice, her story, her acting, her politics, everything about her. I was also aware that Juliette Greco was getting close to her retirement. She'd first sung in the 1940s and her recording and performing career spanned going on for seventy years. In 2014 when she was 87 years old, she embarked on her farewell tour. I noticed that she was going to do two nights at L'Olympia, the theatre where Miles, Judy Garland, Billie Holiday, Edith Piaf, Jacques Brel and Marlene Dietrich had all performed famous concerts. I'm rubbish at booking things online, worse when confronted by a website in French, but somehow I navigated my way through it and booked for Heather and me to see her and we went on the Eurostar.

We stayed in a hotel on the Rue Richer near to the Folies Bergère. That part of Paris is a melting pot of cultures. There are Kosher bakeries, Ukrainian convenience stores, African street vendors and Japanese restaurants and it seems to work. It is a very vibrant district. In the spirit of going to a Juliette Greco concert, Heather decided she wanted to buy a packet of Gitanes. As you walk up the Rue Richer, Folies Bergère is on the right, but before you get there, on the left is a little bar-tabac, a classic Bistrot Parisienne. Like in a lot of French bar-tabacs, the part that sells the tobacco is like a little corner shop with tins and jars and well-worn wooden drawers. We could see through the door to the bar that it was a busy place. They had Belgian Leffe on tap, so we thought it a shame not to try one. The Tabac des Folies is a proper local's bar with a warm welcome for visitors. I won't go as far as to say that it's a pub, but it is a bar and it's one of those magical places that you occasionally stumble upon. The beer was reasonable and the clientele a right old mix. In the space of half an hour we spoke to a photographer, a joiner, an actress and an old man who told us that he had been coming there every day for as long as he could remember. They all seemed to go to the open door for a cigarette together, carried on their conversations on the pavement and then trooped back in together. We told the old man that we were on our way to see Juliette Greco. He started to sing 'Déshabillez-Moi'. When the others encouraged him, he pretended to take his clothes off.

Tabac des Folies is the sort of bar where an old man in a battered beret can sing in a corncrake voice and reckon to do a striptease without anyone raising so much as an eyebrow. The bar is run by Michel and his Moroccan-born wife Myryam. They are lovely people: undisputedly French and very proud of their little place. Michel told me that the bar was one of Paris's historic landmarks and then he spent ten minutes sorting through a load of papers behind the bar looking for a booklet he wanted to give me. It was a guidebook to the old-fashioned bars, bistrots and brasseries of Paris and his place featured in it. The old man who had sung to us told us we should eat before we went to the theatre, because the queues would be shorter. He gave us directions to a place called Bouillon Chartier on Rue de Fauborg Montmatre, just a few hundred yards away. His recommendation was an inspired one. Bouillon Chartier is one of those Parisian dining rooms that are disappearing now. This one goes back to the 1800s and nothing much has changed. The waiters wear long, white aprons, don't write anything down because they have phenomenal memories, and give that Gallic shrug to anything that doesn't suit them. The tables are long which means you share with other diners and the food is homemade, nothing fancy, but delicious and for Paris very reasonably priced.

Heather and I walked down to the theatre. A little fantasy played in my mind for the length of the sidewalks. I am sitting at a table outside the Café de Flore on the Left Bank. The calendar on the wall says 1954 and Greco and Jean-Paul Sartre are blowing the froth off a coffee. They are involved in deep philosophical conversation. A breeze blows the beret from Juliette's head. I pick it up and hand it back to her. She gives me an enigmatic smile. We can all dream.

At L'Olympia, Greco stood in a spotlight for over two hours accompanied by only accordion and piano. She dressed all over in her usual black. She gave a performance of songs by Brel, Ferrat and Gainsbourg, full of charm, wit and passion. It was a dream come true. We called into the little bar on the way back and raised a few glasses more. Then we stumbled back to our hotel.

Heather says that I have eyes like a shithouse rat. Wherever we go, she says I can spot a locals' pub at a mile off. I don't think I can, but I can weigh up an area I'm in and guess what makes it tick. In this way I can usually navigate my way to a decent ale house. My old mate Mick Appleyard, a former miners' union delegate, could find his way round the north of England by looking at the wheels on pit head gears. I can do it by pubs, even when we're abroad.

A favourite landmark abroad is the U Fleku in Prague, an ancient brewhouse famed for its black beer. I'd first gone there back in the days before the Iron Curtain melted, when there wasn't much colour, the food was mainly stew and dumplings with occasional slices of roast goose, and tourists were a novelty. In fact, you could have chucked a blanket over three-quarters of the tourists then because they were all sat at the long tables in the back courtyard of U Fleku. The best communal singing I ever heard in a pub was in that backyard when some young Canadian youth-hostellers improvised a three-part harmony version of

Queen's 'We Will Rock You' complete with handclaps and table banging. I loved the beer in Prague. There wasn't much choice, but you didn't need it when the one beer on tap was that good.

Heather and I decided to take the local train to Pilsen. We worked out that it wasn't that far away and we were longing to try a Pilsner Urquell in a pub near where they brewed it. It took us all morning to get there, the train travelled over rickety rails at twenty miles an hour and it stopped at every village along the way. It was a miserable journey with rain coming down like stair rods through the mucky window. Heather had her camera pinched as well. The sun peeked its head out in Pilsen and we found a place called Na Parkunu. The first sip of the unfiltered beer told us that the journey had been worth it. It wasn't so much a pot of gold at the end of a rainbow, but it was probably the nearest I ever came to finding the perfect pint or at least half a litre of beer.

I was invited to run creative-writing workshops for English Literature students at Changchun University in the north east of China. I kept getting asked out to meals with various academics from the university and we drank little bottles of beer from Harbin in Heilongjiang province with our food. Harbin is, I believe, China's oldest brewery and was the first to use malt instead of rice when they brewed for thirsty Russian railway workers on the Trans-Manchurian railroad. It's not a beer to write home about but it's refreshing, light and palatable. I got used to necking a couple after my work.

One night around the dinner table, as well as the usual teachers and professors, the campus caretaker turned up. He asked me if I would like to try the baijiu. Whenever somebody asks me if I would like to try a drink that I can barely pronounce, I worry. My experiences in Poland with various spirits and in Bosnia with the raki have taught me to be cautious. The caretaker was persistent and when a little pot bottle arrived at the table and he pulled a cork out, I feared the worst. Baijiu is a clear white spirit made from fermented sorghum. I sipped at the little clay cup that the caretaker had poured it into. He laughed and smacked me on the back, beckoning me to whack it down in one. I did, then quickly felt its fire and started to cough and choke. He slapped me on the back again, harder this time and poured me another. I liked the taste of the old baijiu, it's a good job, because they were all up toasting every five minutes. I watched the caretaker's face going redder and redder and felt the flames in my cheeks too. I don't think the cork went back in the bottle that night. I tried to stick to the little dumpy bottles of Harbin after that.

Before I came home from China I persuaded my interpreter to drive me to the mountains on the North Korean border. I had been reading about Heaven Lake which sits atop the volcanic Paektu Mountain. I heard lovely stories that said the Korean people believed they were born out of Heaven Lake and I wanted to see it with my own eyes. The mountain is more than 9,000 feet high, but you only climb the last bit of it. The Chinese have built a road of hairpin bends and cool-looking drivers take you up in SUVs. They wear leather driving gloves, wrap-round shades and they chew on matchstalks while your heart goes in your mouth at every turn of the wheel. It was only when we got to the top that my interpreter confessed that it is very rare to see the lake, because for most of the year it is shrouded in a icy mist. The lake was shrouded in mist that day, like someone had thrown a linen table cloth over it. The interpreter said, 'We shouldn't stay too long, even in summer the temperature drops quickly.' I told her that whenever I arrive somewhere and I'm not sure what to do next, I wait for a bit to see what might happen. We waited twenty minutes and a hole came into the sky above the lake. It was perhaps the most beautiful sight my sore eyes had rested on.

We took directions from a local on the way back. I saw rural China from dirt roads and other roads that were not much more than tracks through woodland. We stopped at an inn in the middle of nowhere. The innkeeper offered us local beer and a plateful of eggs fried with rice and onions. On the bar top were three or four large glass containers with taps on them. I asked about them. The innkeeper told me that it was own brew and he was very proud that he collected the herbs, berries and flowers to flavour his drink from the local woods. My interpreter warned me that it was a type of baijiu and probably very strong. The first glass contained a reddish liquid, the interpreter asked about it and told me that it was flavoured with a type of wild berry. I pointed to the second one, this apparently had more than thirty different herbs in it. The last jar contained a liquid with a slightly milky, opaque colour and had what looked like a thin leek in it. She asked the innkeeper to describe. He became very animated, pointed to me then to his biceps and prepared to turn the tap and fill a glass. The interpreter said, 'Perhaps you will not like that one, it contains the penis of the forest deer.' I tried the one with berries in it.

Some of the best holidays Heather and I have had in recent times have been in Denmark and Sweden. The beer there, despite it being ridiculously expensive, has played its part in drawing us in. We fell in love with Denmark's second largest city Aarhus. It's an old city, one of the oldest in Scandinavia, but it feels young and modern. This might be down to the fact that one in seven of the inhabitants are students. Heather said that no other place she has been to bridges the gap between the tradition and the new like that city does. Heather loved the culture and the art there. The ARoS art museum with its rainbow rooftop walk is a sight to behold. The food is great, a fusion of traditional and ultra-modern. Heather can eat pickled herring until it comes out of her ears. We set off one night in a place called Bodega Theatre, a proper old-fashioned restaurant where you have to book a table even if there are some available. The waiters wear long aprons and tell stories about the menu. We ate seven different types of cured fish and washed it down with akvavit. Someone told us that the Nørregade district was the up-and-coming area. We went up there. Like all 'up-and-coming' areas, the street had its fair share of scruffy shops and what they call these days shabby chic places, but the bar we found there was a beauty. Fermentoren is a perfect example of the craft beer bar. They have about twenty beers on tap, with every brewing style you could imagine, from Imperial Russian stouts to American pale ales, Berliner Weisse beers to English milds flavoured with chamomile. The names are bewildering, perhaps designed to appeal to the iPhone/ Netflix generation. So you get Hobo Chic, Pineapple Unplugged, Warpigs and Full Re Tart.

In Copenhagen we stayed smack bang in the middle of the one-time notorious Westboro district between the back of the railway station and the old meat-packing warehouses. An old hotel had been converted into a hostel for backpackers. It's called Urban House. It's a revelation of a conversion, full of light wood, glass and exposed pipe work. Corinne Bailey Rae and Norah Jones sing from the speakers and you check in using a tablet or smart phone. There's a launderette, a tattoo parlour, a video wall, a room full of beanbags and a cinema room. There is an outside games area called 'The Green Escape' where you can sip the local 'Ugly Duckling' beer at nine quid a bottle. I sat there one morning. A mother with coloured braids in her hair played chess with her young son. He looked about twelve, had on a pair of pink Crocs and a Salvador Dali t-shirt. Older boys with beards and piercings played table tennis with tattooed girls. There was a replica of an old film poster *Attack of the 50 Ft. Woman* and next to it, the old Tuborg poster of Henningsen's thirsty man. Just a street away from Urban House is a bar that has become one of the most talked about brew-pubs in Europe. This is Mikkeller, the vanguard of the craft beer movement. It's a bit too wine bar for my taste and the beer comes from suspiciously wine-glass-shaped vessels, but it does brew great beer; the Warpigs wheat beer is as good as any I've tasted. It is 'craft beer' as opposed to the 'real ale' I'm used to and I'd much rather my beer tasted of beer than lychees or grapefruit, but as the Rolling Stones once sang, 'You can't always get what you want.'

Not long after, Heather and I went to Gothenburg to visit some mates. On a street down the side of the indoor market I spotted a place called 'Olhallen'; literally ale house. The lad behind the bar couldn't wait to tell us that it first opened its door in 1900 and that it hadn't altered much since then. We sat outside to watch the world go by. A tall bloke in his sixties came to sit on the next table. He swung a full rucksack from his shoulder onto the floor and blew out his cheeks to let us know how heavy it was.

'That looks heavy,' I said. That was his cue.

'I am very happy today. It was the last day of Finnish week at Lidl and they were selling the world's best blood pudding at a good price.' He unzipped his backpack and took out a vacuum-packed black pudding about a foot long. 'Mustamakkara!' he said and kissed his pudding. 'I bought twenty.'

It's difficult not to get talking to someone who kisses a vacuum-packed black pudding in front of you.

'I am from Tampere in Finland, this Mustamakkara blood sausage is a speciality of my region. I miss it, so I was pleased to know about the sale in Lidl.'

A big fat man across from us asked the Finnish man if he could have one of his puddings. The Finnish man passed the fat man a black pudding, who then opened his jacket and slid it into a poacher's pocket. This same man then turned to us and told us that he loved visiting Scotland, his cousin played for Dundee United and he knew Sir Alex Ferguson. I didn't know what to say in response so I mentioned that I knew Alex Ferguson was a supporter of the Labour Party. The fat man raised his fist in a salute. 'I am working class till I die, my mother and father worked in the fish canning factory.' I asked him where he went to in Scotland. He said he knew the area around the Moray Firth. I mentioned that I had once worked there and asked him if he had ever tried Cullen Skink. He said that his cousin's wife made the best Cullen Skink in the world.

The black pudding man had heard us mention Sir Alex Ferguson. He waited for us to finish talking about smoked fish soup and then said, 'Hey look!' He lifted his shirt up to reveal a beer belly and a tattoo on his chest. The tattoo was of the crest of Manchester United. All of this happened within the space of ten minutes. As we came away from the bar, Heather said, 'You seem to have a knack of finding them sort of pubs.' I asked her what she meant. 'You know! Full of mad old blokes kissing black pudding and getting their bellies out.'

On a street corner, we found a pub called Olstugen Tullen. It was a traditional-looking locals type of a place, but had a selection of beers and a knowledgeable young bar staff who were delighted to help us make our choice. We tried a beer called Tail of the Whale, another called Electric Nurse and then one called A Ship Full of IPA, which the young woman behind the bar informed us was bursting with flavour from Magnum, Galaxy, Cascade and Amarillo hops. She then told us that the street outside was once a notorious red-light district, but in recent times the reputation was improving. Not through the efforts of the town's elders but through young people with something to say coming there. I'm not sure that you can make an argument for good ale shining a light on the darker corners of society and putting them to right, but things do change on the edge of the wheel. By observing young folk dressed in homemade fashion turning up on bright coloured bikes which they leaned up outside the pub, you could see that the wheel was turning.

Man In A Station

I got a message from Volker at the back end of July in 2015. I picked up his email on a borrowed laptop in my rented room in Changchun. Volker had good news: after twelve sessions of chemotherapy he said that his cancer specialist had told him that his tumour had shrunken to next to nothing. He added that the chemo hadn't been half as bad as the previous course seven years before and that he had come through it all without vomiting or feeling poisoned. He said that he had recently acquired an e-bike and was looking forward to exploring the old tram and train lines in Bergisches Land. I chuckled in my Chinese room, flummoxed by the thought of Volker, a man who travels thousands of miles a year in an American Dodge van, peddling across the north German countryside on a bicycle. He also told me that he planned to visit Britain in the next couple of weeks and asked whether I would be around.

I got back from China on August 3rd. The first email I opened was from Iain Matthews. 'I have two tickets for Cropredy festival going spare if you want them.' Iain was joining with his old band Fairport Convention at their annual shindig in the Oxfordshire countryside. The second email was from Volker. 'I am at Brown's café in Oxford at the moment. I am enjoying Michaela's favourite carrot cake, but the tea tastes like the swimming pools used to do in my youth. Inspector Morse knew this café. I climbed two church towers today, but I couldn't find the record shop I once knew, perhaps it's closed down. Where do you go to buy a Lightnin' Hopkins LP these days?' I wrote back to Volker and told him about the Cropredy gig. I know that he has adored the music of Iain Matthews since he was a teenager. He phoned straight back and said, 'I'd love that. I will drive up from Oxford on Friday, we'll have a pint or two somewhere local and then I'll drive us both back down to Oxfordshire early on the Saturday morning.'

Volker arrived at lunchtime on the Friday. It was the first time I'd clapped eyes on him for nearly three years. In the November of 2012, Heather, our son Edward and I had flown over to Düsseldorf for Jurgen's 60th birthday party. We stayed in a budget motel almost under the legs of the Schwebebahn called McDreams. The party had been held in a bar called Cafe du Congo on Luisenstrasse that we had all known well for going on thirty years. It was a lovely reunion, but there was something in the air that none of us could put a finger on. Volker's wife Michaela looked poorly and frail, the chronic arthritis that she had suffered for much of her adult life had all but stopped her walking now. Volker pushed her to the party in a wheelchair.

Edward had promised to play some Miles Davis for Jurgen and they borrowed a portable keyboard. When it came to it, Edward said he didn't feel like playing. I think he was overwhelmed by a lot of people he didn't know in a bar. He did play, but made so many mistakes trying to remember the tunes that he became frustrated and walked off into a quiet corner. Volker was still the robust and happy lad I'd always known that weekend, though he seemed a bit distant and distracted, but he came to Edward's rescue. He put his arm around his shoulder and said, 'You know what Miles Davis would have said don't you Edward?' Edward looked up at Volker and shook his head slightly. Volker bent down and whispered loud enough for us to hear, 'So what!' Edward smiled.

We spent the rest of the evening reminiscing about trips we had made to each other's hometowns over the years. Volker recalled a visit to Cambridge Folk Festival and remembered something Edward had said that had stayed with him. We were putting up the tents and Edward, who would have been three at the time, struggled with a bagful of bedding. Volker said, 'Can I help?' to which Edward replied, 'I'm a strong lad.' Volker said that he had chuckled at that memory many times and throughout his illness he had told himself 'I'm a strong lad'.

On this Friday, Volker doesn't look like a strong lad anymore. He has lost a lot of weight and those big shoulders that powered him through the water when he was a butterfly swimmer have all but gone. He is a peculiar shade of yellow and his cheeks are sunken. I want to tell him that he is looking fit, but I stop myself, I have never bullshitted with Volker and I don't want to start now. I just say, 'It's lovely to see you lad.' And Volker, doing his Yorkshire accent, says 'And it's lovely to see thee too lad.' We embrace, as we have always done, and I can feel his ribs. I ask him if he's still a vegetarian. 'Only I've got some lovely smoked fish for tea.' Volker says, 'I try to be, but when I am in Featherstone, I will eat what I'm given.'

He echoes something that my gran had told him many years ago when he was invited to Sunday lunch. She had made roast beef and Yorkshire puddings. I forgot to tell her that Volker had stopped eating meat. When we arrived, I mentioned it, but she was already carving the joint. She said, 'Thy's too late with thi barrow, he'll eat what he's given.' Then my grandad took Volker to one side. He said, 'She's been in that kitchen all morning, so when you're here love, you clear your plate.' Volker cleared his plate and told my gran how much he had enjoyed his dinner. He then helped with the dishes. I washed them, Volker dried them and my gran sided them while my grandad wiped his chops with his hankie and went for a puff on his pipe.

After the last best plate was put back into the sideboard we all sat down on my gran's three-piece suite. My grandad asked Volker if he was any good at arm-wrestling. Volker wasn't sure what to say. My grandad said, 'I'll take thee on for ten bob, best o' three.' My gran said, 'Don't torment the poor bugger Eddie,' and then turned to Volker to say, 'Take no gorm on him love, he still thinks he's Rocky Marciano.' I could see that Volker was having trouble keeping up. He understood my dialect when I spoke slowly, but even I struggled with my gran and grandad when they talked fast. My grandad then said, 'Has thy ever heard tell of Max Schmeling? He fought Joe Louis afore t'war.' Volker said that his dad had mentioned him. My grandad saw his chance to do his party trick and listed every heavyweight champion of the world from the bare-knuckle bruiser Hen Pierce to Cassius Clay. When we put our coats on to come home, my grandad helped Volker on with his and said, 'By hell old cock, tha's a grand broad frame on thee.' Both my gran and grandad came to the door to wave us off. When we got to the top of the street, I said to Volker to turn round. We did and my gran and grandad waved us off again. Volker said, 'It's very cold, why do they stand there to do that?' I said, 'It's just their way, they think it's good manners.' Volker looked at me and said, 'I like that good manners.'

We drink a mug of Rington's tea. Volker smiles at the thought that a bloke with a wicker basket still brings it to our door. 'I'm calling this my memory trip. I'm going to visit some places in Scotland that I know and I would like to see some of the pubs we used to visit.'

'Shall we go to The Greyhound at Saxton then?'

'When?'

'We can go now if you want, we've had our tea.'

Volker looks across at Edward. 'Have you ever been to The Greyhound at Saxton Edward?' Edward shakes his head. 'Well it's about time you did then.'

We drive into the countryside towards York. Volker remembers every turn down the narrow country lanes. 'Can you see that big beech wood over there Eddie? That's where Mary Pannel, the last witch to be burned in England once lived.'

'How do you know that Volker?'

'Because every time we come over to this pub, your dad tells me that story!' Volker lifts his right hand off the driving wheel, punches me on the leg and winks.

We bring three pints of hand-pulled Sam Smith's Old Brewery Bitter with creamy heads to a table in the yard. We clink our glasses together and Volker says, 'Get it down lads, it'll do you good.' We laugh at each other's beer froth moustaches. Some cyclists in Lycra pants sit on the next table looking at a folded out map, rooks call to one another from the tops of some trees across the way and a tractor goes past dropping muck into the road.

Volker says, 'I've been coming here for thirty-three years and in all that time a swallow has made a nest in that outside toilet across this yard.' As if to confirm this, some swallows swoop over the outbuildings.

We set off for Cropredy at six o'clock the following morning. We stop just once for a cup of tea in a little café after Volker turns off the motorway. If he can help it Volker avoids motorway service stations, he thinks they are the work of the devil. We were once going down the A1 and got to near Peterborough. Volker said, 'Let's have lunch, do you know anywhere?' I said that it wasn't far to The Bell, a lovely old pub in Stilton. We had lunch there, the platter of six different Stilton cheeses served on a slate with a selection of crusty breads and biscuits. Volker thought it was marvellous that there was such a thing as a selection of six Stiltons, but even more marvellous that such a pub existed a stone's throw from the motorway. He vowed there and then never to eat a microwave Ginsters pasty in a service station ever again.

At the festival site entrance Volker asks me to find out where we can park the Dodge. We are told that we have special access all areas tickets and that we can drive through the crowd on a temporary metal road and park backstage. Richard Digance is singing as we get out two deckchairs from the back of the van and plonk ourselves down in the sunshine. Within an hour we have met up with loads of old friends, many of whom Volker has organised gigs for in the past. Spencer Cozens, John Martyn's keyboard player is here, as is Alan Thomson who toured and played bass with John on many tours that Volker put together. Julian Dawson comes by with Jacqui McShee from Pentangle and Volker is delighted when she involves him in a conversation about an episode of *Morse* that they have both seen. Iain Matthews shows up with his piano player Egbert Derix. He is wearing exactly the same shirt as Volker, they laugh when they tell each other that they shop at C&A. We sit with Iain and Egbert for a couple of hours. Volker tells Iain about how he had done tours for John Martyn, but due to his illness he has been out of the loop as far as gig organising goes for too long and wants to get back to it. If Iain is agreeable he'd like to organise something for him in Germany. Iain tells Volker that he is happy to give it a try. In 1971, Iain Matthews recorded an album called *If You Saw Thro' My Eyes*, a young Volker Bredebusch was turned on to that album by Jurgen's girlfriend, Barbara. It was the start of a musical odyssey that led to Volker becoming a walking encyclopaedia of English folk-rock music and also a highly regarded promoter of the music he adored. Forty-four years later, in a field in Oxfordshire, Volker shakes hands with Iain Matthews and says, 'I'll have a short tour ready for you to play by next spring.'

As dusk fell that evening, Iain Matthews took to the stage with Egbert Derix and played a sublime set. He paused before he introduced his third song. 'I'm going to play you a song by one of my favourite songwriters who is no longer with us, this is called "Man in the Station".' It was as though he was talking directly to Volker in the audience. Halfway through the song Egbert plays a blistering piano solo and then Iain segues perfectly into 'May You Never'. Volker is beyond emotional. I look across at him, a tear glistens in the corner of his eye. Iain carries on with a new song 'Pebbles in the Road' which contains the line 'Me, I do it for the song, I go in hard, I come out strong, but still, I'm just a pebble in the road'. Volker loves that line.

Volker drove us back up to Yorkshire in the early hours, it took ages, there were roadworks everywhere. I was tired, trying to read the map and getting frustrated. Volker reached out his hand and tapped me on the knee. 'No problem lad, it's just pebbles in the road.' We laughed and talked and talked about the gig all the way back to Featherstone. Volker stayed at our house for a couple more days and then went up to Scotland. He sent an email to say that he had driven through Roberton just for old-time's sake to have a look at John Martyn's old house. After that he drove up to Arran, where he and Michaela had spent many a happy holiday. He told me by email, 'I can see the most beautiful sunset above the island.' He called in to see us for one more day on the way back down. I made him a Sunday dinner. He cleared his plate. After that he drove down to Brighton to stay with Beverley, John

Martyn's ex-wife, and their son Spencer. He said Spencer was a talented young man. 'I first met him when he had just got a Kevin Keegan football for his birthday.'

Not too long after, I booked a family holiday in Denmark and Sweden. I had Volker in my mind and felt the urge to visit him, so we organised to start our holiday in Germany and Volker picked us up at Düsseldorf airport. We stayed for a couple of days with Volker at his little cottage in Sprockhövel. It's a solid, stone-built, former toll-road keeper's cottage with roses round the door. Edward was taken with the place, especially when he looked at Volker's music memorabilia. 'Look at that photo there dad, it's John Martyn in his own house.' I told him that I knew and that Volker himself had taken the photograph.

'We should take Edward for a beer at Früh in Köln after breakfast,' Volker announced one morning. 'So make sure you eat well. Me and your dad had an old mate in Featherstone called Sooner. He used to say, "If you want to be a good drinker, you have to be a good eater." Isn't that right Ian?' I spread some leberwurst onto a brötchen and nodded. Volker had laid out a huge German breakfast of four different breads, six cold meats and more cheese than you could eat. There was orange juice, apple juice, boiled eggs and four types of jam and marmalade, two of them from Scotland. We took the train to Köln and made a beeline for the Früh Kölsch pub. Edward loved it, he said, 'That's probably the best beer I've ever tasted, shall we have another?' Volker said, 'Aye lad! When that waiter goes by, say to him, "Noch drei beir bitte!".' Edward reddened up with embarrassment, but gave it a go. The waiter in his blue apron fetched our beers and drank one himself. Edward said to Volker, 'Have I just paid for that beer for him?' Volker said, 'It's the tradition in here, the waiters take a beer if you order a round. It's good to have tradition eh? Is the beer as good as Sam Smith's?' Edward grinned. Later we had a walk by the Rhine and watched an old gypsy musician busking. He played Little Richard's song 'Tutti Frutti' but sang it in an indecipherable language. We joined in with 'awop bap a loo bomp a wop bam boom'.

In the spring of 2016 Volker sent me a CD of the songs of Hildegaard Knef that is only available in Germany. He told me that the tour for Iain Matthews was organised and that because there was a spare date, a gig would take place in his house. I would have loved to have been at that gig. Volker cleared out his front room, borrowed some benches and somehow crammed twenty-odd people in there. Barbara, who Volker hadn't seen in many years, was invited and she came. I guess that a lot of circles were joined that day.

Volker was on a roll again now. He organised a tour for Alan Thomson and Doug Morter during the summer and another for Iain Matthews to start in the September. One Friday I had a message on my answerphone from Iain. 'Hi Ian, we have a gig for Volker in Hattingen in a few days' time, but I can't get hold of him, I think he's ill, do you know anything?' I phoned Iain in Holland. He told me that the last time he had spoken to Volker a week or so before he had sounded really ill and feared that the cancer had returned. I tried to get in touch with Volker by email and mobile phone with no luck. I left messages. I also tried to call Jurgen to see if he knew anything, but he wasn't available either, so I left him a message. On the Saturday, Jurgen called. He told me that Volker was seriously ill in hospital. He said that the cancer had returned and according to the specialist in Essen hospital, it was spreading at an alarming rate, faster than any they had seen. On the Sunday morning, 4th September, my birthday, at around eight o'clock, my phone rang. It was Jurgen. He said, 'I am in the hospital, Volker wants to speak to you.' He put Volker on. I heard him breathing heavily, trying to say something.

I said, 'Now then lad, how are you?' It was probably the daftest thing I've ever said. Volker eventually said, 'Fucking grand. I'm ready when you are Bob.' He was remembering an old advert for Tetley beer that we had both liked and often repeated. Then after a pause that went on so long that I could hear voices in the hospital, he said, 'I'm phoning to say farewell old lad.' He spoke in a hoarse whisper. 'I don't know where I'm going on the next part of this journey, but I'm ready.' I didn't know what to say, I spluttered out, 'I love thee old cock.' I could hear Volker breathing heavily, 'And I love thee too old cock.' He paused for ages, I waited. Then he went on an extended riff about the state of politics, the rise of the right wing and the war in Syria. 'At least we fucking tried!' he whispered. 'You make sure to tell Edward that we fucking tried and that he's got to try as well.' I wanted to cry, but more I wanted to listen to my friend, so I said, 'Can you remember those conversations we had about kismet?' Years ago in a bar in Prague, on one of our adventures, we had somehow got into a conversation about Admiral Nelson. Volker had said that he didn't say 'kiss me Hardy' before he died, he had said 'kismet Hardy'. In the years after that 'kismet' became a special word between us. We used it all the time, in all sorts of situations as shorthand for anything from 'we don't know what the fuck is going on' to 'it's as plain as the nose on your face'. Today when I said it to Volker he laughed a rattling chuckle. 'That's it Ian. Fucking kismet. A simple fucking twist of fate.' Now I started to cry. I asked Volker if he would like to say something to Heather. He would. I took the phone upstairs. Heather had been sleeping, but had woken up when she heard the phone ringing. I said, 'It's Volker.' I stood by the bedroom door and watched Heather trying to gently talk to our mate. She said at one point, 'Look after our Billie when you get there.' I took the phone back. Volker said, 'I'm going to open a bottle with John. I'll see thee old cock.' I said, 'I'll see thee then.' Volker said, 'At least we fucking tried.'

I flew over to Düsseldorf for Volker's funeral. He had been cremated the day before and the funeral director carried the urn of ashes into the crematorium chapel to the strains of Ben Webster's saxophone. Jurgen asked me if I would like to say a few words. I talked about a friendship that had lasted for thirty-four years and the visits that we had made to stay in each other's houses and all the other friendships that had sprung out of our first meeting. There was more music, this time John Martyn blasting from the funeral director's portable CD player. Volker's ashes were placed into a freshly dug hole in the garden of remembrance. We went for lunch in one of Volker's favourite local bars, a former Yugoslavian place near to the old square in Sprockhövel. We raised a glass of Pilsner. After that we went back to Volker's little toll house. In the afternoon sun I watched dust falling down. The house was beyond quiet. I moved around hardly daring to make a noise. On the kitchen wall an old Joshua Tetley wall plaque with the huntsman looked down at me through a monocled eye. There were half-eaten jars of Robertson's jam in the fridge, a souvenir postcard of Whitby pressed behind a cabinet and a collection of *Taggart* box sets neatly placed on shelves in the living room. Jurgen said, 'Volker wanted you to have his John Martyn collection, you should start to put it into boxes.'

I started to place a lifetime's collection of John Martyn records and bootleg tapes into some self-assembly plastic crates. I noticed that there wasn't just one copy of *Live at Leeds* but three. On the back of one of them John Martyn had written in felt pen 'What a Volker' and then, for reasons probably known only to himself, the record's serial number 'ILPS 9343'. My mind went to the last time I had seen Volker. It had been the previous October. We had to take a train from Germany up to Aarhus in Denmark. Volker had booked the journey for us and had woken us up at 5am. He drove us to Bochum railway station in time for the early train. We boarded and looked through the train window. At precisely ten minutes past six in the morning a whistle blew. He mouthed, 'Don't forget to change trains in Hamburg.' Then he turned to walk away. For a moment with my face pressed up near the glass I couldn't tell whether it was the train moving off or Volker walking away backwards and then he stood to wave. A man in a station. We waved back. The train gathered speed and Volker waited. He waved until we were out of sight.

My first great drinking buddy Burt Stephens died suddenly in the summer of 2016. Diane phoned to tell me. I heard her crying on the other end of the line and didn't know what to say. Somewhere in the back of my mind Burt and I sat talking in the back room at The Green Dragon, the beer was a penny cheaper in there in those days. We planned journeys we wanted to make. I could almost hear his voice explaining the theory of logical positivism and then jumping to how he had managed to persuade the landlord in The White Swan to let him have half a gallon of Hull Brewery mild until pay day. Burt loved the incongruities when small-town imagination rubbed up against a desire to travel and understand a bigger world. Diane asked me if I'd like to say a few words at Burt's funeral. I said I would be honoured. I put the phone down and tried to listen more to his voice in my head.

Burt had a humanist funeral at Bishopthorpe crematorium near York. We got there early and called in to one of the village pubs for a couple of pints. Heather remembered the time when Burt came to stop at our flat in Station Lane for a short time when he was in between building sites. He didn't seem to have many clothes then and always wore a red checked lumberjack shirt. One washday Heather said to him, 'If you want to take that shirt off I'll put it in with ours.' He said, 'It's clean.' Heather said, 'But you have had it on all week.' He looked incredulous, 'What you don't know Parky, is that I have got four of these.' Later, Heather bought her own checked shirt. He said, 'I don't know why you're copying my style, it takes a certain type of person to wear a checked shirt, I'm one and you're not!' Diane recalled him waxing his Belstaff motorbike jacket which was his pride and joy. This prompted me to remember when he once borrowed a bike without a grab rail because his normal bike was broken down. I was travelling behind as his pillion and wondered how I should hold on. Burt said, 'You'll have to put your arms round me, but don't start fondling or else you'll be on the fucking bus tomorrow!' We laughed and got another round in and touched our pots in his memory.

At the service a tape of Maria Callas played through the speakers as we walked in. It was 'Un Bel dì Vedremo' from *Madame Butterfly*. Then the officiant read, 'That man is a success who has lived well, laughed often and loved much.' Then I was asked to come to the lectern and speak. I'd prepared a sheet of A4, but decided not to use my notes. I talked about how we go through life looking forward to stuff, but also remembering. How we recall the sunshiny years of our teenage times, our good teachers, workmates, people we travel alongside and especially people who we like. Burt was all of those things to me. I mentioned that how when we were young Turks we drank far more beer than was good for us and ate late-night vindaloos that were far spicier than they need have been.

Sean Tomlinson couldn't make it down to the funeral from his home in the north of Scotland, but I had to mention the story of how Burt had once taken us on a tour of backstreet pubs in Salford. He introduced us that night to a place called The Eagle that only had a licence to sell beer, no wine or spirits. It was a very plain, almost austere place, utilitarian in the extreme, but Burt loved it. He told us that night that pubs don't need to be fancified, gentrified or have inglenook fireplaces. All they need is good beer and someone who knows how to pull a pint, preferably in a bar where they have been doing that for a hundred years. We laughed. Burt said, 'I'm fucking serious!' He loved history, not necessarily the history you can touch or see in museums, but the history that comes in abstract ways through maintaining friendships, socialising, bumping into new people, listening to stories. Burt reckoned that the history of Britain can be found in the taprooms of ale houses in the backstreets. I think Burt, Sean and I made it our mission from that night to uncover as much of that history as we could drink in.

Burt was the one who said to me when I told him I was giving up the building sites to become a writer, 'Well you can't be any worse with a fucking pen in your hand than you are with a shovel.' He loved to tell the story of how me, Heather, him and Diane, who was eight months pregnant with their daughter Jess at the time, blagged our way into the Nostell Priory rock festival by telling a daft security guard that we were Van Morrison's roadies. The security lad narrowed his eyes and said, 'Are you sure?' Burt said, 'Well you were drinking Theakston's Old Peculier last night with us at that complementary bar.' The lad said, 'Oh, all right then, I'm sorry I didn't recognise you.'

He loved far-off places and travelling to them. Jess told me that one of his last big trips had been a long hike up the North Western seaboard of America and how delighted he had been when the locals had advised him to store his food in bear-proof containers.

I finished off by saying, 'Life is a journey, isn't it?' Burt relished that journey. You go through life with a lot of stopping off as you go. You make many acquaintances and friends along the way, some of those friends are special, you know that they will always be your friend. Burt was one of those.

There was a reading of a William Wordsworth poem, the line, 'Though nothing can bring back the hour, of splendour in the grass, of glory in the flower,' sticks in my mind still. Then through the speakers came Van Morrison singing 'Sweet Thing'. I looked across at Jess, in her thirties now, married and with a good degree. I chuckled inside at the thought of her being in her mam's belly when we went to see Van Morrison that time at the Theakston's music festival.

Our friend Sean Tomlinson has become one of the undisputed heroes of British brewing. I recall vividly a moment up at his house in Queen Street in Pontefract. He had brewed some home brew using a kit. We got stuck into it one night whilst listening to Elmore James on the record player. It was all right so far as home brew goes, but not something you'd want to sup on a regular basis. Sean said, 'If I can't make a better beer than this there's something wrong.' After that he went down to Fawcetts Maltkilns and persuaded them to sell him a small amount of malt. I think he got the yeast from the bottom of a few Guinness bottles. And his beer was glorious.

When all the pits shut down, it was inevitable that the companies that made coal-cutting machinery would follow. Jeffrey Diamonds started laying people off. Sean didn't wait to be asked, he volunteered for redundancy and moved to work at a chemical factory. He got made redundant from there as well. Redundancy became an occupational hazard round our way in the 1980s and 90s so Sean decided he would go into brewing full-time. He made a peculiar request. In lieu of redundancy pay he asked if he could have steel and copper instead. He wanted to start right from the beginning and build his own brewery. He found premises in an old bakehouse in Pontefract and created Tomlinson's Old Castle Brewery, the second part of the name coming from a long lamented brewery of that town called Pickersgill's who went out of business in the 1930s. Sean named his beers after aspects of Pontefract history. He brewed one called De Lacey, after the man who built a castle after the Norman invasion, and a bitter called Sessions after the local court house. Sean brewed beautiful beers and won a lot of awards from the off. Within a couple of years of starting, his Hermitage Mild, named after a local historic landmark, won champion beer of Britain in its category at the CAMRA awards. He then combined Pontefract's other culinary claim to fame, liquorice, with the malt and hops to make a beer called Three Seiges that gained a national reputation. It was the best creative use of liquorice since Charlie Chaplin ate his boot and laces in the film *The Gold Rush*. He even got a beer on the handpumps at the bar in the Houses of Parliament. Sean's wife Tracey brewed one called Femme Fatale and they launched it on International Women's Day. There's a great photograph of Mo Mowlam, Margaret Beckett and the then speaker Betty Boothroyd toasting each other with glasses of the beer brewed at Sean's little brewery in Pontefract.

Sean relocated to Scotland in the 1990s and found work helping others to set up breweries. He was head brewer at Caledonian for a long time and won many more awards with innovative beers. He now consults on brewing and with Tracey runs a beer shop in Inverness. The awards keep coming, the shop has won the award for best beer shop in Scotland. I'm very proud of my old mate. It's a long way now from our musketeer drinking sessions, but Burt and Sean are never far from my mind when the subject of beer comes up.

Peeling Back The Years

In 2010, Tetley Dave introduced me to a bloke called Neil Midgley and his partner Maureen. Neil told me that he was planning to buy a derelict pub in Castleford town centre that had been boarded up for a couple of years. This was The Junction. It stood decaying on a street corner opposite Castleford parish church, looking to all the world like it had served its last pint. Neil had a vision to let it become what it once was. The sort of pub that existed before Sky Television, microwave lasagne, piped music and free WiFi. He wanted to strip back layers of identikit pub interior decoration and introduce robust wooden furniture, open fires, and try to create a pleasant meeting place where conversation thrived and you could buy a good pint of real beer at an honest price. Neil Midgley has a philosophy that beer is the drink of the working man and pubs are the last bastion of the gathering places of the working classes. He also believed that you don't need to reinvent the pub. 'It's already there, you just need to lift off everything that's been added over the years and bring it back that way.' I liked listening to what Neil was talking about. It was like a breath of fresh air. With twenty-odd pubs shutting down in this country every week for the last twenty years, I'd heard all sorts of hare-brained schemes about how you might turn the tide. Here was a bloke not trying to reinvent the pub as a coffee house, a theatre, a dining experience or a nightclub. Neil had a simple mission and it started with good ale.

Neil opened The Junction a long time before he'd finished turning his vision to something real. You had to watch where you were going at first, because there were sawn bits of timber all over the place. But he did manage to get the ale right straightaway. He sourced it from local brewers, like Malcolm at the Five Town's brewery and Bob who brewed a magnificent beer that he called Chardon-ale. He then went into an agreement with Simon at the Ridgeside brewery in Leeds. Ridgeside brewed some of the best beers I have tasted and The Junction always featured three or four at a time.

I went in The Junction one Friday afternoon, not long after Neil had installed an old fire range with an oven at the side. Something smelled good. I asked Neil what it was. 'I'm testing my oven, I've got rabbit stew on the go.' In one of the back parlours were piles of parquet floor blocks. Neil told me that he had bought the floor of an old chapel in Derbyshire and that he intended to lay it in his bar area. The problem was the parquet blocks had been laid on pitch when they were put down, perhaps a hundred years ago. When they were lifted, the dried black pitch came away with the wood and needed to be scraped off before the parquet could be re-laid. 'It'll be another long job, but I'll do a few at a time,' Neil said. He didn't seem to be outfaced by anything. He was already scraping layers of paint off the exterior walls to reveal the original blue-glazed tiles from Beverleys brewery circa 1920s. He was doing it with the edge of a coin every time he went out for a fag. The parquet blocks stood gathering dust for weeks after that.

My lad Edward was in between fifth form and college. He told me that he could do with a little job, but nobody wanted to employ someone who was going to work for a few weeks and then pack it in to do A-levels. I happened to mention to Neil that if he was prepared to let Eddie loose on his wooden floor blocks, he might have a go at cleaning them for a bit of pocket money. Neil said, 'Well there's no harm in letting him have a go, but does he realise what hard work it is?' I took our Eddie down to the pub after breakfast one Wednesday morning and we worked side by side scraping. When we got home, I said to him 'What do you reckon?' He showed me his hands. He was blistered on every finger. Up to that point Edward's experience of work had been a gentle bit of sweeping up in a hairdressing salon owned by a friend of ours. He said, 'I'm not sure I want to go there again.' I said, 'Tell me in the morning what you think and I'll let Neil know.' When he got up he said, 'I'll try again Dad but I think I'm going to put a pair of gloves on.' He did and for a good few weeks after he went nearly every day to scrape the blocks, determined to finish them all, despite blisters like grapes, and he did. On that day, Neil announced that to contrast with the lighter wood of the beech he might like to have a dark wood border when it came to laying the floor. Eddie looked at me and whispered, 'Will they want scraping as well?' I said they probably would, Eddie's face was a picture. Eddie was sixteen at the time he prepared the parquet floor. Neil said to him, 'On the day you are eighteen, you will have your first legal beer in here and I will buy it for you.' Of course on the day Eddie was eighteen we went to The Junction to celebrate. Neil stuck to his word. Eddie is proud that he stuck to his task and every now and then when he comes to the pub he'll say. 'That floor looks well doesn't it, Dad?'

Neil had been preparing for his vision for a long time. Twenty years before he came to The Junction he had bought a bank of Gaskell and Chambers beer engines that had come from a long-gone brewery called Melbournes. He thought that one day they might come in handy. Ten years after that he bought an entire Victorian bar when they knocked down the old Haddon Hall pub in Leeds. Again with the thought that it might come in one day. Now Neil started putting his jigsaw pieces together and the pub started to take shape.

He was painting the windows outside on a scaffold one Saturday. I climbed up to have a chat. 'Do you know,' he said, 'I think the original signage might be under all of this plastic and wood.' We prised some of the boards off. He was right. Underneath we saw golden lettering in a beautiful art nouveau typeface. The lettering said the name of the pub and the name of the brewery 'Beverleys'. This was an old Wakefield brewery that sold out to Watney's in the 1960s. In this way, lovely tasty beers that were brewed just eight miles down the road were replaced by Watney's bloody Red Barrel. Of all the indignities thrust upon drinkers in those stupid times, this was the biggest of them. Neil knew that he could strip back all of this nonsense and reveal the true pub underneath. There were never any big strides toward this vision, just little tiptoe steps, but with every step Neil was getting to something like the place he wanted his pub to be.

I play dominoes every Friday afternoon there with some old lads: Alan and Dave are both eighty, Barnsley Brian is in his seventies. All three sup ale like it's rabbit gravy. Brian likes to reminisce about his days working at the power station and when they sent him to Finland to work. Alan tells us how many bricks he could lay in a day when he worked on the building sites. He'll show his hands, 'Bricklayers hands them.' When Dave is that road out he'll place his dominoes on the table, look at the other two and announce, 'Look here, are we playing bloody dominoes or clocking on?' I take our Edward down for a game occasionally. I want him to learn how to play Fives and Threes from blokes like Alan, Dave and Barnsley Brian. There is strict pub etiquette, you only get a game if invited to play by the regulars and only then once you have 'put a knock on', which means you're required to knock the table like you're knocking on a front door. It took ages for Edward to pluck up the courage to knock the table and when he finally did, Dave turned round and said, 'Hey up young 'un, who does tha think thy is knocking?' Edward went as red as a beetroot. Now our Eddie gets a game regularly. He's still not too sure when he partners up with the older men, but they reassure him, 'Just play your natural game kid.' When Dave or Alan drop their dominoes on the floor, Edward picks them up. One week, Dave dropped his top set of teeth out. Edward heard the click on the floor but didn't realise until he had the teeth in his hand that it wasn't the double blank he'd been feeling under the chair for. He handed them to Dave who put them straight back in and said, 'Is it my drop?'

Neil started picking up awards for his beer and for the pub. He built up a good custom amongst locals. Some of these had known the pub for sixty years. Others came by bus and train to find the place after its reputation started to spread. The brewers too wanted to be involved.

I stood at the bar with Neil one afternoon. We'd just come

back from a brewery at Southport. We had been to collect an award-winning beer called Golden Sands. Neil was disappointed that the beer was in a plastic cask. He said, 'Beer ought to be in wood. Not because that's the traditional way, but because it tastes better.' He then told me that there are things in wood that puts flavours into beer as it undergoes its secondary fermentation. I wondered aloud if it might be possible in this day and age to have a number of wooden barrels that could be sent to small breweries for washing and filling. Within days of that conversation, Neil contacted a master cooper called Alistair Sim. He commissioned Alistair to make him dozens of wooden casks. The Junction found its unique selling point. All of the beers it sells are now drawn from wooden casks. The Junction may be the only pub in the whole world that does this. When Elland brewery won the champion beer of Britain award they won it with a recipe from 1872. The beer was called 1872 Porter. It was rightly celebrated as a great beer, but only The Junction served it from the wood.

Beers from the wood are now becoming fashionable. Brewers are using a bewildering array of mature casks to impart new depths of flavour; sherry casks, whisky casks and giant oak casks from the Portuguese port industry. The hipsters are already into this new phenomenon. The interesting thing is that this didn't start in some trendy inner-city brasserie with overpriced so-called craft beers. It started in a working-class boozer in an unfashionable town, where the landlord was trying to find a way back to good honest beer for locals. It's also the only pub I have been in where the first prize for winning the quiz is a jar of homemade piccalilli. You have to bring the jar back though, because Neil and the lady who makes it are both serious recyclers.

Who could have foreseen the revival in real ale and the appreciation for the traditional methods that go towards making a great beer. When you come to a junction you decide which road you are going to take onwards. Sometimes it pays to just sit down and wait. Good things can happen to those who wait.

My lad Edward likes to have the occasional pint with me these days. We go down to The Junction at Castleford. He's already reminiscing in his pub conversations about the time when he blistered his hands helping to prepare the parquet flooring for the pub. I like to show him some of the pubs that I frequented with Sean and Burt. Now and again we go over to The Greyhound at Saxton. I tell him about the adventures I had in pubs with them back in the day. He yawns as though to say 'Tell me the old old story' but the last time we were there together I took a great delight in his company, I was overjoyed when he came back from the outside lavatory and said. 'You'll be pleased to know Dad, that swallow is still nesting in that corner under the roof.'

I raise a glass to Burt and Sean, to Volker and Jurgen, our Heather, Tetley Dave, Martin, Sooner, Paul Windmill, Peter Green and all the others I have had the pleasure to drink alongside since that first taste of beer I had in the colliery welfare club opposite the pit where my grandad worked. I believe it tasted nutty.

Ian Clayton is an author, broadcaster and storyteller from Featherstone, West Yorkshire. He is a traveller, a collector, a gatherer and is passionate about finding the voice of the common people. He still lives in the town where he was born and lists his hobbies as tap-room conversation and gentle subversion. His stories are about making sense of where we come from. His books include *Bringing It All Back Home*, a bestselling book about music; *Song For My Father* about his lifelong search for a father figure; *Our Billie* about loss; and *Right Up Your Street*, a collection of his weekly columns for the *Pontefract and Castleford Express*.

For more on this book, please visit:

www.ianclaytoninfo.wordpress.com
www.route-online.com